Jana Cruder

OKSANA MARAFIOTI

American Gypsy

Oksana Marafioti moved from the Soviet Union when she was fifteen years old. Trained as a classical pianist, she has also worked as a cinematographer. She lives in Las Vegas, Nevada.

american Gypsy

american Gypsy

OKSANA MARAFIOTI

FARRAR, STRAUS AND GIROUX   NEW YORK

Farrar, Straus and Giroux
18 West 18th Street, New York 10011

Copyright © 2012 by Oksana Marafioti
All rights reserved
Distributed in Canada by D&M Publishers, Inc.
Printed in the United States of America
First edition, 2012

Library of Congress Cataloging-in-Publication Data
Marafioti, Oksana, 1974–
    American Gypsy / Oksana Marafioti. — 1st ed.
        p.   cm.
    ISBN 978-0-374-10407-8
    1. Marafioti, Oksana, 1974–   2. Romanies—United States—Biography.
3. Immigrants—United States—Biography.   4. Marafioti, Oksana, 1974– —
Childhood and youth.   5. Romanies—Soviet Union—Biography.   I. Title.

DX127.M37 A3 2012
305.891'497073—dc23   2011047075

Designed by Abby Kagan

7/2012
3 855 8653   www.fsgbooks.com

1   3   5   7   9   10   8   6   4   2

To protect the privacy of certain individuals, the names and identifying characteristics of
several people have been changed and composite characters have been created.

For my parents

We are all wanderers on this earth. Our hearts are full of wonder, and our souls are deep with dreams.

—ROMANI SAYING

AUTHOR'S NOTE

There are well over five million Romani people living in every corner of the world today. We are bound by thousands of years of common history, but our culture is as diverse as our customs and dialects. Although there are many similarities between the clans, the stories in this book are mainly those of my experiences growing up in the Romani community of the former Soviet Union.

american
Gypsy

AMERICAN CHEESE

The woman on the other side of the desk scribbled in her files. I studied her with interest: perfectly manicured nails, killer perm, and a beige pantsuit with the American embassy ID clipped to the left breast pocket. She warmed us now and then with one of those smiles that make you want to ask its owner to be your child's godparent even if you've only just met. She didn't look like someone who held the fate of my family in her hands.

Before the interview that morning, Mom had instructed Dad not to speak, for two reasons. First, he couldn't complete a sentence without swearing. And second, but more important, he always said the wrong thing.

The woman looked up from her paperwork and turned to my father. In a version of Russian that made me feel like I was teetering on a balance beam along with her, she said, "Mr. Kopylenko, tell why you want exist in United States?"

I stared at Dad's fedora, thankful that at least he had given up his earrings for a day. Mom tightened her grip on her purse, and my eight-year-old sister, Roxy, stopped swinging her legs.

Dad straightened, cleared his throat, and said in equally

precarious English, "I want play with B.B. King. I great Gypsy musician and he like me. When he hear me play, we be rich. Here, I great musician, but nobody know. We live in 1980s, but feel like 1880s. Russian peoples only like factory and tractor. I no drive tractor. I play guitar. Her name Aphroditta. Also." He lifted his index finger to stress the importance of what was coming next. "I super-good healer. I heal peoples. If you have hemorrhoid, I fix. I take tumor with bare hands. In Russia, I not free. I go to jail, you understand?"

I was mortified, my eyes jumping between Dad, the awfully quiet American, and my mom, who'd plastered on a smile like a fresh Band-Aid.

"We want our girls to have a better future," Mom said in Russian, after recouping from the awkward pause. "You understand."

Years of managing a Roma performing ensemble had taught my mother the schmooze side of business. She closed many impossible deals over black caviar and bottles of Armenian cognac, items she couldn't bring to our interview, though not for lack of trying. That day, November 18, 1989, Mom had put on a periwinkle wool dress, a fox-fur coat—we had waited in line outside the embassy for three hours—a pair of Swedish-made boots, and not a flicker of jewelry except for her wedding band. She had made sure none of us looked too rich or too poor; it was important to appear like the average Soviet family. This was tricky, since, as far as Americans knew, the USSR did not have a middle class and was not supposed to have an upper class, which we happened to belong to.

This wasn't Mom's first trip to the embassy. Her brother Arsen, who had moved with his family—including two of my favorite cousins, Nelly and Aida—to Los Angeles three years before, sent us a visa that was short an important form: his agreement to sponsor us when we first arrived in the States. The visa might as well have been blank without it. But Mom didn't give up, even though it took her years of networking, bribing, and entertaining in the classiest restaurants to finally get our file going. This last family interview was the key, quite literally, to freedom.

Thankfully Dad had kept quiet, and the American asked only Mom questions from that point on. Soon the two women were swapping locations of the best butcher shops in town. "On Wednesdays, go to Komsomolskaya Ploshad. Ask for Borya. Tell him I sent you," Mom said, voice low as if the room were full of strangers waiting to snatch her secret.

It still felt then as if we were bargaining like prisoners caught between an unfair sentence and a pardon, but I could hear that freedom. In my ears, bells were ringing, that huge music they belted out from the towers of St. Basil's Cathedral in Red Square.

The woman flipped the pages of our file and addressed my mother in measured Russian: "I'd read here that you drink?" She lifted an arm to her lips and curled her fingers around an imaginary bottle. And a needle scratched across my sound track, exactly the way you hear it in movies.

The four of us halted like toys unwound.

Mom drank often. This was after Dad had nearly died of alcohol poisoning and renounced booze as the religion of choice, and before Mom started drinking every day. But what if Americans didn't drink? Ever. I hadn't considered that possibility.

With a look of complete mortification the woman said, "Oh goodness. Sometimes my pronunciation is bad. You sing, right? You singer."

All the Kopylenkos in the room showed signs of life for the first time in at least fifteen seconds.

"Yes, yes, I do!" Mom laughed and we joined in, somewhat maniacally, as I recall. In Russian, "drink" and "sing" are a letter apart.

At the end of the hour, the American finally stamped our

papers. She blushed while my parents took turns hugging her, all three talking as if they were going to be neighbors once we moved. Even when we walked out of the office I couldn't breathe, too afraid she would change her mind and rush out to take back the good news.

Once we had our permission my parents didn't waste time packing. In their desperation to leave they didn't pause to consider the difficulties they might encounter across the ocean. They just knew that everything would be better in America.

The days leading up to our departure seesawed between too much activity and too little sleep. "We're finally getting out of this hellhole," Dad told anyone willing to listen. He practiced his guitar with frenzied dedication, for that fantasy meeting with his hero, B.B. King. It never crossed his mind that maybe he couldn't walk up to any old music legend and dazzle him with killer technique.

Mom sold or gave away most of our valuables because Soviet customs employees weren't shy about confiscating anything that turned a profit on the black market. Even our house had to go. According to Soviet law, we had to surrender all real estate before emigrating. Mom's relatives talked her into giving it to one of her distant cousins. It was better than seeing it go to a stranger. My parents had friends who put their names on waiting lists for years for an opportunity to buy Moscow real estate. As connected as Mom was, it had taken her two cases of cognac and fifteen thousand rubles to bribe a housing authority official to bump up her name for a fifty-year-old house with cracked shutters.

Our house was located near the city limits, where oak and maple trees commanded the streets, making human structures look insignificant and fragile.

Muscovites preferred the city high-rises, and I didn't know that only the old folks and the Gypsies still lived in those old houses on the outskirts until one of my fourth-grade classmates educated me.

"It's like I read in my dad's newspaper," Nastya said, pushing a mop around our classroom. We had floor duty every Tuesday after school. "Our leaders built these new apartments for everyone to live in. The old people got smart eventually. But the Gypsies set up tents in the courtyards and said they liked to sleep and pee outside. Can you imagine? If you ask me, I think they just didn't know what to do with all those walls and doors. Like, if you bring a mouse inside, it's always looking for a hole to jump into."

"What does that have to do with houses?" I asked Nastya, taking care with my words. When I started first grade, my parents, without much explanation, told me not to mention that I was part Roma. To Nastya, I was Oksana Kopylenko the Ukrainian, because all Soviet last names ending with *nko* traced their roots to Ukraine.

She leaned on the mop's tip and whispered, "They're closer to the dirt that way."

After school I marched home and demanded to know if Nastya's story was true.

Dad was in the garage mixing paints—neon yellow and torch red—to use on our car. Mom stood inside the doorway, eyes fixed on Dad, arms crossed like a pretzel high and tight over her chest.

"It took those cretins five years to get all of the Roma off the grounds," Dad said. "They were so used to people obeying that Gypsy insubordination was big news, headlines in all the papers."

"It's not true." I was appalled. I had hoped Nastya had lied. "Why wouldn't they want to live in a house? It doesn't make sense."

My reaction sent Dad into a fit of laughter.

"You think everyone lives like us? Nice place with modern

amenities? In some cities those charity apartments don't even have heating or water. You squat behind a tree and wipe your ass with newspaper."

My parents loved that house. They had put in parquet floors throughout, except for the kitchen, where Mom preferred marble. Both bedrooms had sleek Swedish furniture, while the living room, the center of all gatherings, boasted curvy Queen Anne–style couches and Persian rugs.

"We'll buy a mansion in Los Angeles," Mom assured everyone who called to ask after her mental health. "And for dirt cheap."

Dad left a number of albums with his sister, Laura, for safekeeping. Featuring my grandparents' beautiful voices, they were produced during the height of Roma popularity with the Russian public and signified an irreplaceable legacy. He wrapped them with painstaking care in soft towels, laying them inside a small

Grandpa Andrei's first Gypsy ensemble, 1936. Grandpa Andrei is seated in the middle row, with Grandma Rose to his left

wooden chest. "It's only for now," he had told his sister. "I made copies on these tapes in case you want to listen to them. The needle scratches on that damn record player."

My eight-year-old sister bragged to all her friends about the move. She had recently developed a crush on George Michael and had been making plans of her own, which included locating, ensnaring, and eventually marrying the pop star.

I spent most of those last days in an emotional limbo, uncertain of how I felt about the impending metamorphosis. Petrified to part with the comfort of familiarity, I still couldn't deny my excitement at living in a place most of the world believed to be paradise. A few years back, a drummer from our ensemble had taken a trip to Las Vegas. When he came back, his eyes were as lit up as the fabled Sin City billboards.

"You get free soap in all the hotel rooms," Vova had exclaimed in our kitchen. My parents, along with a few musician friends who came to hear about the States, wrapped their ears around Vova's stories. Sometimes, like in the case of the free-soap claim, they would burst into a debate. "I don't believe it," somebody said. "Why should anyone need free soap in Vegas?" Another added, "To wash their ass with, after they shit all the money away."

Roxy and I had lurked in the corners of the kitchen that night, trying to stay undetected. But when Vova produced a piece of something yellow covered in filmy plastic, we forgot about the threat of bedtime.

"What is that?" Roxy asked.

"This"—Vova held the delicate sheet between his forefinger and thumb—"is American cheese."

Our cheese came in thick blocks, so heavy they could kill a man. Even when sliced, it never turned out so thin.

My father, always the smart-ass, interrupted the momentary

glorification of the cheese. "Are the Americans rationing food? I thought the war was over."

"No, man," Vova said. "It's like this on purpose. You put it between two slices of bread and cook it on a skillet until the cheese melts."

"What about the plastic?" I asked.

"Here." Vova placed the cheese into my palm. "You pull this edge up and remove the wrapper."

A collective "Oh" went around the kitchen.

My father shook his head, still unimpressed. He turned to Mom and said, "See? I told you. Anybody with half a brain can become rich in America."

But all I thought was, My God—singly wrapped cheese; so exotic, so needlessly luxurious. As Vova continued to list the marvels of everyday American life, I couldn't help but daydream of what living there would be like.

I even got a special haircut for the big move. It was called the Lioness.

In the USSR, all haircuts had names. The Lioness looked identical to Jon Bon Jovi's hair except fluffier. Tamara, Mom's hairdresser, had suggested the cut to offset my eyes, which, she claimed, appeared unnaturally large compared to the rest of my face. If it's good enough for Jon, I thought, it's good enough for me.

For my arrival, I wore an outfit that you could appreciate only if you grew up during the eighties. In that case, you would be sick with envy over my aquamarine sweater and neon-pink corduroy pants, purchased on the black market for three hundred rubles. I had even put on makeup: a touch of green eye shadow and pink lipstick. I felt like a movie star. My Wednesday Addams personality nearly vanished behind the trendy Oksana who was about to move to the land of opportunity. I had no doubt I would fit right in, wearing clothes in the tradition of the MTV music videos

I had studied. Perhaps this Oksana could pass for a girl with an average family, instead of a Gypsy one.

Funny: I really thought it would be that simple.

For the first fifteen years of my life, my parents performed in a traveling Roma ensemble the size of a circus. They had little choice in the matter—my grandparents ran it, and it was a family affair. Although my mother was Armenian by blood, once she married my father, she may as well have been Roma.

We led a spur-of-the-moment kind of life, always on the road touring and adjusting to schedules and local customs. Officially we lived in Moscow, but by the age of ten, I had traveled from the Mongolian deserts to the Siberian tundra; I had become adept at sleeping on the worn-out seats of old train stations and during show rehearsals.

Even after I started school, I tried to spend every possible moment on the road, in part to hide my inclination to forget homework assignments or to ditch school for a matinee of a foreign flick. But a bigger reason was fear. For the first five grades I'd done well as the Ukrainian Oksana. Then, one day, a classmate stuck a piece of paper to my back. I didn't notice it for some hours, and by then it was too late.

Gyp.

The classmate was Aleksey Moruskin, Nastya's boyfriend. Later, when he and I sat in the principal's office, his hair and face stained magenta-red as he sulked at the floor between the principal's desk and his feet, I knew his pout had little to do with guilt and a lot with the fact that I'd dumped a bowl of beets on his head during lunch. It was the only time I was grateful to the school cooks for making home-style vegetables every day.

Timofey Timofeevich, who sometimes punished students by

making them kneel on a pile of dried beans in the corner of his office, sat across from us like God come down for Judgment one day early.

"*Raskazivay* (Tell me)," he said to Aleksey.

The boy mumbled, "Nastya heard her"—a nod at me—"grandmother singing on the radio," then stopped and swung his legs like a kindergartner.

"I don't have all day, boy." Timofey Timofeevich sang bass with an a cappella quartet called Bright Sunrises. His voice reached places.

"The announcer guy said she was a . . . you know . . ."

"Where's that bag of kidney beans I've been saving for a special occasion?"

"Hesaidshewasagypsy," Aleksey pinballed in a single breath.

The bag was opened, the beans scattered. Aleksey cut me a look that hissed of revenge. He kneeled down, cheeks puffed to hold in the sobs. You'd have to kneel for a while before it went from uncomfortable to painful, but he still cried.

"My dad is a *Ukrainian* Rom," I said to Timofey Timofeevich, as if he were about to confiscate my last name now that the Gypsy part had been revealed.

"In that case," the principal said, back at his desk now, "you ought to act like a lady, no matter the unfortunate choices your Ukrainian ancestors made with all this mindless mixing." The principal's admonition of my family's unsavory behavior was quite common in the Soviet Union at the time. As the Stalinist cleansings made horribly clear, certain nationalities were considered second-rate—proof optional. Gypsies came third. We were quite new in our role as model citizens, a bit clumsy at it, and it seemed that even a few centuries of domestication couldn't fully smother our nonconformist ways. We questioned too much, followed too little. Therefore, "trouble" and "useless" remained synonymous with "Gypsy" in a country that tooted solidarity from every slogan.

I lost most of my friends, my Gypsiness proving too much of a deterrent to their popularity, and whenever I could, I joined my parents on the road. The hectic stage life never allowed much time to dwell on school politics.

When we relocated to Los Angeles in the summer of 1990, we thought of it as another tour stop. "Here goes nothing," Dad had said when we landed at LAX, winking like he was about to set off on some grand adventure. Never mind the fact that we barely spoke English. Since I spoke more of it than the rest, I knew that in case of an emergency, the task of communicating would fall on me. The prospect hurried my steps ahead of my parents across the crowded airport. Mom's brother, my uncle Arsen, had assured us that he would wait outside to pick us up when she called him before we left Moscow. Nevertheless, we would have to make it from the gate to the passenger pickup without having to utter one English syllable.

In fifth grade, my foreign-language teacher, Ludmila Ivanovna, taught our class a traditional Scottish folk song called "My Bonnie Lies over the Ocean." She wrote the lyrics on the chalkboard, expecting us to memorize them. Ever since then I had been obsessed with the English language, which sounded like spoken silk to me. For my eleventh birthday, I had asked my parents for a Russian-English dictionary, and I read it like a novel, though I didn't understand most of it.

But now that I had a chance to practice what I'd learned, I couldn't remember a single word. It didn't help that once outside we discovered that Uncle was not there. An hour later, at one forty-five in the morning, we were still waiting. Roxy slept slumped over the mountain of our belongings: canvas bags and leather suitcases.

Thanks to an entire can of hair spray, Mom's hair, also styled in the Lioness, didn't move at all as she paced the sidewalk and peered into every passing car.

"Should I call them? Maybe they got the dates mixed up."

"We'll hail a taxi." My father sat on the bench, smoking. He shook his head side to side, slowly. I couldn't see his expression from under the brim of his fedora, but I heard him whisper *"Hahs amareh khula* (May he eat shit)" in Rromanes. Like most Russian Roma, Dad's primary language was Russian. But when it came to swearing, he'd often make an inadvertent switch to the language of his ancestors, as if that somehow authenticated his complaint.

At the tail end of another hour a gargantuan vehicle dawdled to a stop in front of our bench.

Uncle Arsen lowered the passenger window and leaned out, grinning, his tall, wiry frame bent at an awkward angle, head nearly touching the ceiling.

Moments later we were speeding down the freeway, and I was amazed that even at this hour I could see into the depths of the city, thanks to its billboards and traffic. Moscow at night had the softness of a child's bedroom illuminated by a night-light. Los Angeles didn't seem like a city that would ever be caught sleeping.

"Will you help?"

My sister's question dragged me away from the car window. "What?"

"To find George Michael. Will you?"

"Go back to sleep, Roxy."

Outside, like a beacon in the dark of an unfamiliar ocean, the Fox Studios' sign shone over the freeway. It was beautiful.

"What do you think?" Uncle glanced around expectantly. "Bought it last week. It's called Cadillac Eldorado."

In Moscow, where traffic rolled down the streets like mince

out of a meat grinder, cars weren't a necessity; hop a bus or a trolley, get a taxi, or use the metro that stretched below the city in a subterranean spiderweb. Dad had bought a car mostly to transport his instruments, and it was a special occasion each time we mortals could ride in it.

"Very big," Dad volunteered, with Mom adding "Oh yes," as if they were speaking to a child.

"It sure is," Uncle said, although his shoulders had fallen in response to the thin praise.

Uncle Arsen's one-bedroom Hollywood apartment had no wallpaper—I was shocked, thinking they hadn't the money to properly finish it. Later I'd learn that the spit-up color on its naked walls had a name—eggshell white—and that most dwellings in America came with bare walls and carpets stapled to the floor.

Uncle's wife, Varvara, met us at the door with a lukewarm smile, briefly flashing discolored teeth as she attempted to hug my sister and me.

"Oh, look at you, Roxy." She smooched her lips into my sister's cheek. "So skinny, like a stick. And Oksana. Practically a woman, isn't she, Arsen?"

I remembered my aunt with thin dirty-blond hair, peering hazel eyes, and an omnipresent smile at the corners of her mouth. But three years in the States had loosened her at the waist so much that she resembled a nesting doll, the kind Russians put atop their samovars. On the other hand, my two teenage cousins hadn't changed at all. Nelly's straight blond hair and fair complexion stood in stark contrast to her younger sister's curly black mop and uninterrupted eyebrow.

We stayed up all night gossiping, reminiscing, planning—talking about everything and nothing at all. The adults gathered in the tightly furnished living room, drinking cups of Turkish coffee like it was water.

Aunt Varvara had set the kitchen table with a variety of cold dishes served in tiny crystal saucers. There was the delicious ruby-red Vinigret—a robust salad made with fresh beets, peas, and carrots tossed in grape-seed oil. A dish of homemade sauerkraut spiced the air next to a mound of shredded carrot salad sprinkled with ground walnuts and raisins. Estonian and Krakovskaya kielbasas took up the center stage like a big mama duck surrounded by her little ducklings. Though not an actual meal, the spread worked for a late-night snack when accompanied by many bottles of vodka.

Not wanting to be disrespectful, I ate, but the lack of American food sorely disappointed me. In Moscow, before McDonald's had officially opened their first Russian restaurant in the late eighties, hamburger stands had begun popping up all over the city because some entrepreneur believed that hamburgers equaled wealth. Young people loved the idea of trying something American, even if older folks disapproved of any influence from the evil place across the ocean. Not much to look at, the hamburger still signified a threat. But my friends and I gladly paid two rubles to sample the Devil's treat.

Thin buns concealed a sheet of overcooked meat smeared with some red stuff and a sliver of dehydrated pickle. It did not put fear in our hearts, and it failed to fill our stomachs. But despite its shortcomings, we devoured this poor relative of the fast-food superstar as if we'd never eaten meat and bread at the same time in our lives.

BRINGING DOWN THE WALL

At my uncle's house old habits and new converged into a patch-work of delirium. I itched to learn everything at once.

"What is this?"

"A water dispenser. And here's the ice maker."

"How come your legs are so smooth?"

"In America, girls shave their leg hairs with a razor, and their underarms, too. No one here likes to look like a yeti."

"Our pillowcases don't fit any of your pillows."

"That's because pillows here are not square like in Russia. Who makes square pillows nowadays, really! That's so seventies. Real pillows are rectangular."

When my cousins went to school, Roxy and I watched TV, enraptured by flawless women and men promising instant miracles during the advertisements. I hadn't realized how many important things our previous existence lacked.

We had owned a VCR. One had to have money to afford a VCR. Most came from Japan via the black market, and ours was a gift from a Japanese journalist who had come to stay with us for a while. Electronics equaled status; if you had them, you would never fall short of friends. But even as my parents boasted about the JVCs and the Panasonics to many close friends who appreciated all of the name brands, one huge difference set them apart from truly having it all: sixty channels of cable television.

I can't recall much of what my parents were up to during those first weeks in America. Looking back, I see their absence had a definite cause: something awful had begun brewing between them. And I either chose to ignore the signs or was too overwhelmed by pepperoni pizza and *Murder, She Wrote* to notice.

Truth be told, my parents' problems had started years before our move. Back then Dad claimed he couldn't stand Mom's drinking; this even while he drank himself. Mom insisted that he had driven her to it by cheating on her with her friends. In Moscow, they used to get into blistering fights, too wrapped up in each other to notice the destruction they were wreaking on Roxy and me.

Once when I was about twelve, I was in my bedroom, reading Russian fairy tales and waiting for my parents to stop wishing each other dead. Earlier I had made a mistake of coming out. Dad was chasing Mom with a butter knife. What he thought he could do with such a dull weapon, I can't say. They yelled for me to get back inside my room and shut the door, and I scampered away and tried to calm my sister down while listening to the ruckus outside. Roxy kept crying, and it was well past midnight when I finally read her to sleep in my bed. My eyes drooped, but I struggled to stay awake in case I needed to call an ambulance. A terrifying silence fell and I sneaked out to make sure no one was dead, tiptoeing on the freezing parquet floor down the hallway toward the only source of light streaming from the living room. My heart galloped ahead of me. I heard voices coming from behind the cracked living-room door, and I peeked around it.

Mom was sitting in a chair with Dad kneeling in front of her, the butter knife still in his hand. They were both crying.

"Don't you know I love you," he said. "Why do you torment me like this? Don't you know how much I love you?"

Mom didn't say a thing. Just curled her fingers in his hair and sobbed.

I felt like an intruder, but after I ran back to my bed I fell asleep within moments; I had heard my father's words, and I believed in their truth. The memory of that night had always made me think that we would be okay, even in America.

But I was wrong. One day we were an immigrant army of four, ready to take on Hollywood; the next, my parents were lashing out at each other with accusations of infidelity and abuse.

"Don't lie to these girls, Nora. I never planned on staying with you." My father had a booming voice. "You're nothing to me."

Mother's hands flew to her hips, her eyes enraged and glassy. "I'd like to know where you plan on going, then. Where? Where will you go?"

"Oh, I'll be taken care of."

Mom halted as if she'd swallowed too much water and was about to choke. And then the words tipped over. "If it weren't for my brother sending that visa you'd be playing Moscow clubs with your drunken buddies—"

"Your brother didn't want us here. I know that's why he left out that paper. They've always been jealous of us, your brother and his wife. It'd make them deliriously happy had we been denied the entry and stayed to rot back in Russia, waiting for them to bless us with their packages of American crap. That's what they wanted."

Out of the corner of my eye I saw my aunt hiding behind a potted fern while she punched a number (probably Uncle's at work) into the kitchen phone.

"You should be thankful," Mom continued as if he hadn't said a word, "that I brought you here, that I didn't leave you after the shit you'd put me through all these years."

My father exploded. "Thankful? You were a nobody, *derevnia* (country bumpkin). I showed you the world, gave you the opportunity to work onstage. I could've had any woman. They lined up, one knockout after another."

"Oh, I see now. The only reason you came with me was to bring your slut to the States. Is that it? Why didn't you just stay with her?"

"She's more of a woman than you'll ever be. Look at you. You're nothing but skin and bones!"

"I should've run away from every one of you when I had the chance," Mom shouted, and I knew that if someone didn't intervene soon, my parents would start throwing things. That's what happened once Mom grouped all of us into one category. Suddenly she wasn't fighting just Dad but the entire population of the world, her children included.

"I gave you all my life, my youth."

"Stop the melodrama. What about *my* life?"

"The girls are going to hate you for this."

"You've made sure they already do with all your bad-mouthing."

I couldn't take it any longer and burst into the living room. Wasn't there any love left between them?

"Will you guys stop? Split or make up, but stop yelling. Talk like normal people, so you can hear each other for once."

Dad's face turned redder than it already was. "Unless you can stop your mother from harassing me, I have no use for you."

"Don't call our daughter useless."

"With you as her mother . . ." Dad shrugged.

I stood in between them, confused; it was difficult to tell if the argument had something to do with me now or if my parents threw my name in to piss each other off. All I remember is that with each day, their arguments intensified, and consumed everybody around them.

Apprehension pulled at Roxy and me like rubber cement. Had our family really traveled all this way just to lose one another?

CROSSFIRE

We had been in America for two months when a recurring dream of drowning in a churning black ocean began to chase sweat down my back at least once a week. I flailed in the howling charred waves, skyscraper-size with ashen tips foaming, but I always woke before the ocean claimed me.

A very bad sign.

One morning Roxy and I woke up and Dad was gone.

"Where did Papa go?" Roxy asked, rubbing her eyes and climbing on Mom's lap.

"Good morning, *sladkaya* (sweet)," Mom said.

I said nothing. A few minutes earlier, I found a pile of photographs in the garbage can under the sink. I picked up one of Mom, Dad, and me taken in a studio when I was three. We were dressed up, our hair all the same length, just above the shoulders, and I was holding a stuffed rabbit in my hands. I think I was smiling in that picture, but I couldn't tell. Dad had cut out my head along with Mom's.

Not long after, Aunt Varvara demanded we leave her house.

Aunt Varvara was the only woman I'd ever known whose brows

furrowed even when she was playing patty-cake, but still, until the day she ordered my uncle to fetch an apartment guide from the gas station a few blocks away, I loved her. The rest of the world might not have seen past her brusque exterior, but as a kid I listened to her recite children's rhymes from memory, convinced that she was a fairy with the power to bring them to life.

When Uncle came back, he tossed the magazine on the table and walked out of the house again, mumbling, "I don't want to get involved in women's business."

Even years after the incident, the two women kept the reasons behind the falling-out to themselves, but it must've been something worse than cancer or world hunger, because within a few days Mom, Roxy, and I were gone.

My sister and I had expected our movie-star mansion at last. But when I saw the building and the neighborhood that was to be our new home, I almost dropped my canvas bag of clothes. Lexington Avenue was more concrete than grass. More sickly palm trees and dilapidated housing than the expected year-round California perfection. It looked as if a hurricane had barged through and no one had bothered to pick up. Our first American apartment was located on the second floor of a very noisy complex, a two-story dove-gray structure with a gated pool shaped like a cashew in the middle of a cement courtyard. Music spilled out of the windows, unfamiliar melodies bouncing off one another in decidedly non-American flight. Bars covered the windows, and graffiti crawled in bold strokes along the walls. I told my mother I had never imagined living somewhere identical to Butyrskaya Tyurma (Butyrka Prison) back in Moscow. "At least it has a roof," my mother said as she squeezed my shoulder and bravely passed through the front gates.

Uncle Arsen had arranged for the deposit and first month's rent. He hardly said a word as he helped carry the suitcases up the stairs. Mom unlocked the door and swung it open so that he could walk inside without bumping into her, which he did with tight lips and long strides. He dropped our things in the corner and went back to his car for more.

"Is Uncle gonna help hang my posters?" Roxy asked. Once inside she had immediately unzipped her bag and pulled out the rolls of George Michael posters she had brought from Moscow.

"No," Mom said.

"But why? He's a boy and you said only grown boys like Papa are allowed to touch nails and hammers and Papa's not here and when Uncle leaves who'll hang them then?"

Mom stood over the threshold peering into the courtyard.

"He's not a grown boy yet," she said.

Uncle left with a soft "Bye" and a softer "Sorry."

I almost immediately caught my little sister trying to grab a cockroach in the palms of her hands. "Ew, Roxy, let it go!" I shouted. The creature dashed in crazy zigzags toward the fridge, disappearing under it.

After the initial shock and much frenzied clothes-shaking and closet-inspecting, we finally felt safe enough to hang up our things and put away the linens. We tried to make it a home over the next several days, all the while wondering if we had actually moved to Los Angeles or had somehow landed in a third-world country.

Despite my anger at the way we'd been treated, my yearning for friends brought me back to my cousins' house. Basically I chose to ignore the tendency that life has to cuff you in the face. I would walk the four blocks between our places almost every weekend, expecting Aida or Nelly to be as I remembered them, but they never answered the door even if I could see them tiptoeing behind the curtains.

Once Aunt Varvara actually opened the door and thrust a

plastic bag at me. "Here," she said. "I don't want anything of your *alcgolichka* (alcoholic) mother's in my house."

I obediently brought the bag home. When Mom opened it, I saw the silver coffee set she had given Aunt as a gift upon our arrival. She had to pay the customs officer a nice sum for letting it pass the gate. Mom stuffed the set back in the bag, hands shaking. "Take it back and tell her it was a gift."

I did, three more times: a reluctant messenger caught between two emotionally charged alphas.

"I said I don't want it." Aunt Varvara's slitted eyes narrowed at me. She took up most of the love seat. Cousin Aida came into the room and somehow managed to squeeze in next to her mother. Aida used to read during her meals. Growing up, I thought it was a sign of great wisdom. That day, I felt sure that she'd talk sense into both our mothers. Then she put on her best foo dog grimace, and I blanched.

Aunt ordered for me to sit down and folded her meaty arms across her meatier chest.

"We have allowed you into our home, found you a place to live, done everything to make you comfortable. Tell me, why is your mother so ungrateful? Does she think just because she's family it's okay to bring her problems here?"

Her words froze my insides. "What are you talking about?"

"Don't act stupid, Oksana. I shouldn't be surprised, now, should I? That's what your mother gets for marrying a Gypsy. Did you know we had to keep him secret from our friends? For years! She didn't really believe they would have a normal life together, did she? Arsen was right not to want you people here in America, with us. He warned me you'd be trouble."

A cold weight pressed down at my heart. Had my father been right about Uncle Arsen intentionally leaving out the most important document in the visa application? Aunt Varvara went on.

"They thought because they lived in Moscow, and because they were artists"—this last she spit out like bad tobacco—"that made them better than us. But because your mother knew all these important people didn't make her better than us. We actually had to work for a living!"

"But you never worked," I almost pointed out, then decided this was unwise.

"I told Arsen not to send that visa. I knew you'd be a burden, an embarrassment! We can barely make it here as it is without more people to take care of."

Aida, my cousin, my friend from childhood, and the one person I believed to be unshakably good, said, "Grandmother took such good care of you half-breeds when your spoiled parents went off on their tours. She made sure you got the best caviar and the biggest birthday parties. But we are her grandkids, too." Her eyes shot resentment. "Didn't we deserve caviar, Oksana?"

Grandma Rose, a matriarch of my mother's family, had risen above poverty after being orphaned at the age of three and became a successful accountant. She had made one great mistake in her life: she had allowed her kids to think she owed them something. Every time one of them found themselves in trouble, Grandma came to their rescue. With time, they grew to expect it.

If it were up to Grandpa Andrei, my dad's father and the manager of the troupe, kids would never be permitted on the long tours that took the performers all over the fifteen republics; but most of the performers had no one to leave the kids with, and Grandpa grudgingly gave in only when he had to. For this reason, Mom sometimes had me stay with Grandma Rose in the small Armenian town of Kirovakan.

I remember only one birthday party from my entire childhood. I was turning five and Grandma had made me a dress with an orange-pink satin bodice and a tulle tutu so huge I couldn't see my feet over its starched skirt. It made me look like a blooming marigold. I remember the barbecue fires infusing the air with the aroma of grilled beef and lamb, tables creaking under the weight of food: trays of *horovatz* (barbecue), pickled vegetables, dolma with garlic sauce, crusty *matnakash* (bread), crystal bowls full of walnuts and raisins, and sweet rolls called *gatah*. A crowd of guests, including my aunts and uncles and cousins, lifted their wineglasses to my health and happiness, and Armenian music rose and fell in a rhythmical lilt of *duduk* (Armenian oboe) and drums. And I clearly remember twirling around the dance floor until my head spun. I love my grandmother for that memory.

Years later, when I retold the events of that horrible day at Aunt Varvara's to her, Grandma Rose laughed, her plump middle shaking, and said, "For goodness' sake! I fed you so much caviar because your optometrist had said it would help with your vision problems." I was born with a condition that rendered my left eye nearly blind. The doctor had thought that caviar and carrots could remedy that, and although I loved eating both, that eye, to this day, is there only for decorative purposes.

Now, when I replay that scene at Uncle's, I come up with all the right things to say, but back then, I just stuttered.

Only when I stepped into the blinding sunlight did I allow myself to cry. By the time I took the steps up to our apartment, I had a migraine and my nose ran like an open faucet.

Mom met me at the door, her eyes searching for the bag of silver. "Did she keep it this time?"

"I threw it away in an alley."

"*Gospodi* (my God), Oksana! That set was nearly two hundred years old. What . . ." She saw my face. "You look sick. What's the matter?"

Mom held me while I tried to tell her what happened.

Although Uncle and Aunt never openly admitted that they

didn't want us in America, they did try, indirectly at least, to stop us from coming. Was the Gypsy side of us so unbearable that they would find any reason to dismiss us with such ease? At fifteen, I assumed that was it, even while it confused me. For the longest time I tried to solve the riddle of that day's events, but I'm no Indiana Jones. One day I gave up.

It was the last time I knocked on my aunt and uncle's door.

SURVIVING AMERICA

We didn't own much furniture: a rickety kitchen table with chairs, two cots, and two small couches Uncle had bought for us from a furniture warehouse downtown. At first I'd thought he did it out of guilt, but then I learned Mom had to pay him back as soon as she could.

Our father had disappeared, and all Roxy and I knew was that he'd gone to Russia for something our mother avoided discussing but cursed about whenever she vacuumed the couch cushions.

"That's why he wanted to come to America so bad," she'd say. "Used me, used my brother. *Babnik* (skirt chaser) arranging his own fresh start, is he now? *Shtob on provalilsya* (May the earth swallow him up). *Shtob on sgorel* (May he burn). *Shtob on sdokh* (May he drop dead)!"

I was glad Mom had her cushions to vacuum, and the floor-to-ceiling living-room window to keep washing, and the fridge decorated with Roxy's drawings to clean out daily. I was glad, because all the activity kept her from blurting out the truth about Dad that I wasn't ready to hear.

Often in those first few weeks, I felt an unsettling tug of

nostalgia—for Dad and, incredibly, for Russia. I'd started a journal, using one of the two graph-paper notebooks Mom had
brought over. On its cover I wrote "Journal Number 2"; I'd left the
first one with my Romani cousin Zhanna, daughter of my dad's
sister back in Moscow, imprisoned at the bottom of her dresser
until I decided what to do with it. It contained the old life, and
I wasn't sure how much of it I wanted to bring over.

Zhanna was the only person I trusted not to read it because
she'd lived most of the events mentioned in its pages along with
me. We were the same age and spent a lot of time together during
concert tours.

Once we boarded the train to Estonia in the middle of the
night, twenty-five of Grandfather's musicians and their families
stuffed canned-food-style into the last three cars. When the ticket
agent at the Moscow central station found she was dealing with
Gypsies, all the good tickets mysteriously sold out. We were stuck
riding in the back, where everything swerved and rattled and
swayed from side to side like a shark's tail.

Inside our private car I fell asleep to the mechanical heartbeat
under my ear. Say what you will, but a train is an insomniac's
paradise. You can complain about the drafts and the sheets with
stains as old as the Kremlin, but once your head hits that pillow,
the train song reaches for you.

The only reason I woke up early the next morning was
Zhanna's voice outside our compartment door. On the bunk
above, my father snored in harmony with the train, and Mom was
already up and making her rounds. As the band's administrator,
she was a mother hen to twenty-five fully grown adults.

I slid open the door.

"And then you cut up the goat balls and add them to the salad,"
Zhanna was saying.

"Is that so?" The conductor was a woman shaped like a barrel with two sacks of flour hanging off the front. She stood with her hands behind her back and did her best to sound nice, but I could tell she was ready to find Zhanna's parents and lecture them on how to raise a proper little girl.

"Yes," Zhanna continued, and nodded to me for support. Her golden hair gleamed in the sunlight. "But you have to make sure they're fresh, not shrively. That'd be disgusting." She made a face.

"Little girl. Your language is inappropriate and you shouldn't make up such stories."

"But I'm not, am I, Oksana? Don't our parents make goat-ball salad all the time?"

At eight years old I was looking into the mischievous eyes of a best friend. I puckered my brows at the barrel woman.

"All the time. Goat, sheep, even ferret balls." The conductor cringed. "They're a delicacy all over the world. Even in Italy."

In a Russian's eyes, especially a Russian woman's, Italians are gods. "Girls, you are horrible . . . But really?"

We nodded in unison.

"How do the Italians eat them?"

Zhanna's expression was innocent, clean of doubt, even though her mom had stepped out of their compartment and seconds remained before she came to investigate and we got punished for the rest of the tour. "With spaghetti sauce, of course."

The pain of missing my cousin was so tangible I felt like I could quite possibly extract it with tweezers, like a splinter of glass, had I been able to reach that deep inside myself. To ease the longing, I figured I should create a list of things I missed about Russia and then one of everything I didn't. Lack of sanitary napkins and tampons, for example. (We used to have to wrap gauze around bulky wads of cotton, which was responsible for a number of bloodstained skirts and pants. Also, it made you walk like you'd spent one too many days in the saddle.)

Me, Aunt Laura, and Zhanna in Moscow, 1988

I never thought I'd be homesick for a place I had been eager to leave, but the oddest things went into the "missed" column: the soothing glow from the rose-patterned lampshades of our Moscow living room, and the irritable cat we left behind, named after Michael Jackson. I missed the mashed potatoes Dad used to make, the ones I refused to eat because of the lumps, and the way my mother's Climat perfume lingered in our house for hours after she'd left for a business meeting. Surprisingly, I also missed the snow. Blended with the scent of the freshly cut fir trees huddled behind FOR SALE signs near metro stations, the snow smelled like Christmas.

Moscow snow, though, reminded me bitterly of my first school fight. A month after Aleksey Moruskin pinned the Gyp sign to my back, he sidled up during the sixth-grade school party and asked me to dance.

"No," I said, suspicious of his motives.

Nastya saw the exchange and rolled toward us, knocking people aside like a bowling ball.

"You Gypsy skunk," she shouted. "Why don't you go back to

begging with your folks at the train station instead of stealing our boys?"

"Don't call me that."

"What? Gypsy or skunk?"

"Say it again and you'll be sorry," I said.

"Let's see you try."

We made arrangements to meet behind the school in ten minutes. Like a duelist with star power, Nastya brought an entourage of six girls. I waited alone, the winter night biting my skin. Nastya and I stood ten feet apart, our breathing already uneven. The girls cheered louder and, spurred by their enthusiasm, Nastya and I rushed at each other. She slapped my face, and the pain bit harder than the cold. I wished she'd used her fist, because that seemed less degrading. The girls' voices flocked into the black sky. Nastya landed another one on my face, and then, as if possessed, I roared and punched her in the middle of the chest. She fell in the snow, gulping for air.

The girls circled their friend, helping her stand as she pressed her hands to her breast. Panic rounded her features into a caricature of herself.

I took a step closer, my ears loud with the beginnings of hysteria. I didn't want Nastya to die.

"Get her!" someone screamed.

I tore across the field behind the school, sinking deeper in the snow with each step and my lungs burning hot. When I finally crossed the field, I sprinted home, but they caught up before I rounded the last corner.

One of them yanked me back by my coat and shoved me forward face-first onto the ice-covered sidewalk. I rolled over and lay there stunned, surrounded by my classmates.

"Well?" Nastya said, peering at me. "Did you girls see how she almost snatched Aleksey as soon as I wasn't looking? That's what Gypsy whores do, because they start having sex at like ten and then they can't stop."

"My mom said they grow boobs and curly hairs faster than normal people," one of the others volunteered.

Nastya leaned down. "Not so fast now, are you?"

"You can have your fat Aleksey," I spit out, rising as the cold from the ground fizzed into my bones. The night grew darker, even the streetlamps seeming to fade.

"She's bleeding!"

They were gone as the blood crept down my face and over my eyes.

At home, Mom pressed bandages soaked in hydrogen peroxide to the cut several inches above my hairline while Dad demanded to know what happened.

"I fell down," I said.

"You were walking and suddenly fell down?"

"Leave her alone," Mom said. "Be useful and fetch that chocolate bar from the fridge." She had read in a scientific journal that eating chocolate helped the body produce more blood.

"Are you out of your mind, woman? She's going to have a scar. I want to know how she fell down, that's what I want to know."

Mom dabbed iodine around the cut, and I leaned my head into her hands, a bit dizzy.

"We should call the ambulance?" Dad hovered, trying unsuccessfully to make me talk, but I was afraid that the truth would drive him to Nastya's parents' doorstep. Dad had experienced his share of racial confrontations, which usually ended with something straight out of *Romeo and Juliet*, with his cousins and friends going after the offender, who in turn recruited his own family to battle the mad Gypsies.

I hadn't missed my family's frequent thespian adventures, and like an old woman I now wanted only peace and a certain amount of predictability.

I wasn't the only one adjusting. My newly single mother moved about the apartment with restlessness and unease. Still, she laughed and joked with us, and made sure to cook our favorite meals, like the eggs over easy with tomato slices for breakfast, or *pelmeni*, Siberian dumplings, for dinner. Only sometimes did I glimpse the pain living behind her eyes.

Since we didn't have a TV, a clock radio served as entertainment.

"Is that Eagles?" Mom exclaimed if a good song came on. "Ooh, turn it up. That's a great song. 'Velkom too khotelle Caaaaalifornya. Soshalovah playz, soshalovah playz.'"

"Mama. Those aren't the words," I'd tell her. "It's 'such a lovap ace, such a lovap ace.'"

"Oh, what do you know? I performed this onstage millions of times." And she'd continue singing in her scratchy alto as she filed her nails or put away the dishes while I rolled my eyes at her horrifying accent, relieved that no one but Roxy and I were around to hear it.

Mom had indeed sung that song before, though probably in even worse English. When my parents toured the Soviet Union back in the seventies and eighties, their repertoire had consisted largely of Soviet and Romani songs. Everything else, especially American music, had been banned from concert halls ever since I could remember. But my parents and a couple of the younger ensemble members shared a passion for rock and roll, and managed to sneak away to gig the underground clubs, where the managers took bribes in exchange for silence.

Only a year before, Dad had attempted to jot down the lyrics of "Dancing Queen." In the kitchen of our Moscow house, he stopped the tape and rewound a single line over and over until he could somewhat decipher the words screeching out of his boom box. As neither of my parents spoke English then, the lyrics they performed were usually a nonsensical jumble. But the public loved it anyway and sang along with enthusiasm.

Youkondanz. Youkonjyiy
Haveeng ze tyne ofur lie
Ooh see zegyol, watchatseen
Diging ze donseekveen

There was the ever present risk of someone ratting the place out to the officials; the possibility created an atmosphere of nervous excitement. Perhaps that was why Soviets drank as if celebrating their last day of freedom.

I remember watching from a table in the back on many occasions, my parents crammed on a tiny stage of some dive along with the drummer, the bassist, and the equipment. The musicians regularly complained about everything: the location, the acoustics, especially about the drunks who climbed onto the stage in an attempt to grab Mom's mike and sing along. But they always found more illicit places to play.

Dad and the other guys wore wing-collared polyester shirts and bell-bottom pants, giving the eighties the finger. They played as if there were no audience, tweaking their sound during songs and making appreciative signs at one another by tossing their manes whenever a particularly juicy chord change occurred. But Mom had more fashion sense: her custom-made dresses were enhanced with patterns of sequins she'd carefully sewn on herself. And she had more people sense, too. When she sang, each person believed she sang for them. There was always at least one lush who'd ask Mom to run away with him or to marry him, and she'd let him know that she was flattered but that she'd done both already and no, thank you, but please you must come see another show.

At school, I bragged that I knew the lyrics to many pop songs by heart, and some kids, despite my Gyp status, begged me to write them down. When asked to translate, I'd improvise. Anything to keep them talking to me. Elton John's "I'm Still Standing" was a tale of a heartbroken man lost in a country of joyful people in vibrant leotards, and Queen's "I Want to Break Free" was about women finally getting fed up with housework.

Russia had plenty of great music of its own, but the bulk of the Soviet music on the radio eulogized our country and its working class. There was an immense difference between the Soviet formula and the Russian. Even Soviet love songs were first and foremost propaganda, ballads of metalworkers or farmers who loved their country first and each other second. But there also was another, more authentic community of incredible poets and songwriters who barely got any radio play because they weren't Soviet enough. People like Vladimir Vysotsky, a Russian bard who'd reached amazing underground popularity in the sixties and seventies, despite strict censorship.

Vysotsky sang of politics and love with equal passion, his voice leaving you bleeding for either freedom or kisses. His words eventually got him killed because they made people restless to see change. Some people maintained that he died of a heart attack, while others suggested drug abuse, but my parents, along with many other artists of the time, claimed to know better. To this day, his death remains shrouded in controversy.

Growing up, I never fully grasped the amount of danger that surrounded my family. Their overly progressive political views put them on the secret police's radar more than once, and only money and connections kept them out of the interrogation cells. We lived under a strict regime, but I was too young to comprehend what that meant. To me the Soviet government was inside the pages of my history book, in small print and not very interesting. My parents had a good friend, Albert, who was a doctor by profession. He was also an "extrasense," a kind of psychic with an ability to diagnose patients by running his hands over their bodies, like an X-ray.

Albert's skill was considered witchcraft and therefore was illegal. Still, people sought him out. A year before we moved to America, his body was found floating in the Moscow River. Soviets didn't advertise their special abilities or anything that could be labeled unpatriotic lest they end up like Albert.

I heard stories like Albert's often enough that I began to wonder if this was the reason people hid themselves inside luggage in the cargo bays of planes to get out of the USSR.

Dad relentlessly and foolishly clashed with the Soviet government. So did Mom, by association. Once, Dad spent a night inside a *militzia* interrogation room for calling the director of the Ministry of Culture *khren morzhoviy*, or walrus dick. As always Mom came to his rescue with bribes. Our house was searched, attic to basement, for American propaganda after an anonymous "good" citizen tipped off the secret police about having seen my parents receive suspicious-looking packages from America, which turned out to be nothing but my uncle's presents.

But my parents managed to navigate the political circus of the time without letting Roxy or me feel the threat. Thanks to Mom, we were now far away from it all. And though our present circumstances screamed downer, one thing I knew for sure: Mom had survived the Soviet Union, and she would survive America, too.

WHEN IN DOUBT, COOK!

Roxy, as could be expected from a nine-year-old, seemed oblivious to our predicament. She made friends with most of the Hispanic kids playing in the courtyard with no regard for the language barrier. One day she was sitting on the stairs watching the kids cannonball into the pool, the next she was getting into trouble for splashing pool water at the neighbors' windows right along with them.

She knew where everyone lived and what kind of food they had in their fridge, and soon the neighbors started to send gifts back with her: a basket of a sweet bread called *pan dulce* or a plate of homemade enchiladas. At first, Mom was wary of eating things prepared by strangers. In her mind it was "stuff that looks like food but is made entirely of millions of germs from un-washed hands." But she eventually grew too curious. She'd often pick the food apart to see how it was made and then try to make it herself.

Roxy's chirpy mood bounded in counterpoint to my own. We were surrounded by foreigners like ourselves. Where had the Americans gone? Sometimes I braved the world outside the gate to see if I could spot one. Little by little, I wandered farther until I found the DollarDream Market, a convenience store owned by two Hindu brothers. Their parents, Raj and Shubi, spoke as little English as I did, but they always grinned. They ran the business, but their only responsibilities seemed to be ringing up customers while always keeping one eye on the Bollywood musicals blasting from their TV.

I strolled through the aisles, amazed at the crowded shelves and the abundance of products made in China. I began to notice things I'd seen before, inside the packages Uncle Arsen sent when we lived in Moscow.

Every time I'd gotten a package from Los Angeles, I gained new friends. They loved the gum that came in crinkly, see-through wrappers, and the shiny hair clips with Disney characters. I had clothes with Michael Jackson and Elvis and Marilyn on them. For my seventh birthday, Uncle sent me the "Thriller" jacket, like the one in the video, red with black stripes. My friends drooled over it. Having an entrepreneurial spirit, I took reservations for the privilege of wearing it and charged ten kopeks a day.

Inside the DollarDream those gumballs sold at ten per dollar, and the hair clips inside the giant buckets by the cash register were a mere quarter each. There were the three-dollar watches with grinning Mickey Mouse dials, and the celebrity T-shirts, a bargain at three for ten dollars.

Had everything Uncle ever sent us from America come from the DollarDream Market? Later I discovered that wasn't so. The "Thriller" jacket was from a swap meet two blocks up. As an expert bargainer you could get it for twenty bucks.

When I told Mom, she didn't seem surprised. "It's the effort that counts, not the cost of things."

I remembered with how much care Mom had wrapped the antique tea service in terry-cloth towels and crumpled-up newspaper, the fight she put up when the Soviet customs officer fussed over it. "Why didn't you bring a couple of *matryoshka* dolls for Aunt Varvara, then?"

"That would've offended her," she said, "and I have more class than that."

I'd learned long ago that food is a beautiful language.

When my parents first got married, Grandma Ksenia, dad's mom, hated my mother, and she measured that feeling with food. In Romani culture, multiple generations live together, and for a long time Mom found herself under a hostile roof. Ksenia avoided her daughter-in-law, refusing to eat at the same table with her. (To be fair, she scoffed at eating with the rest of the band when touring, always requesting a tray of food be delivered to her dressing room.) If they saw each other by chance around the house, she'd say things like "You're getting fat. I'm not here to support a leech, so make sure to stay away from my pantry."

During the first months my parents were together, Dad often sneaked sandwiches into the bedroom. In the morning, Grandma often noticed the missing loaf of rye or the pitcher of milk half full, and she never hesitated to comment on it. Mom's solution was to start cooking for herself. The first time she made *kotleti* Armenian-style, with lots of onions, potatoes, and dried basil in the minced beef, the aroma beckoned Grandma into the kitchen. The second time, Grandma waited until my parents had left for a show before swiping a *kotleti*. The third, she said, "How do you make them so juicy?" It took years for Mom and Grandma to get along, but the first step was made over a plate of savory minced beef.

My favorite of Mom's dishes was *tort-salat*, or cake-salad in English: a salad composed like a layer cake. Every time Mom made it, I'd be in the kitchen. Mom never used cookbooks or written recipes, and she eyeballed the ingredient portions and estimated the cooking times.

"Mom," I'd say, "let me make *tort-salat* this time. Write down the steps and I'll follow."

She'd hardly look up from her cooking, hovering like an alchemist over potions. "The best way to learn is by observing the cook."

But that proved more frustrating than not knowing. When asked how many potatoes to use in *podzharka*, Russian beef stew, she'd say, "Enough to last four people two days, because it's always best the day after you make it."

"When do I place the chicken into the frying pan?"

"Not until the melting butter stops hissing at you."

"How do I know when the borscht is done?"

"When it smells done."

Mom picked up many of her cooking skills on the road from other Romani women, and maybe that's why her methods seemed so chaotic. Soviet hotels didn't come furnished with kitchenettes, and no performer could afford to eat out while on the road for six months at a stretch. Even if we had the means, restaurant fare in most of the towns we played would make a dog puke. But cooking in hotel rooms was strictly forbidden. I remember Esmeralda, Zhanna's older half sister, hurling a perfectly good pot of chicken and potatoes out the hotel-room window while the hotel manager banged on the door, shouting, "I smell meat!" As she passed me on her way to the door, Esmeralda pressed a finger to my lips and pinched my cheek. "Our secret, okay?" She opened it, relaxing her curvy figure against the doorframe like a star of the silver screen. The manager's Brezhnev-like eyebrows unfurrowed, but his nostrils flared as he tried to sneak a look past her shoulder.

Like Esmeralda, the women in the band hid hot plates in their luggage; a single burner and a pot was all they needed to throw together mouthwatering dishes. And they made quick work of it. Onions had to be chopped with mad speed, eggs fried until just runny, toast buttered and swallowed before we were discovered. Mom and I spent many an afternoon watching some Romani do her magic over a tiny electric stove. In fact, it was the reason I'd started keeping a journal in the first place.

I was nine and my first entry described the way Esmeralda made tea and how she'd managed to turn the brewing process into a magical spell.

"To make proper *zavarka* (essence), you need five tablespoons of loose-leaf Ceylon tea in a white teapot." The leaves formed into mountains as she measured them out. "Then, hot water to just below the spout." After this step, she'd fetch a tall heatproof glass and fill it halfway with the essence, pour the liquid back into the pot, and repeat it thirteen times.

"What are you doing now?" I asked.

"Marrying the essence with the water," she explained. "If you want to catch a good man, pay attention."

"Oh, is this how everybody does it?"

"Smart women do whatever's necessary. It's simple. The leaves won't infuse the water if both are standing still and not putting effort into it. Leaves by nature are lazy, and water's too proud. So you, the tea-maker, help by creating motion between them. Every time you pour from one vessel to the other, the liquid gets stronger, richer. That's what every relationship needs."

"Strong-smelling tea?"

Esmeralda tousled my hair. "How much sugar?"

"Three lumps. So why do it thirteen times? Is that like a magic number?"

"It's *my* magic number. You'll have to find your own."

For a while I'd stopped adding new recipes to my collection.

Other matters, like getting used to living without a father and learning to answer the phone in English, took precedence. But in my mother's tiny L.A. kitchen, I started up the old habit, finding its familiarity comforting.

According to my notes, the first step to making *tort-salat* was to boil some beef the same way you would if making beef broth. Mom would then put it through a meat grinder she'd purchased at the local Russian market. At the same time, she'd cook eggs, carrots, beets, and potatoes in water until they were soft but not soggy, and then grate them. Next, she'd start building the salad: a layer of potatoes, followed by a layer of beef, eggs, and the rest of the vegetables. A little mayonnaise, spread between each layer, kept everything moist. Mom would repeat the process several more times, and sprinkle some grated cold butter and a generous amount of parsley, dill, and cilantro on top.

I'd been known to eat *tort-salat* every day for breakfast, lunch, and dinner, so Mom always made extra, or guarded it from me if guests were coming.

During those first months in America, we found solace in the familiar foods or in the songs Mom sang under her breath, many of them centuries-old Armenian melodies.

Ov, sirun, sirun. Inchu motezar?
Sertis gahtnike inchu imatsar?
Mi unmech sirov, yes kes siretzi
Isk do anyraf davachanetsir.

Oh, my beautiful. Why did you come near?
Secrets of my heart, just how did you hear?
With an innocent love, I have fallen for you
Shamelessly betrayed, your love so untrue.

We often sat on our cots and read out loud from the books we'd brought with us. Mom's sister, Aunt Siranoosh, lived in Kirovakan with Grandma Rose, and the walls of their living room hid behind enormous bookshelves stuffed with classics, large and leather-bound and intimidating. Aunt Siranoosh used to send me parcels of books from her collection a couple of times a year.

I'd brought several of them with me to L.A. *Alexander der Grosse*, by Fritz Schachermeyr, read like an epic adventure of courage, something we needed now. Every time I reached the part when Alexander tamed Bucephalus, his legendary horse, Roxy would exclaim, "Victory!" and shake her fists in the air.

Our neighborhood looked and felt nothing like the America from my father's friend Vova's stories, with houses the size of Iceland and flower beds that bloomed year-round. But maybe this was how people started out before they got their dream. Maybe living in a dump, on a street with cracked pavement and skeletons of cars, made them tough and ready for all that glory they would experience later. I felt determined to find out.

RUNNING AWAY

Most Romani don't give a rat's ass about fitting in. Instead, they shape the world around them, bend it like a spoon. But it mattered to me, and it mattered to my mother even more. Once in America, she wanted nothing to do with her Romani past, which had been anything but typical. For Roxy and me, she envisioned a more conventional future, and soon after Dad left, she developed but one goal in addition to having the most spotless apartment in our building: finding wealthy American husbands for her two girls. Like any devoted immigrant mother, she suffered for the sake of her offspring. "You are Americans now," she often reminded us. "You don't need any of your father's nonsense. I didn't sacrifice my youth, my status, for you to turn out like his brood. I had more admirers than stars in the sky, decent men . . . and who did I end up with?"

"Yes, Mom," we'd say.

Mom's eyebrows would lower into dangerous angles. "I curse the day I laid eyes on your shit-eating gigolo of a father. The bastard lured me in with his guitar and smooth tongue. I won't let you two make the same mistake. You'll marry nice American doctors or lawyers."

I woke up one morning to find Mom ironing one of her dresses on an ironing board in the kitchen. In Moscow, sheets, socks, underwear, and mounds of handkerchiefs regularly underwent this treatment. The last time she ironed was when she got a call from an old friend from Moscow who wanted to let Mom know that Dad had bought two return tickets to America. One for him and another for his mistress. My father, being a real spoon bender, didn't move across the ocean to change. He knew that no matter what, he'd always be Rom, but that at least in America, nobody cared. He took his outsider status to even greater heights by getting engaged to his longtime mistress, a notorious fortune-teller with eyes the color of chimney smoke and a soul a shade darker. The day my mother heard that Dad was bringing his fiancée to the States, she steam-ironed all the curtains in our apartment.

Now she was at it again.

"Are you going somewhere?" I asked.

"When your sister wakes up, get her breakfast, don't forget. And make sure she doesn't stay at the neighbors' too long. She could eat what I cook for once."

I went to the fridge to get orange juice. The way that dress was being ironed, I figured the farther away from her, the better.

"Your father and I are getting a divorce," Mom said to the dress.

She looked up at me, and I dropped onto a kitchen chair.

"He's bringing his hussy over from Russia. I bet that's why he disappeared before we even moved out of Arsen's place. Didn't have the decency to wait."

"You've been married seventeen years."

Mom's cheeks were flushed, and she concentrated on the areas around the buttons of the dress as if she were setting a diamond into a ring. "He's running," she said. "Wish I could run, too, but I have you and your sister to look after. He's my punishment for walking out on Leonid all those years ago, I know it now. No matter. I won't let you make the same mistakes. I will keep you safe."

I don't think she would've ever told me who Leonid was if it weren't for my habit of rummaging through her dresser for money. One day in Los Angeles, I was looking for change for a pack of rubber bracelets and came across a picture, hidden beneath Mom's nightdresses, of a handsome man with blue eyes. I thought it was Montgomery Clift and took it into the kitchen, where Mom was shredding cabbages for homemade sauerkraut. Completely overlooking the fact that I wasn't supposed to be going through her things, I said, "Can I put him up on my wall?" Mom snatched the picture from my hands and gave me a halfhearted lecture on stealing. She didn't ground me, though, seeming distracted by my find. My curiosity kept me after her for weeks. Her confession shocked me.

Handsome and a well-respected member of the intelligentsia, Leonid was a music professor at a university in Krasnodar in southern Russia. He'd had the bad luck of falling in love with one of his students, who came from a well-to-do Armenian Greek family. They loved each other, my mother told me, with the tenderness and modesty one finds in old black-and-white films.

Once married, Mom left the university to avoid a scandal. Leonid built a boat as a wedding gift to her, and on the weekends they sailed the Kuban River, fishing, talking about philosophy, and planning to see the world.

The marriage lasted a year. Then a traveling Gypsy ensemble came to town, bringing my father with it.

In the USSR, art belonged to the masses. That's why our ensemble was officially called a collective or a troupe; the members worked for the government, their official job to entertain the public. Every corner of the country, no matter how isolated or poor, boasted a performing arts center where concerts, plays, and exhibits took place. But who got to perform where was up to the government. All fifteen republics had an arts branch that oversaw artist placement in their cities. An artist's reputation depended on these placements. To gig in Moscow, you had to be either brilliant or very well connected.

Leonid was appointed as the fine arts inspector in Krasnodarskiy Krai—the area between the Black and the Caspian seas. His job consisted of auditioning the hopefuls to determine the quality of their performance, and it was he who happened to audition my grandfather's ensemble.

Leonid and my mother, who often accompanied him, were standing in the hotel hallway, talking business with Andrei Kopylenko. The man was a giant, close to seven feet tall. He had a long beard, a booming voice, and piercing green eyes.

That's when my father sauntered into the frame, and as she tells it, her heart stammered. With his catlike amber eyes and long hair, he looked to her like Edmond Dantès from *The Count of Monte Cristo*. Two giggling women hung on his arms. He held a half-empty wine bottle in one hand and a seven-string guitar in the other. As he passed, his eyes ignited her, and she was lost.

That night, she tells me, I was conceived.

Mom divorced Leonid, and she and Dad got married a week after the papers came. Her relatives were in an uproar. Dad's Romani family protested his decision to marry a *gadjee*—a female outsider. Though not a common practice, some Roma men found wives outside their culture, and these women were often kept at a tense distance by the rest of the community. On the other hand, if a Romani woman married a *gadjo*, she would most likely be cut off forever and even her children would not be considered Romani. Dad's own mother, Ksenia, was Russian Greek, and she never quite gained Romani trust. Yet, instead of siding with a potential friend, she objected the loudest.

Since circumstances surrounding my conception had begun with an affair, all kinds of questions arose. The main one being, whose daughter was I, really? A question that haunted my father for a long time and Grandma Ksenia for even longer.

Grandma could've written a manual on proper diva behavior—she accomplished it with aplomb—and as divas often do, she reigned from behind the closed doors of her dressing room. To her, my slanted eyes were too . . . slanted. She speculated that, considering my mother's wanton tendencies, my real father could've been a Chukchi from eastern Siberia. The Chukchi are indigenous to the area around the Bering Sea, their isolated and nomadic lifestyle similar to that of the Eskimos. For a long while Grandma Ksenia wanted nothing to do with me.

The parallels between Mom's and Grandma Ksenia's stories are remarkable. Grandma had been eighteen when she met my grandfather in Krasnoarmeysk, Ukraine. She was a singer in an all-girl trio at a local day club, an equivalent of an American USO club. "I had followed her voice from the street," Grandpa once said, "and found a diamond to be worshipped." But her parents, a Russian schoolteacher and a Greek-born general in the Red Army, wouldn't suffer a marriage between Ksenia and a Gypsy eleven years her senior. My grandparents ended up running away together. It might sound romantic, except that the news had devastated Grandpa's wife, a full-blooded Roma named Gala, and their four kids.

My father claims that because of Grandpa's decision to marry a *gadjee* and break his Roma family, we remain forever cursed by Baba Varya, Grandpa's mother and a notorious Romani practitioner of black magic. Every misfortune to befall our clan since came as a direct result of that curse, and my father believed this so fully that in his twenties he began to dabble in an effort to find a countercurse.

"Baba Varya collected dirt from where stray cats fought," Dad once told me, "and would sprinkle a pinch inside my parents' bedsheets. They'd end up quarreling for days."

Baba Varya had once tried to poison Ksenia with a homemade *piroshki*, a stuffed fried bun, which made her vomit violently. She spent days at the hospital. Later, Grandpa asked if she'd taken any food from Baba Varya.

"Just one *piroshki*," Ksenia had said.

Grandpa had a terrible fight with his mother and ordered her to never touch the stove again.

When I heard that particular story, I couldn't help but wonder how much truth there was to the poisoned apple in *Snow White and the Seven Dwarfs*.

I don't know if Grandma Ksenia's desire for the stage eclipsed my mother's, but it must've been close, since she'd given up an easy life to hop a train with a Gypsy musician, and endured ridicule and scorn from the Roma. Her yearning must've been immense, because adventure wasn't in Grandma's nature. She had the manners of a princess, knew a fork by its course, and worked at little, preferring to have things done for her. And so she never assimilated, her talent as a singer remaining the only link to her husband's culture. She was the star, the one people came to see, and the Roma grudgingly accepted at least that.

My beautiful grandmother Ksenia

But it didn't take my mother long to gain the Roma trust. I always suspected it happened because she was so much like them.

At first, Dad wouldn't let Mom perform—despite his own promiscuities he was the jealous type and believed his new wife would benefit more from embroidering his costumes than from doing shoulder-shimmies—but eventually she coaxed him into it. Turns out, she was an average dancer, but she made every rehearsal on time and, unlike half the performers, sober. The Roma, and especially Grandpa Andrei, took notice of her tenacity and of the fact that she acted like part of the troupe. With time, Mom became the band administrator, which, considering all the trouble the members were constantly getting into, was a feat.

WAR AND NOT SO MUCH PEACE

When I was five, Dad had a run-in with a group of skinheads at a club. It all started when a man in the audience made a request for a well-known Nazi tune.

"Hey, Gypsy cock! 'Horst-Wessel-Lied' for me and my friends," he shouted across the dance floor.

"Up yours," my father said into the mike, and was promptly asked to step outside and have a smoke, which was code for "fight."

There were two others waiting in the alleyway. One in a leather jacket was ready to leap at my father, who'd pulled out a knife he always carried at his waist.

"Stop this," said a man my father hadn't noticed yet. He was short and bald. Gently he pushed the other two guys out of the way. "Don't need violence to solve this, do we, Gypsy?"

"I'm ready either way."

Shorty swung his brass-knuckled fist up into my father's jaw. The back door opened and a waiter came out carrying a bin to the Dumpster. Using that distraction, my father took off.

"They had a gun," he said later that night on our way to the hospital. I'd stubbornly climbed into the ambulance, certain Dad would die without me. Rather than make a scene, Mom climbed in next to me and we were off. Dad looked furious as the nurse tried to assess his condition, and he kept explaining to Mom that he wanted to fight, really, but was outnumbered. Ditching a fight humiliated him more than being called a "Gypsy cock." The nurse carefully tugged at his lower lip to find that his jaw had been cracked down the middle. The left side of his gum line was higher than the right, the teeth like bone stairs.

The doctors stapled Dad's jaw together and packed it with medicine and gauze. He drank soup for days, but once he had healed he went back to that club with five of his largest cousins. The Roma and the skinheads trashed the club that night, and Dad lost his gig, but that was the way of things. On the surface, the Soviet Union was a picture of order, when in reality it was ruled by gangs. Some powerful, like the KGB mafia, others of the smalltime-crook variety. Their influence depended on the city they operated in and their financiers. The Roma were no different, because if you didn't have "brothers" to watch your back, you were asking for everyone else to stab it.

The men in our band went around with daggers and guns. They knew firsthand that order could be as delicate as ice on a lake: rock-solid under your feet until a hairline flaw sent you plunging into the waters. Ironically, the *gadjee* weren't the only ones to worry about.

Like the cultures of India, considered by many Romani to be our motherland, we are still divided into castes. There's no peace between them, and many confrontations I remember were nothing more than reactions to centuries-old prejudices.

Grandpa Andrei, for example, wouldn't accept Roma artists of Hungarian descent. Tzigane, or Russian Gypsies, called them Lovari. "Lovari make trouble," he said. "Reading palms backstage after the shows." (This wasn't entirely fair, since anyone in the

Soviet Union with the knowledge of divination read fortunes when short on cash, which was most of the time.)

In turn, most Lovari considered Tzigane to have sold their souls and their culture to the Soviet government. The majority of European Roma clans considered our dialect of the Rromanes language to have been watered down by Russian, a threadbare blanket with too many holes.

Russian Roma, which include many clans of their own, are very different from the rest of the European clans, some of whom remain nomadic to this day, often because the communities they are in force them to move. The last nomadic Russian Roma settled during the seventies, when Khrushchev had ordered the building of all those neat apartments. One thing we *were* known for, even within the clans, was our music.

The majority of the Roma I grew up with were performers. Not so glamorous, considering how even the most acclaimed artists made very little money—the average monthly salary of a top-paid actor in the eighties was about 300 rubles, or 480 U.S. dollars—but everywhere they went, people shook their hands as if they were national heroes. They performed because they couldn't imagine doing anything else, knowing full well they'd never come close to the superstardom of Western celebrities. More often than not, people with serious money worked for the government. My own grandparents, who held the title of National Artists of the USSR—an equivalent of the Lifetime Achievement Award in the States—fared better than most, but they also saved every *kopeika*.

To the European Roma, we were court jesters, doormats, quacks, but the mainstream society still considered us feral despite our polite handshakes. At the first sign of trouble the old stereotypes reappeared.

I recall one particularly explosive brawl between the band

members and a group of taxi drivers in front of a Moscow train station. (Soviet *taxisty* had the look and the punch of your best mixed martial arts fighters, and they were also one of the biggest mafias around.) When I asked my father what had started the fight, he claimed, "One of the assholes called Stepan a shit-eating Gypsy invalid. I couldn't stand by and do nothing."

Dad and Stepan knew each other from the postwar streets of Kiev, back when they ran with a gang of Ukrainian kids, searching for food like the rest of the half-starved population. Once, Stepan dug up a can of food that turned out to be a grenade, which exploded, blowing away half his hand. Despite the injury, he became a virtuoso guitar player.

All I remember of that evening, besides the Russian fur hats called *ushanka* flying in the air and men rolling in mud-smeared snow, is Mom sneaking hundred-ruble bills to the *militzia*, the Russian police, to keep the Roma boys out of jail.

When my parents' tour bus crashed into a bulldozer parked illegally on a country road one winter night, Dad spent four days in jail for thrashing the bulldozer driver, who'd decided to take a booze break in the shrubbery and had forgotten to turn on the emergency lights. The bus driver had died upon impact, and Grandma Ksenia had broken both legs. The next day, the Roma were urged by the town's administration to either take the stage or not get paid. When they did, looking like war casualties, arms in slings, faces lacerated by broken glass, the audience started to laugh. "Look! The Gypsies were fighting again!"

My mother said into the mike, "We had a terrible accident last night and lost a friend. This first song is dedicated to his memory." The subdued audience behaved for the rest of the show, and later several locals brought food and drink to the hotel where the Gypsies were staying. A peace offering at a time when food began to disappear from markets and restaurants due to one of the worst recessions the Soviets ever experienced. This act of generosity from people who might not have had a full meal in months made Mom teary-eyed, while Dad rallied the band and the unlikely guests for an all-night *vecherinka* (party).

God knows Dad needed constant supervision, otherwise he'd spend more time in jail or intensive care than onstage. And Mom was all too happy to keep rescuing him and his spirited brood, as if she thrived on pandemonium. Her flair for diplomatic magic staggered the Roma, who by nature trusted no one and whose tempers put wildfires to shame. My mother never ran out of occasions to exercise her skills.

JOURNAL NUMBER 1

Just weeks after my parents divorced, Mom resumed molding Roxy and me into Americans in case we ran into a brain surgeon or two.

The three of us were sitting on our cots one night, and Mom stroked my hair as she described her vision of my wedding.

"I'll string your hair with natural pearls, one for each strand, and you'll wear a diamond-studded gown embroidered with real golden thread. And I'll fly in our family and friends from Russia and Armenia to sit on our silk-cushioned chairs and eat escargots from our golden spoons."

Roxy, who'd been brushing Mom's hair this entire time, said, "What if her husband doesn't have enough chairs?"

"He will, because he'll adore his mother-in-law and do anything to make her happy."

Like most girls, I grew up playing house with my dolls. Every type of divination Zhanna and I tried evolved around a single question: Will I get married? We read the tarot, but most often, we used the pendulum. All we needed were a needle and a thread as long as a child's forearm. I'd hold the thread by the tip, steady, with the needle pointed at the ground. "Will I get married to the handsomest man in the world?" I'd ask, and silently beg the needle to swing in a circle, a sign for "yes."

But in America, I was no longer obsessed with marriage. I had convinced myself that I'd grow old and sprout hair on my face (like most females over fifty in my family) without a man to push my wheelchair or tweeze my chin. Truth is, I had known a boy once who owned not a single golden spoon. For him I'd have stitched a thousand wedding dresses.

Ruslan and I met on a concert tour when I was six and he nine. The ensemble had performed the last show of the evening in the Ukrainian city of Uzhgorod, and most troupe members had returned to the Hotel Friendship. It was close to eleven, but on account of a raucous poker game going on inside our room, I was able to sneak out to explore the building, which, from the outside, looked like a flying saucer.

I crept down the stairs to the second floor, and about ten feet away saw a woman beating a boy. He rolled into a fetal position as her fists flew into his ribs and face. I stood in the middle of the barely lit hallway in my pink pajamas, my feet momentarily growing roots. My parents never hit me, but I'd witnessed plenty of battles on the road, so I did what I'd seen other women do time and again.

I rushed the boy's assailant with a screech, waving my arms in the air. Shock registered on her face and that tiny reprieve gave him a chance to crawl out of reach. I grabbed hold of her arm and bit down, and the woman struggled to shake me loose. I remember still digging my fingertips into her flesh when somebody jerked me away from behind. Next thing I knew, my father had me up in his arms.

The woman hollered, "I'm bleeding!" I recognized her then. Kristina, a dancer Grandpa Andrei had recently hired.

"You'll live," my father said with a glance at the tooth marks on her forearm.

People crowded the hallway. Their voices soon rose in argument.

"You could've killed your own son," someone said. "Have you no shame?"

"He's stronger than he looks," Kristina said.

I wrapped my arms around Dad's neck, my eyes on the boy as he ran a sleeve across his nose, smearing blood over his face. He stood, one hand on the wall for support, and dipped his head at me in acknowledgment.

Ruslan and I spent whatever time we could together. Only I knew that sometimes he slipped drops of valerian into his mother's glass so that she slept through the night without chasing him with a knife, and no one but he knew I once stole a cucumber from the school cafeteria kitchen on a dare.

It was not unusual for the Roma boys to perform (many preferred that to going to school), but Ruslan was obsessed, practicing his guitar for hours. Whenever he had to sit a number out, he'd pace until allowed to go back up. That's how he was. Once he set his mind on something it swept him like an avalanche.

The first time Dad auditioned him, everybody grew quiet and the people rehearsing nearby drew closer to listen.

"He's a wunderkind," Dad exclaimed later while Mom attempted to shorten the sleeves of his magenta stage coat with my father still in it. "It's like fire shooting out of his fingertips."

"That's all the boy thinks about," Mom said. "Not healthy. And now he's dropped out of school! Again!" Ruslan had dropped out at the age of nine to beg on the streets, per his mother's instructions. He went back, but struggled through every day.

"He's not good at academics, but with fingers like his, who needs algebra?"

"He should have other interests, kick a soccer ball once in a while."

When I was nine and Ruslan twelve, Grandpa Andrei ordered

Kristina to leave. She had a habit of stealing husbands or, more often, borrowing them for a night. Ruslan's father was a mystery many band members often and without shame bet money to solve. Kristina was also a heroin addict and Ruslan often suffered the rage that came with the high.

When Ruslan's mother left, she didn't say goodbye. He himself showed no emotion as he watched her get into the taxi from the hotel window. He had decided to stay with the troupe.

Later I found him sitting on a ratty yellow couch down in the hotel lobby with his guitar case propped against the wall. He was softly tapping a rhythm with the heels of his scruffy shoes. I couldn't tell if he was going to cry or rip the couch in two, so I sat down on the other end, hoping he'd do neither with me there.

"The next show's in three hours," I said.

He scrutinized the people walking about as if he'd never seen anything more interesting.

"You just gonna wait here this whole time?"

"Don't feel sorry for me," he said.

But how could I not? If my mother had up and left, I would've been terrified.

"I'm not," I said, so nervous he'd grow silent again. "We'll take care of you."

He stopped tapping.

"Oh yeah?"

"Sure." I shrugged. "Now we're your family." But I wanted to say "I'm your family." One day I was a nine-year-old with the musings of a nine-year-old, the next I'd sit through two shows to see him play for a minute or two. Over the next four years Journal Number 1 grew fat with love notes:

> Before going onstage last night, Ruslan winked at me. I will die
> if he does it again. God, please, make him!

Ruslan showed me more dance steps today. I lost count. Twice. And walked out even though he didn't laugh at me. Now I'm stuck in this hotel room, too embarrassed to show my face.

I have to go back to Moscow in a week, and he won't even notice how I love him.

Six months after my thirteenth birthday, during our tour of Uzbekistan, Ruslan asked if I wanted to tag along to buy guitar strings at the music shop a few blocks away in downtown Tashkent.

"On the way," he said, "there's something I need to ask you."

At the shop, the bushy-sideburned salesman peered at us like a toy terrier after a bath. "Young people these days. Barely weaned and already doing God knows what. Running around together, unchaperoned. Aren't you a little too young to be out with this fella? How old are you?"

"Thirteen," I said.

"Young man?"

Ruslan jabbed a finger at the packets of strings that hung on a hook above a poster of Lenin preaching to a sea of soldiers. "Two of those. If you're not too busy."

"*Vonuchie Tzigane* (rotten Gypsies)." The old man plucked the packets off the hook and tossed them in a paper bag. "But such are the times. Let everyone do as they please."

I couldn't understand it. Our clothes were good quality, our faces clean. We paid with rubles and displayed good manners. How could a stranger tell us apart from everyone else?

On the way back to the hotel, Ruslan squeezed the brown bag into a ball, and I nearly had to run after him. We passed a park where a small gathering of old men were arguing over a game of chess. The sidewalks bustled. We tried to shoulder our way through a crowd boarding a trolley, each passenger fighting for their right-ful place.

"Are you all right?" Ruslan asked. He took my hand so we wouldn't get separated.

"Are you?"

A sharp nod, and he pulled me to the other side of the street.

"He's old," I said. "He didn't mean it."

"You notice how it's never just 'Gypsy'? It's always 'dirty' or 'rotten' or 'stupid.' They mean it, Oksana, never doubt that. And the old are most dangerous. You can't change their thinking."

"Nothing we can do about it," I said.

"In Romania, right now, Romani our age are fighting back."

I'd heard of rallies going on in Romania at the time. Romani all over Europe told stories about women being sterilized without consent; there were rumors that no Romanian Gypsy could get documents in order to work. Some of the younger Gypsies were becoming restless.

"As soon as I save up enough money I'm going to join them," he said.

"In Romania?"

"Important things are happening there."

"But we need you here, too. Probably even more."

He laughed. "Yeah, the show would fall apart without me."

I found the entire conversation terrifying.

"Funny how the old man thought we were dating," he said.

"Hilarious," I said. "Do you want to?"

He cleared his throat and his ears flushed. "Want to what?"

"We can go to the movies together sometimes. I mean, do you like me that way?"

How could I have said those things? He was practically my brother. Uncle Stepan had taken him in, treated him as his own son. Mortified, I couldn't wait to get to the hotel room, where I'd lock myself in the bathroom and drown in the toilet.

"It's okay," I said. "We're really good friends and—"

He stopped, curls of his shiny black hair caught in the wind.

"Okay," he said.

"Good. I only said that because I don't like going alone."

"Do you want to go steady with me?"

"Yes," I said.

"Thank you."

"No problem."

In Mom's eyes, Ruslan's lineage made him unacceptable, and Dad would never allow his daughter to associate with a moneyless dropout except during performances. Ruslan was as close to a leper as a young Rom got.

The night Dad caught me and Ruslan backstage, our heads bent over a pamphlet on the Romani equal rights movement in Romania, Dad chased him around the entire theater.

"The boy is a bastard!" he later said behind the closed door of our hotel room.

I remember wishing for the building to cave in before the entire band heard my father's voice in the hallways. Mom was making beef stew on a single burner that she wasn't supposed to have.

She shook a serving spoon at me. "There's bad blood in that family tree. What kind of future does he have? No money, no way to take care of a wife—"

"Wife? We were reading," I said. In truth, *I* was reading. Ruslan had asked me to help him practice his reading and writing, and I said yes before he was even done. It amazed me that he couldn't string together the simplest of sentences on the page. He jumbled syllables and words, and knocked the books away in frustration.

Dyslexia was something neither of us considered, since we'd never heard of it, but I've wondered since why none of his teachers had caught the signs.

"His own mother didn't know who knocked her up," Dad said. "No decent woman will want him."

"It doesn't matter. He's too old for me anyway."

"See? You're thinking about it, but beware, my daughter. If I catch that *govnyuk* (shithead) anywhere near you, I'll rip his head off."

I knew that by "rip his head off," Dad meant "He'll be fired and on the streets."

Six months later I turned fourteen. We were back in Moscow, the band on a three-month hiatus. I was so afraid that Ruslan would lose his job that I made certain Dad had no reason to fire him. Instead of going to the movies, we wrote love letters. Zhanna took Ruslan's dictations and carried the contraband between us like a partisan dodging unfriendly fire.

The night Ruslan came to talk, Zhanna and I were staying at Esmeralda's flat. He wouldn't come in but had asked Zhanna to fetch me.

The landing was dark, with only the elevator buttons blinking on the wall. When I saw him, I knew something I wouldn't like was about to transpire. He wore a suit with a black tie over a white shirt. Roma boys dressed like that for official matters ranging from weddings to gang disputes. He was also carrying a briefcase. Next to him I felt distinctly unofficial in my bathrobe and slippers.

"I missed you," he said. That's how he started every letter: *I miss you. I want to embrace you. I want to be near you.* Every sentence started with "I" and ended with "you." Without much fuss, the letters evolved into declarations and promises made by both of us and intended to be kept.

"You look handsome in that suit," I said. "I love you."

"And I love you. It's one of Stepan's."

He balanced the briefcase on one raised knee and clicked it open.

"I brought something for you," he said, pulling out a thin strand of a necklace. "It's not very expensive but it's silver. I figured if I give you a ring, your dad will send you to a convent and I'll never find you."

"Very funny. You came here in your suit to give me a present?" My voice betrayed the edges of worry. "I don't want presents. Come in for tea."

"I have three hundred rubles saved up from the tour—"

I pulled the robe tighter around my neck, my fingers stiff like twigs.

"I have to do this, Oksana. When I come back I'm quitting the band. Maybe get a part-time gig at the Teatr Romen."

I was seriously considering wrapping myself around him, hanging there until he missed his flight. I wanted to beg and to scratch my face, to scare him into staying.

"Romania is so far from here. The letters will take very long," I said.

"Will you wait for me?"

Placing the briefcase on the floor, he walked over and draped the necklace around my neck. Then he kissed my cheeks. The tip of my nose. My fingers came alive. I seized the collar of his jacket, not out of passion but to keep him from leaving. He kissed my chin. Then lips, burning his mouth to mine.

"When we're husband and wife," he said, "we'll kiss every morning, after breakfast, at noon, midday nap, and many times in the evening."

"Stepan won't let you go alone." But I knew that at seventeen Ruslan was perfectly able to travel unsupervised.

He looked at his watch and pushed the elevator button. "I'm off. As soon as I get to Bucharest I'll call."

The elevator heard my pleas and refused to budge from floor twelve, but Ruslan was onto us, and turned to take the stairs. I was still holding on, barring his way.

"Please, Ruslanchik. Please. When I'm sixteen we'll go together. Just wait two years."

He kept entreating me gently to let go. He had so much to do in Romania. If anyone heard that his girlfriend made him stay they'd laugh at him. He'd be gone for only a couple of months. On the ground floor he pried away my hands and kissed them while apologizing for hurting me.

"That's fine," I called out to his receding back. "Romania can have you and your promises."

But two weeks later, I was planning our wedding. Sure, I'd refuse at first. After what the bastard did, he'd have to drag his knees for days in front of me, begging forgiveness. I'd act non-chalant, perhaps go visit Grandma Rose in Armenia for a couple of months before saying yes. I already knew my parents wouldn't approve of our plans. We'd have to wait until my sixteenth birthday, but no matter. More time for me to drive him crazy, make him see that he'd made the wrong choice by picking a country over me.

A month later I began to worry. No letter had reached me. Had the politics seduced him, leaving no time to jot a quick note? I could ask around, but I'd go to Hell before hounding for information like an obsessed girlfriend.

I didn't have to. Instead, Hell came to me.

My parents were celebrating a good friend's birthday. Ivan had been a band member for years and was like a brother to my father, who believed that anyone who'd back him up in a fistfight against five angry crane operators was family. Esmeralda had arrived earlier to help Mom make *solianka*, a spiced soup. She had brought Zhanna along—a great idea, since my parents threw parties on a weekly basis—and once the talk of work turned to politics, I was inevitably ordered out of the room to watch Roxy.

At one end of the table Roxy and I were listening to Zhanna tell a story about an abandoned church outside Leningrad inside of which people claimed to have heard a woman crying.

"I heard it on TV today," she said, dipping a chunk of rye bread into the soup. "A man peeped through the boarded-up window, and you'll never believe what he saw."

Seven-year-old Roxy covered her ears. "Don't tell it if it's gonna be scary."

"Well?" I urged.

"A flying apparition of Mother Mary!"

I lowered Roxy's hands. "What a fairy tale. Mother Mary's flying about like she has nothing better to do."

"I'm telling you, it was on the news," Zhanna said. "Now people are going to camp out around the place. I bet all of Russia will be there soon."

"Won't she get tired of flying?" Roxy said.

I was going to add something smart-ass when a conversation between Ivan and Dad caught my attention.

"Stepan is coming back with the body day after tomorrow. What a tragedy."

"I had no idea." Dad pushed aside his bowl. "How did it happen?"

"How do you think? They caught him alone, beat him, dumped him in the alley. It's not like the cops are eager to volunteer information."

The din around the table softened.

"What's this?" Mom said.

"Stepan's boy was killed yesterday," Dad said.

Ivan had only the skeleton of the story. After one particularly explosive demonstration, Ruslan and a few local Romani got caught up in a fight with some *gadjee* boys. No one knew who instigated the fight, but it ended with the participants scattering to escape the police. Later Ruslan was found dead behind the local pet clinic. He'd been beaten to death.

Mom's hand flew to her mouth, but Esmeralda and Zhanna were already sobbing as if someone had turned on a switch.

Ivan's hands lay clasped on the white tablecloth as he attempted to answer all the questions. Being the bearer of bad news was never a good thing for the bearer.

Zhanna hugged me and her sobs filled my ears. But I had no tears of my own. I felt like I'd been given a drug that was slowly pulling me under. I propped up my elbows on the table, rested my chin in my hands, and thought, If I faint right now and my face lands in my mother's *solianka*, could I drown in it before anyone reaches me?

I refused to go to the funeral.

"I don't believe you," Zhanna said to this. "Where's your soul? I thought you loved him."

My parents had had one of those fights that left holes in our kitchen walls, so I was staying at Esmeralda's for a couple of days, and Roxy was at Grandma Ksenia's. Earlier Esmeralda had gone to meet with Stepan to arrange the three-day vigil. She was also in charge of the music (Romani often hired small bands to escort funeral processions into the cemetery).

"Go to the vigil at least. We'll go together after midnight. Stepan's not even staying home tonight, but he's leaving it unlocked for visitors."

I leaned on the windowsill, stories above the kids playing dodgeball in the yard, where spring blew kisses from tree to tree.

"No," I said.

"Are you being such a bitch just to piss me off or what?"

"You got it. All this is for your benefit."

After several very long minutes I felt Zhanna's arms wrap around me. She rested her chin on my shoulder.

"You can cry if you want."

"I am," I said.

That night I told Zhanna I was going home—it wouldn't do to have her think she had swayed me. Since Stepan's place was an hour away by metro, I took a taxi. As a rule I'd never get into a car driven by a man with a barely healed gash on the side of his face, but I honestly didn't care if anything happened to me. Nothing compared to what had happened already.

Inside Stepan's flat, the living-room furniture had been pushed against the walls. There were candles burning in large sconces, the only source of light. Normally I enjoyed the scent of candles, but that night their sinister spitting made the air too thick. From my spot in the living-room doorway I dragged my eyes to the coffin in the middle, raised up on a platform. It was dark brown with fake-silk lining that looked like frothed icing.

I came near Ruslan. So close, I saw the details of his suit, the red carnation peeking out of his breast pocket, the spattering of hairs on his knuckles, and the makeup someone had tried to cover his bruises with. They had combed Ruslan's curls straight down the sides of his head. He looked like a choirboy ready for "Ave Maria." I unwound the scarf from around my neck and wiped down the side of one cheek, and continued until his face came alive with color, the bruises almost black in the candlelight. I never expected that the last time I'd see him would be like the first, his body marked by violence.

It was the strangest sensation to sit the night through in the presence of my first love's death, and yet I remember so little. At my great-aunt Ophelia's funeral, relatives threw themselves across her coffin and screeched at the sky for God to love her. A Romani funeral is never a shy affair. It's meant to celebrate a life lived and secure a smooth passing between two worlds. I'd heard in some countries that the Romani lay their loved ones in tombs furnished with their most precious belongings, and others bury them standing or sitting, a sign of ultimate liberty from life's oppressions. For Ruslan, songs would be sung, Christian prayers recited, and tears would flow for the next forty days, the time it takes for a soul to depart from earth. *Pominki*, memorial meals, on the ninth day and the fortieth, would ensure his safe passage.

But all this involved a crowd of people when my only wish was for us to be alone.

I pulled up a chair, adding several cushions, and sat next to him. Had I been stronger, I could've forced him into the flat, imprisoned him, and looted his pockets of the three hundred rubles. I could've flung them out the window for all the neighborhood drunks to catch.

Before I left Ruslan early the next morning, I tucked my scarf under him, but I still didn't cry.

Zhanna was furious.

"*Ti shto, s oomah soshla* (Have you lost your mind)? Do you *want* his ghost to haunt you forever?"

"It's already done." Ask any superstitious Romani and they'll tell you that entrusting personal items to the dead or keeping anything of theirs can bring bad luck.

Zhanna shook a finger at my face. "You go to that funeral and get it back."

But I didn't, and the scarf descended into the earth with Ruslan.

I began to ditch school and walk miles without direction, sometimes getting lost in the woods nearby until a passing hiker pointed out the correct path, and I did whatever I could to get expelled from school. My parents' influence made it tricky, but I persisted.

I stapled Ruslan's many pages in my journal and begged Zhanna to take his letters because I felt them breathing in my room at night. Besides, I had memorized the words long ago.

The necklace I kept. It carried his touch.

Inside Journal Number 1, I continued to make entries, careful to avoid the sealed pages but reluctant to start a different notebook. I was fourteen brooding on seventeen, my writing an abandoned land mine. On a really bad day, I spent hours in a dreamlike state in which I'd float outside my body and watch the motions I went through with detached curiosity. I called it the "Black Sleep."

I felt a deep sense of abandonment. Odd, since my parents were still together and tried their best to give Roxy and me a semblance of a normal family life. When not flinging ashtrays at each other, they were almost normal. On one of those days I heard Dad mutter, "Baba Varya's curse is to blame for this strife, but in America everything will change. The curse can't reach across the ocean."

After the interview at the American embassy, on the day our plans to come to America were finalized, I wrote my last entry: "This hurt can't reach across the ocean. I will leave me here and find me on the other side."

THE CURBS OF BEVERLY HILLS

I once heard a rumor about immigrants who, unable to read English, had mistaken cat food for canned tuna. That unwelcome image was wedged in my mind as Mom and I stepped through the sliding doors of the local supermarket on our first official shopping trip alone. When we moved out of Uncle's, the Russian Immigrant Outreach Program brought us groceries, but their services ended after a month or so.

"First things first," Mom said as we pushed our cart down the bright aisles. "We need butter." Her black pumps echoed against the canyon of freezers stuffed with food. She wore a gray dress with intricately carved silver buttons down the front. With her freshly curled and styled hair, she looked like a Mediterranean Jane Seymour. When she'd spent an hour dressing up, I had complained, worried we'd draw too much attention. I was right. People stared, not only because of her opera-ready makeup, but also because she shouted in Russian to me as if we were miles apart. The heels and the crimson nails weren't too bad. We came from a culture where outside excursions meant people would be checking you out, forming opinions behind your back. You absolutely had to look your best. God forbid you went to the downstairs bakery in your sweats and slippers; eventually the neighborhood would learn of your poverty. Party invitations would be withdrawn and rumors of mental illness would circulate.

It was the volume of my mother's voice that drove me to pretend I didn't know her that day. For the first time, I was ashamed of my language.

"Do you see butter, Oksana?" Mom bellowed.

Anybody familiar with Eastern European cooking practices will understand the value of good butter. If you don't use a stick of the stuff in your recipe, you're either a miser or a lousy cook.

We had found the dairy section, and with it, our first dilemma: too many varieties. Butter, according to *Merriam-Webster*, is a solid edible emulsion obtained from cream by churning. How many different ways of churning are there? How many kinds of cream?

I missed the days when I'd walk up to our local market's dairy counter, ask the brightly lipsticked Elena Leonidovna for a kilo of butter, and be on my way.

"Oksana. What does this mean?"

I squinted at a beige tub Mom pointed to, studying it with the curiosity of an archaeologist. "'Fat-free.' I don't think that's good."

"Why not? What does this 'fat-free' mean?"

I envisioned a golden cloud of creamy mass floating in the sparkling sky, blobs of fat swirling around it in fancy-free abandon. "It means it has way too much fat. Fat has complete freedom. It has taken over this butter."

"Oh . . . then we don't want it."

In the produce aisle I almost forgot about my mother's vocalizations. I had never seen so much food in one place, not to mention so many off-season fruits and vegetables. The neat rows of unreasonably large strawberries and glossy apples made me think they must've come from a factory instead of a farm.

We couldn't splurge with the thirty dollars we had allotted for food that week, so we bought potatoes, bread, bologna, cheese, milk, and pasta. I did get the strawberries, but Mom drew the line at the apples, which she said smelled like candle wax. It took a good two hours, but in the end, we left with a sense of great accomplishment. And that night Roxy and I sifted sugar over our tasteless strawberry giants while I told tales of the market: not just a market but a *supermarket*.

The next task made me a bit more nervous: paying the rent. The landlady, Rosa Torres, lived downstairs in a unit tucked into the corner of the courtyard. Mom had officially elected me as her interpreter, though I could say little more than "My name is Oksana, I am fifteen years old."

At age twelve, with help from my tattered Russian-English dictionary, I had started writing songs with English lyrics. I performed this one at a school concert.

> *Today, me not to think of in the past.*
> *Stars to burn how fires.*
> *Them show to me way*
> *To fairy-tale valley full happiness.*

Only when I came to America did I laugh at those lyrics. Hurriedly I'd acquired a used Russian-English dictionary from one of the workers at the Russian Immigrant Outreach Program to replace the one my dad had taken when he left. Every day I opened to a random page and scanned the words, saying them out loud, trying them on for size. The ones I found especially beautiful I wrote down in my journal. "Transparent" was the first, then "shenanigans." I'd stand in front of a mirror and have conversations with myself in a language that still felt like a pair of new shoes. Or I'd repeat things I heard on TV, memorizing phrases like "buy one, get one half off." In front of that mirror I interviewed Madonna. In public I stuttered while buying milk.

"You know plenty of English, Oksana," Mom said as I knocked on the landlady's door, hoping for no answer. "At your age I spoke Russian with barely an accent." Russian was the official language of the USSR, but you could tell which of the fifteen republics a person came from by their accent when they spoke it.

I haphazardly pieced together all the useful words I could think of, and forgot them the instant the door opened.

"Jes?" Rosa smiled at me above the door chain. Her bleached hair shrieked next to her dark, pockmarked skin.

"Hello. We pay rent. Please. Thank you."

"Come. I'll give ju a receipt." Her apartment, rich with dark furniture against very pink walls, smelled strongly of beans, onions, and spices I didn't recognize.

We carefully counted out the money on top of Rosa's polished dining-room table: $450. But we didn't leave right away. One hour passed, another, and the three of us . . . talked. A true conversation. Rosa, an immigrant herself, had come from Mexico with her husband and daughter, Maria, six years before. Like Mom, she was now divorced. As it turned out, Maria and Roxy had met only days after we moved in and had without hesitation become best friends. And it wasn't long before our two broken families became very close.

Once Rosa saw the inside of our apartment she began to visit regularly. Almost every day, she walked up the stairs carrying a shiny toaster, or a chair, or some curtains for the bedroom windows.

Mom kept refusing the gifts, uncomfortable with the idea of taking handouts—especially since back in Russia, she'd been the one handing them out.

"*Mija*. This stuff is free and ju need it."

"Free?" I asked.

"Rich people gets rid of things. Good things. They leave them on street in front of their houses."

"To throw away?"

"Jes. But dose are good things: furniture, clothes. Expensive. I go to Beverly Hills and pick up for my garage sales."

That weekend Rosa talked Mom into going to Beverly Hills with her. Roxy, Maria, and I piled into the back of Rosa's purple 1978 Buick Regal, with Mom and Rosa in the front. We drove past unremarkable houses, but as the neighborhoods changed, those houses blossomed.

"Maybe my George lives here," Roxy said, staring out the window in fascination.

"Or not," I said.

"You're such a grump, Oksana. We should ask somebody."

We stopped at our first curb, where cardboard boxes overflowed with clothes and vibrant fake flowers. Rosa kept the car running. She tossed the boxes in the trunk and jumped back in, driving away quickly.

"It is okay to take them?" I asked. The process felt too much like stealing.

"Is fine. They jes don't like to see us do it." While Rosa stuffed the car with merchandise, I admired the grandeur of the impeccable lawns and the plentitude of Mercedes-Benzes. This, I thought, was the America I'd expected. Unfortunately, I was scavenging from its garbage.

We went to Beverly Hills regularly, raking in carloads of stuff Rosa later sold. Each time her Buick passed the Beverly Hills sign, we entered a universe most people glimpsed only on TV. On both sides of the spotless streets, beautiful palms swayed their model-thin necks. The houses lay scattered about like multicolored beads. Everything here glimmered with that special, extra-golden sunshine. And for the few hours a week we spent ragpicking, we, too, got to bathe in its rays.

A PREMIUM IDEA

Dad called our apartment a week before Christmas. Several months had passed since the last time we'd heard from him, and during that silence I'd tried to make sense of his actions. What did Roxy and I do to make it so easy for him to abandon us? Why did he never try to help?

Roxy had picked up the phone first, and we took turns talking to him in hushed voices while glancing in the direction of the kitchen, where Mom was battling with her hand-cranked meat grinder.

"You girls okay?" he asked in Russian. "How's school?"

I cupped the phone with the palm of my hand. "Everything's fine." He didn't need to know that although Roxy had been going to Marshall Elementary for the past month, I had refused to enroll in the local high school. "Where are you?" I asked.

"Are you coming home?" Roxy interrupted, sticking her face into the receiver and fighting to grab it as I pushed her away.

I hadn't asked him that question because I knew better. When I'd heard him tell Mom that he loved her that night in Moscow, I'd believed he'd always live by those words. Yet he'd walked away from us as if our family had been a temporary arrangement. Some part of me wanted him back, but the stubborn me refused to let him know that.

"I'm sorry I didn't call you on your birthday," he said.

I wanted to tell him how he had ruined it for me. "No big deal," I said.

I'd turned sixteen a month earlier, in October. Mom had made brownies from a box. We'd never heard of brownies before, and she wanted to surprise me with an authentic American dessert. She'd ended up burning the mix into the pan. After dinner we scraped the remains off the sides. They tasted like dried fertilizer, and my birthday wish was never to have to eat brownies again.

Dad cleared his throat. "Is your mother there?"

I turned to check and found Mom drilling holes in me with her eyes. "Who is that?" she asked, but the question sounded more like "It better not be who I think it is."

Roxy jumped up and down in the middle of the living room. "It's Papa. It's Papa!"

Mom flew out of the kitchen, hair bouncing. She yanked the phone out of my hand, ordering us to leave the room, and shut the door.

Roxy and I ran to the bedroom and then listened with our ears pressed against the wall.

Growing up, I suffered from what I now call a split nationality disorder, never quite sure if I was Romani or Armenian. I was an impostor; a half-breed trapped between two vibrant cultures, never allowed a choice without guilt. My parents' breakup was feeling eerily familiar. I didn't know whose side to be on, and they made sure I couldn't choose both.

After some customary bickering my parents finally came to an agreement on the subject that was the reason for Dad's call: the holidays. The winter season ranked high for both sides of my family, and even the worst rivalries were often temporarily put off to celebrate it. Roxy and I would spend Christmas with Dad, and New Year's at home with Mom. A truce, however shaky.

The following day, Dad picked us up in a dark blue van with pictures of howling wolves on its sides. No surprise there. When I was nine, he'd painted eyelashes around the headlights of our Volkswagen Beetle and a tail in the back. Mom had refused to get in when she saw what he had done, but I'd thrown my arms around it and called it Sipsik, after my favorite stuffed toy.

It felt like years instead of months since I'd last seen Dad. He wore a leather jacket and pants, and had dyed his long hair to cover the gray. We managed a clumsy hug. Dad was never big on affection. Also, neither of us knew how broken families were supposed to act. Roxy, as always, had too much energy to be awkward. She jumped into Dad's arms and gave him two sloppy kisses on each cheek. "Papa, can I show you my George Michael book?" She reached out and grabbed a handful of Dad's ZZ Top beard.

Divorce was the new "empowered," or so my mother had been trying to convince me. But the moment I saw him, it became clear that we'd been lying to ourselves. I was glad to see him and mad at myself for being glad. On the way to his West Hollywood house, Dad made conversation as if nothing weird had happened, and even though I felt betrayed by his actions, I was happy to have him back.

"Girls, I have great news," he said. "I've got a few gigs booked for next year. What do you think of that, eh? Your old dad, back on top."

"You bought new equipment?" I asked.

"Not yet," he said, and I knew I shouldn't have asked that question. He grew quiet, shaking his head. "Remember my Gibson?

Now, that was an instrument to befriend the Devil for. No other guitar had such a juicy sound, like a ripe watermelon in July. Scored it off a Finnish tennis player."

"I know, Dad." A twinge of sadness made me want to wrap my arms around his neck. Before leaving Russia, Dad had sold everything except for his father's guitar. He had moped around for days as if he'd lost his entire family. And now he had, by his own choice.

He slapped a hand on the wheel. "No matter. I found a way to make extra cash. It's a premium idea. If everything goes well, we'll be rich by spring. I had a dream."

Here we go again, I thought. Dreams were my family's version of the *Farmer's Almanac.*

Every morning in Moscow, after Dad had dragged his feet into our kitchen, his hair Einstein-wild, he'd sit at the kitchen table, sigh, and complain about his insomnia, and then proceed to tell Mom about his dreams.

"I'm a spider," he once said. "Inside that new restaurant on Arbatskaya. And I'm biting my legs off. Then I see Elvis. He's a spider, too, except instead of legs he has guitars. And he's calling me to follow him onstage. Now, what do you think it means?"

"You should cancel that gig," Mom said, and then added as an afterthought, "Thank God you didn't listen to Elvis." Everyone knew that if you followed the dead in a dream, you'd soon perish.

There in the van, I didn't know what to say. Both my parents had hatched their share of ingenious plans that often backfired. Like the time Dad convinced Mom to sell homemade *oladushki* (pancakes) on the side of the Medvedkovo metro station. At first Mom laughed. "Why would people pay extra for our *oladushki* when they can make their own?" "For convenience," Dad said. We learned that Russians still preferred their own pancakes to those of strangers.

For this reason I didn't ask about Dad's latest scheme or the dream that had inspired it. Better not to encourage him, I thought. Roxy, on the other hand, began to list dozens of luxury items she would need Dad to buy with his millions. Even at a young age she knew that every courtship must begin with toys. Surely George Michael would not be able to resist a pink fairy bicycle with a matching helmet.

Immaculate houses lined both sides of Dad's street. This neighborhood was a galaxy away from ours.

"It's no Beverly Hills," Dad said, "but it's all I can afford right now."

On the outside, the house had a flat-roofed Spanish design, but once you stepped across the threshold, it resembled the interior of a traditional Romani wagon. Richly hued rugs swallowed every inch of the floor, some even continuing up the walls and to the ceiling. Everywhere I looked, I found yet more rugs and wall hangings. It would be very difficult for one to get hurt surrounded by so much wool. Red-and-gold shades predominated; there were burgundy-framed pictures, red statues of Hindu men on top of gold-colored elephants, and a number of bright-red pieces of furniture. I tried not to stare at the garish decor, but my eyes would not obey as they attempted to find a moment of peace.

Dad hadn't decorated on his own. One thing he couldn't stand was ethnic or folksy art on his walls. "Modern" was his motto. Our Moscow house had images of British flags painted on the bathroom walls, Miles Davis above the fireplace, and Japanese concubines in the kitchen. He had a style all his own. All signs pointed to one thing—my father's mistress was in the house—and before I had time to imagine myself charging at her with fists on the ready like a cocksure Irishman, she floated into the room to greet us.

"Girls, welcome. I am so happy you are here! Sit. Sit now, and

I will make tea." Her dress sparkled like a Vegas showgirl's. Threaded heavily with sequins, it fell to her feet. Golden hoop earrings clinked through a mass of long black wavy hair. When she grinned, two golden teeth winked out of her mouth. She hugged Roxy and me zealously, an assortment of golden bracelets jingling on her wrists.

People often comment on Gypsies' obsession with gold. Sometimes you can pick out Romani by the amount of jewelry they wear. This habit comes from a time when the wandering caravans didn't possess the freedom to settle anyplace long enough to grow roots, so wagons, forests, and riverbanks became their homes. But the wagons were often vandalized by outsiders, most of the forests belonged to uncharitable nobles, and the rivers were as unpredictable as the towns around them. The Romani learned to trust no one. They developed a tradition of carrying their wealth in the safest place they found—on themselves.

"How did you get here?" I blurted out, not expecting to see Olga, our old family acquaintance from Moscow, in my father's living room.

She flashed a diamond ring, and grinned. "We're married."

"What?" Roxy and I shouted in unison. This was the woman my father had gone back to Russia for? Olga was eighteen years Dad's junior, and besides the fact that she was not our mother, her reputation didn't stand out as exemplary. Olga was one of those Romani women whom tourists are warned about before their overseas trips; the kind *we* were warned about by Grandpa Andrei all our lives. She told fortunes for a living and would do anything to rid people of their money short of actually digging in their pockets. You'd never find her losing sleep over an unpaid bill or planning for retirement. If she had money enough to invite twenty guests for dinner, she would, even if it meant that she would have to eat cheese sandwiches for the rest of the month.

Many of my Romani relatives considered her attitude too risky for modern times. But Olga always said, "You can't plan life." A street-reared Romani, she'd come from a family that practiced but one motto: "Survive the day by all means necessary and start over tomorrow."

Although Olga danced fairly well, my grandfather had refused to have her in his shows, claiming she reinforced the stereotypes he'd worked to eradicate. So how did my father end up married to her?

It was about five years after my parents' divorce that I learned their affair had gone on for years before our move to the States. When Mom found out, just months before coming to America, Dad promised to stop seeing Olga. Turned out he'd been planning to bring her over all along and had waited until after the move to ditch us and send Olga a tourist visa. The marriage my mother was hoping to save was the furthest thing from his mind. Of course Olga had no intention of going back to Russia, but long-term resident visas were almost impossible to get. With a tourist visa Olga had a chance to come to America and get lost in the system.

My own father, an adulterer. In the past, every time Mom had accused Dad of sleeping around, I hadn't wanted to believe it. But the reality, I knew, was that many women thought of him as a catch. He was not only good-looking but also rich (at least in terms of Soviet-era Russians) by way of his parents.

Sitting around the kitchen table, Dad, Roxy, Olga, and I were soon drinking black tea together as if this were the natural order of things. On the outside, I was doing my best impression of a girl with manners. On the inside, I was a hunter with a fresh kill. I was dragging Olga by her hair out of the kitchen, across the scratchy living-room carpet, into the front yard, where I could skin her with my curved dagger. This Oksana was uncharacteristically ruthless, and I almost felt remorse until my mother's face came to mind. For Mom I was ready not only to mount Olga's head above a fireplace but to do so with Dad watching.

Olga had arrived in Los Angeles a few weeks earlier but had already come to the conclusion that Hollywood was a place with broken hearts galore. Plenty of immigrants meant great business potential. The woman never changed her ways—you could drop her in the middle of the Bible Belt, and she would not only find a way out but inevitably make cash doing so.

"I have already placed an ad in the local Russian paper," she told us through a cloud of Marlboro smoke. " 'Famous Gypsy fortune-teller Olga, with extraordinary abilities to predict the future, will help you in your quest for happiness. Call, and see your troubles fly away.' "

"It's coming out next week. It'll be premium," Dad added, sitting between us and her at the head of the table. He bit into an open-faced salami sandwich, a trail of bread crumbs in his beard. Then he smiled at Olga. "You did a great job, my little sparrow."

They exchanged sweet looks. I was speechless and a little sick to my stomach. My father had never spoken a word of lovey-doveyness before.

"Ah, I can't wait to begin," Olga said.

I wasn't sure if she was exuding such enthusiasm for our father's benefit or ours. I had heard that she lived and breathed everything occult, as much at ease channeling spirits as she was shopping for shoes.

"But it's the holidays," I protested.

"Exactly. The best time for hooking the shunned, the desperate, the hopeful, and all the rest of the assholes who want miracles for pennies. Plus, the nights are more favorable for séances around Christmas and New Year's—you know that."

"But you were going to start playing again, Dad. You said you were buying equipment."

He shrugged. "Too many musicians in L.A. We're like rats scampering after a crumb of cheese. Remember my plan? This is it. I've got three gigs booked in February, and I need my instruments before that. But I can see already that no matter how many gigs you have, you can't make a decent living playing *gadjen* weddings in L.A. In this city, you need serious money to survive."

"But, Dad . . ." I said, still uncomfortable with the idea of Olga's psychic business. In the Soviet Union, practicing occultism or paganism was against the law.

Occultism might have persisted more in Russia than in the rest of Europe because we never truly experienced the Renaissance or the Enlightenment. If it weren't for Peter the Great introducing French culture to his country, ordering his ministers to shave off their "heathen beards" to appear more civilized, Russia might not have discovered progress for centuries to come. But Russians are stubborn people. Two hundred years after Peter, many still followed their ancestors' traditions steeped in thousands of years of superstition. Some believed in both Christianity and paganism, the practice called *dvoeverie* (two faiths), and I first encountered it when I was thirteen. Mom used to go to this ancient woman for readings, and if I insisted enough, she'd take me along.

Agrefina lived in a *derevnia*, a small hamlet, two hours north of Moscow. She was an oracle of sorts, a seer, but she never read for money. Mom brought her sacks of groceries one could find only in large cities. Toblerone chocolate bars were Agrefina's favorite. She'd cut them into chunks and share them with me.

I remember first seeing her house and thinking that I'd stepped into a fairy tale. It was made of logs, with a rooster-topped ridge-pole on the roof and ornamental woodwork around the window-sills and doorframes. I thought they were for looks until Agrefina explained they were symbols of protection. The most important was a circular carving with a six-petaled rose in the middle, called *gromovoi znak*, or the thunder sign. It belonged to Rod, a pagan god of light and creation. Inside the house, a candle burned next to an icon of Jesus set high on a shelf. A large hand-carved cross hung over the threshold, and from it dangled a number of talis-mans in the form of gems and dried-herb sachets.

Having never seen anything like it, I asked Agrefina about the cross. She patted my head and replied, "The Lord minds not how we pray so long as we mean it."

I'd immediately drawn my own version of *gromovoi znak* in my journal. People like Agrefina fascinated me. Like Romani, they adapted to changing reality while retaining their beliefs. But what Olga had in mind had little to do with tradition and a lot with making money.

I didn't want Dad to be a part of it, especially not with Olga, whose Devil tarot depicted menacing figures with impish eyes. But she'd hooked him on the idea, and I could tell by the anima-tion in his voice that he couldn't be persuaded to give it up. At least not by me. Maybe not even by his own father, who'd always been against divination.

Many Roma found Grandpa Andrei's attitude strange, par-ticularly since his own mother, Baba Varya, had been a notorious magicker who performed spells in addition to being a healer and a midwife.

The very first thing I remember hearing about Baba Varya was that she was a giantess. The second, everyone was afraid of her.

But according to the stories I'd collected over the years, she wasn't always a witch. She'd led a rather normal life as the wife of a farmer. They had three children who all helped tend the family plot. But one day her husband died unexpectedly and everything changed.

Grandpa Andrei said that after that, his mother withdrew from life for a very long time. She wasn't able to tend the land on her own and spent her time in a roomful of black-magic books. She started doing spells for the townsfolk, barely making enough money to support the family. Eventually they lost the land. All three kids left school to work, but they never lived as well as they had when their father was alive. All the stories after this painted Baba Varya as a *vedma* (black witch).

But then I heard this from Aunt Laura: during World War II Grandpa Andrei went to prison in Siberia for faking food-ration tickets for his Roma band; the Communists didn't consider Gypsies to be model citizens yet, and the rations were issued first to those loyal to the Red Party. The sentence was ten years. Grandpa and a couple of inmates attempted escape from their labor camp in Gulak, but got lost in the tundra for days. By the time the authorities found them, Grandpa had developed gangrene in his frostbitten toes, and the prison doctor gave him no more than a couple of months before his feet would have to be amputated. Grandpa sent Baba Varya a letter. At this time, Baba Varya traveled with various caravans and only the Roma knew her whereabouts. They used something they called *Tziganskaya pochta*, or Roma mail, to contact one another. Even those Roma who didn't travel in caravans visited with relatives throughout the year. It wasn't unusual for grandparents to stay at each of their kid's houses for months, and the local Roma were always aware if someone new showed up in town. The mail was passed from hand to hand without the need for postal service. That's why Grandpa's letter was addressed to:

Varya Nikolaevna,
In care of the Roma at the central Kiev marketplace

Baba Varya immediately set off for Siberia, carrying a jar of homemade ointment, and once at the prison, she bribed the infirmary medic to allow her entrance. Grandma Ksenia claimed that the jar's contents were pure black magic, made from puppy fat, but it could have been a simple folk remedy. No one knows for sure. Black magic or not, Baba Varya saved her son.

Still, Grandpa Andrei had constantly lectured his employees about the harm that practicing occultism could do to their reputation as legitimate artists. Society didn't know the difference between gifted practitioners and scam artists. Once, he found out about Dad's spirit-channeling sessions; Dad defended his actions by claiming that he had the "gift" to help him lift the family curse. They got into a terrible fight over it and didn't speak for almost a year.

And now Olga had rekindled my father's fascination with everything occult.

"Girls, I know that the business will do well. I have seen it. Besides, your father is too old for the stage," Olga said, a sly glint narrowing her heavily penciled eyes. "Isn't that so, my honeylamb-shank?"

Roxy's face lit up. "He's, like, Santa's age! It's true."

Olga winked at Dad. "Hey, Valerio? Those picks getting too heavy for you?"

Dad dropped his sandwich on the table with an indignant frown. "Who's old? Me? Your dipshit ex-husband is old, that's who! If I have to, I can wrestle a bear."

"Lucky for us there are no bears in Hollywood for you to terrorize."

Okay. So they acted like they had been cozily married for years; so what? I smiled politely, not completely sold on this show of domestic incivility.

"Oh, come on," Olga said, catching the lukewarm set of my lips. "I'm kidding. Your dad is a great musician. I'll bet you right now he'll soon be playing until his fingers fall off. I only think we can make more money by doing this on the side."

"Yeah, right," I said. "Nobody's going to pay you for reading their palms. This is America."

"So what? Everybody wants to believe something else controls their lives. That way, we don't have to feel responsible for what happens to us."

"But you can't lie to people to make them feel better."

"Who said anything about lying? I tell them what they want to hear. Like a head doctor, no? But instead of giving people pills, I have them sprinkle dirt in their husband's shoes and pray he will stop cheating."

"Dirt does not have superpowers," I said.

"No, but faith does."

NO JOAN OF ARC

My parents were married for seventeen years before they split. During that time, my Armenian and Roma families tolerated each other, but barely. Though not openly hostile, each side secretly regarded itself superior to the other, more cultured and sophisticated. Ironically, love of superstition was the biggest thing they had in common.

The Armenians spit over their shoulders and knocked on wood, while the Romani crossed themselves when yawning, to prevent evil spirits from entering their bodies, and poured salt around the foundations of their houses to keep them out. Every time Mom and I got on the train from Kirovakan, her hometown, to go back to Moscow, Aunt Siranoosh splashed water from a ceramic bowl onto the platform to ensure a safe journey.

At wakes, my Romani relatives poured vodka shots for the deceased so they would not feel parched on their way to Heaven, and my Armenian relatives covered the mirrors with swaths of black cloth so the dead wouldn't get lost by walking through them into the realm of the living and become ghosts.

In each culture, nearly everything was construed as a sign. Back in Moscow, if Dad missed a turn on the way to a party, he'd turn around and drive home. No one sat at the table corners unless they didn't want to ever get married. If you dropped a spoon on the floor, a woman would come calling soon; a knife signified a man; and if it happened to be a fork, the powers to be were not 100 percent sure on the gender. The signs are endless and move inside me like mice in a wheat field. To this day, I catch myself skimming tea bubbles off the top of a steaming cup and dabbing them on the crown of my head in hopes of acquiring a large sum of money.

According to Russian Roma legend, the period between December 21 and January 14 is when spirits come down (or up, depending on your viewpoint) to walk the earth in celebration of the winter solstice. If you dream of discussing Macbeth's foolish ambitions with Shakespeare himself, your chances of success increase greatly during these magical days.

The season is marked by ceremonies to divine, cleanse, and renew. The enthusiasm with which the Roma carry out these acts can be contagious, especially if there's a chance of seeing what your future husband might look like.

At well past midnight, Dad, Olga, and I sat in a tight circle around the table. A candle burned on top of the kitchen counter, next to a sink full of dirty dishes and a bottle of Jack Daniel's. In my opinion, it conveyed great disrespect to summon spirits amidst the pungent smell of fried carp and the slowly gyrating curls of cigarette smoke coming from my stepmother's lips. But I did not voice these thoughts, preferring to watch Dad watch Olga with great interest.

A piece of white poster board lay on the table. In the middle, all the letters of the Russian alphabet were arranged in a wide circle. Olga placed a small white plate marked with a single arrow at one edge in the center of the circle. "Porcelain," she said. "The purer the material, the better the reception."

I'd seen the plate before. It was one of the few items Dad had brought with him from Russia, where he had kept it locked away. Any object used in divination was off-limits to kids. As a little girl I once made the mistake of playing with Esmeralda's personal tarot deck. When she found me gently lowering the king of hearts onto the roof of my newly built house of cards, she moaned, "How could this have happened?" as if I'd stolen bonbons out of the special Richart chocolate box she opened only for dates with the most "marriage" potential.

I gathered the cards. "I was careful. Didn't even bend them, see?"

With a sigh, Esmeralda kneeled on the floor next to me. "They won't work anymore, sweetie. I'll have to buy a new deck."

"I broke them?"

"Cards are part good, part bad, God and Devil all in one. Kinda like grown-ups. They need both in order to work, but kids

Esmeralda's cards, after I'd ruined them

are all good, you see? So when you played with the cards, they lost their Devil."

No one was allowed to touch Dad's plate, kid or adult. And now Olga pawed it while discussing its quality. As I got ready to say something wicked, she closed her eyes, touched her fingertips to the plate's rim, and began to chant along with my dad.

I knew what was coming, had seen this done numerous times before. It was kind of like using a Ouija board without having to pay $19.99 for the fancy lettering. But to my family, it wasn't a game.

When I was eleven, I'd overheard my parents and some of their friends channeling one night in our Moscow kitchen. I didn't see spirits, only Dad reading an incantation from a tattered book with a black leather cover. It had belonged to Baba Varya. At that age I knew her only as a *vedma*, so seeing my father use her book terrified me.

I used to love driving to the outskirts of Moscow with my mother to visit Agrefina or watch some other ancient Russian crone predict our future using stagnant water. Mom nursed not an ounce of skepticism for these peculiar practices, as if she were taking in a doctor's diagnosis. Even our own priest discussed the future with a fortune-teller's poise. I grew up with God and the Devil and every other idol in between at my doorstep. Opening that door was just a formality. Every December I participated in various divination ceremonies, and on Christmas Eve, Zhanna and I made sure to place saucers of springwater under our beds, hoping to dream about our future husbands.

At Dad and Olga's table, my heart thrashed like a cat in a sack, with a mixture of anticipation and fear. Channeling, to me, has always been like deep-cave diving: a daredevil sport.

The air around my shoulders wavered. Chills ran up and down my arms. I scooted forward in my seat just a touch.

Dad raised his head, hair shining in the abruptly frenzied candlelight. He opened his eyes and looked up to the ceiling. "Spirit, I thank you for responding. I am Valerio, and I do not bind you by any act of artifice or vengeance. Will you choose to confer?"

The plate slid to "Yes." Olga's fingers barely touched it.

My pulse drummed inside my ears.

"Thank you," Dad continued, exchanging a satisfied smile with Olga. "What is your name?"

"Avadata," the plate spelled out.

A quarter of an hour later, we knew a lot about Avadata, although it did not make me any less scared. She had been born in 1888, but would reveal neither where nor any of the details of her death. According to her, the afterlife consisted of seven levels, number seven being Heaven and number one, Hell. A soul worked its way up by aiding the living and being generally virtuous. Presently, Avadata resided on level three, which, she informed us, was "a dastardly place." But she wished to raise her status and so had been searching for ways to increase her chances. She adored cats, and often took possession of people fond of liquor and opium, a habit she had been trying to break herself of.

I glanced nervously at the half-empty whiskey bottle, then back at the plate, which was crawling to "No" in response to Olga's question of whether she'd soon become a millionaire.

"Ask her something," Dad said to me. "We don't know how long this connection will last."

"Like what?" I asked.

"Anything. How about your past life? You're always asking me about it."

I cleared my throat. "Ms. Avadata, could you tell me who I was in the past life . . . please?"

For a while, nothing happened. I began to think, with some relief, that perhaps Avadata had grown bored and left. But then—

"It's moving," Dad whispered, and leaned closer, stringing the letters into words as the plate slid around the circle. "1943. Le-nin-grad. Or-pha-nage 72. Head. Mis-tress."

"How glamorous," Olga said, clapping her hands.

I had hoped for Nefertiti, or at least Joan of Arc, but the head-mistress of an orphanage?

"Maybe she's making stuff up, like the way *you* do," I suggested to Olga.

"No, it makes sense. That's why you're always bossing Roxy around. So cool, so serious, like a gendarme. I bet you wore your hair in a tight bun and everything. A whip and a ruler are in your blood, my girl."

"How would *you* know? You're not our mother."

"Stop that," Dad interrupted. "You're acting like children. Concentrate or the spirit will feel the discord and leave."

I shot Olga black looks as if she had had something to do with Avadata's ridiculous claim.

"Ask another," Olga said to me. "Ask who you're going to marry. Chicken?"

My hands pulsed with the urge to hit her. Even if no real animosity marked her attitude, she had this annoying habit of always looking perky and amused at someone else's expense. I had to keep reminding myself that she meant no harm. Or else I'd wind up giving her the opportunity to replace the rest of her teeth with gold nuggets.

"Don't be a baby. Come on."

"If you call me a baby one more time, Olga, I will cut off your hair and make a stuffed cat out of it."

She roared with laughter. "So you're not all spineless Armenian like your mother. You've got a temper after all. I was wondering where you were hiding it."

"Don't talk about my mother."

"That, right there," she said. "That's your Roma fire, girl. Don't keep it caged up."

"I'm only half Gypsy. In case you haven't noticed, we're Americans now."

"Darling, you're no more American than pizza. Your father is Rom, and that makes you one, too, whether you like it or not. Be proud."

Her words rang true, and I hated her for it. "It's late," I said, standing up, not caring about hurting even the spirit's feelings anymore.

Olga pelted me with laughter like a skillful bully with a slingshot.

"Leave her be, woman," Dad said.

Without waiting for a response, I stormed out of the kitchen.

That night, I lay wide-eyed and restless on the living-room pullout couch, seriously considering leaving my father's house for good.

I wished Grandpa Andrei were there to talk sense into Dad.

Perhaps he'd remind him about all those times the band members got arrested in marketplaces because the police assumed that no Gypsy could resist the urge to read a palm when in public places.

Of course not all Soviets held these views.

During World War II, wounded soldiers often found refuge among the Gypsies. Many a time Romani aided the partisans by carrying messages between military posts across hostile territories; Roma mail became of much use. *Romancy*, Russian songs that were a vital element of Russian culture, were a fusion of Roma and Russian styles. Great writers like Tolstoy and Pushkin had been known to disappear with the caravans for weeks. Tolstoy mentions it in his writings more than once. Every time he

Russian kids watching one of Grandpa Andrei's
earliest shows, Kiev, 1939

feels dejected, it's off to party with the Gypsies. Pushkin was en-
amored with their romanticism, their wildness, and their bond
with nature, and even dedicated an entire narrative poem to them,
The Gypsies.

> *The Gypsies in a boisterous throng,*
> *through steppe of Bessarabia wander.*
> *Their dingy camp is pitched along*
> *The bank above the river yonder.*
> *How free, how cheerful their tents lie*
> *With tranquil dreams beneath the sky.*
> *Between the wheels of carts half slung*
> *With tapestries and threadbare rugs,*
> *The meal is done, the bonfire's blazing,*
> *The horses in the field are grazing.*

There were Soviets who proudly confessed to having "the blood" in their family tree, and there were those who clutched their purses as soon as the word "Gypsy" grazed their ears. According to my grandparents, the country had always been divided this way. But so were the Russian Roma.

Zhanna and I came across a group of Roma women once, right after Zhanna had turned fourteen. It was a beautiful spring day and we had decided to take the metro from my parents' house to Esmeralda's on the other side of town, which would give us a chance not only to people-watch but also to show off the new French denim vest Zhanna got on her birthday. At the Tretya-kovskaya station we followed the midday crowd outside, where we were suddenly surrounded by a flock of women in colorful skirts. They were Roma, although their dialect, as they admired my gold earrings and Zhanna's vest, sounded slightly different from the Rromanes my family spoke.

"Beautiful girl," one of them addressed me. She wore a scarf that only partially covered a bruise on her neck. "I'm a famous Gypsy fortune-teller. Let me tell your fortune." She accosted my hand and with one finger drew a circle in the middle of my palm. Next she pressed a pocket-size mirror into it. "You have five rubles? If we put it under the mirror you'll see your future husband's face." From the corner of my eye I saw another young woman place an identical mirror in Zhanna's palm, and I heard my fortune-teller tell Zhanna's fortune-teller, in Rromanes, to hurry it up before the next train came.

"Do you know us?" Zhanna said with a kind smile.

"Yes, yes." The woman extended her other hand. "I'll only borrow the money."

"We're Andrei Kopylenko's granddaughters."

As soon as the women heard that, the mirrors returned to the pockets of their skirts and they let go of our hands.

"*Devlo,*" my fortune-teller exclaimed. "You Romani girls? We had no idea. Why didn't you say so?"

We gave them money anyway, because we knew that most likely they had husbands back home who'd beat them if they didn't return with enough earnings for alcohol and cigarettes. We'd also give the change in our pockets to the Roma kids begging near churches. We knew where the scratches and the bruises on their skinny arms came from.

I was so afraid that my father, like those women, would pigeonhole himself. I'd hoped that when we moved to America, we could avoid those kinds of assumptions about us, as long as my family behaved.

Only now, instead of moving away from the one thing that could hurtle us out to the fringes of society, he was preparing to announce it to the entire population of Los Angeles.

HONEYLAMBSHANK

The next morning I walked the six miles home. I'd shaken Roxy awake, but she pulled the covers over her head and rolled onto her side, snoring before I was even dressed. Sneaking out of the house was a breeze because Dad stayed up all night and usually slept all day. Apparently so did his new wife. No doubt Mom would begin her interrogations the moment I came through the door, but better that than waking up to Olga's loaded comments about our little spat.

After I'd seen Dad's nice new place, the reality of our situation became that much more apparent. We were living in the Dumpster of Los Angeles. But if I told Mom, she'd go nuts, especially if she heard about Olga renting a house around the corner from Beverly Hills. And who could blame her? It didn't seem fair that we had to live in a shithole while the witch was enjoying the good life in a house she'd nearly suffocated with her rugs.

I bet Olga doesn't have to deal with roaches, I thought to myself as I shut the front door after a quick survey of the floor. I dropped my backpack in the corner, looking forward to getting some actual sleep. Something whistled in the kitchen. As I tried to sneak by, Mom turned and cleared her throat, holding a steaming kettle in one hand. "What happened?"

"Nothing," I said, which in teenage language means "Everything."

"You hungry? You look starved. Did they not feed you at all? Is Roxy eating all right? Is she with you?"

"She's fine. She's gonna stay for the rest of the week."

"Well, all right." Mom looked disappointed. "Goodness, you have such bags under your eyes. Sit down. I'll make something light."

I took a chair at the kitchen table with a sigh, bracing myself.

"I thought you were going to stay until New Year's."

"Change of plans."

Mom placed a plate of toast in front of me and sat down.

"If you don't want to tell me what happened, you don't have to."

"Okay."

"I don't care to hear anything concerning your asshole father anyway." She eyed me from over the rim of her coffee cup.

"That's good."

There was a very long moment of silence. I munched on my toast. Mom's staring meant the conversation was far from over. But for a little while neither one of us spoke.

"We need to talk about school," she said out of the blue.

"Nothing to talk about. I'm not going."

"Oksanochka. We came all this way for you to have a better life. Don't start it as a high-school dropout."

"I read, I write, I know my numbers," I said. "What can I possibly learn that I don't already know?"

"You're right," she said.

I hadn't expected that and made the mistake of looking surprised.

Then she continued with "But . . ."

"We just moved, Mom. I need time to adjust."

With a skeptical huff, Mom got up and poured herself another cup, adding a splash of brandy. "It's a matter of principle. We must show everybody that we can make it in America. You need to have a goal, Oksana, and you might not think school is so important, but wait until you're thirty and cleaning toilets because of a stupid mistake."

"What's wrong with cleaning toilets?"

"Absolutely nothing," she said. "As long as you're doing it by choice."

Pride wouldn't let me tell her that my not wanting to go to school had nothing to do with school itself but with the other people there. And I wasn't against having goals. As a little girl, I was convinced that I'd grow up to be a famous dancer.

It was only when I started school that I realized the foolishness of dreaming so big. My goals diminished in size and grandeur down to one: Don't get beat up. Who was to guarantee that Hollywood would be any different from Moscow?

Mom sighed. "Does my suffering mean nothing to you?" she said. "Look at how skinny I have become. If it wasn't for my coffee and cigarettes, I'd be walking on crutches by now. Oksana, you must try. To give me hope in these hard times. To show me that there is someone in this world who cares for me."

I hated it when she said things like that, especially when she used that small, defeated voice accompanied by melodramatic sighs. She could've written *The Idiot's Guide to Ruining Your Child's Life with Sighs.*

"Fine. After the New Year," I said. "Happy now?"

When she sat back down, her eyes sparkled, like she was congratulating herself on her theatrical outburst.

I was ready to lock myself in the bedroom for the rest of the week, but she was staring again and I knew I wouldn't be able to leave the kitchen without telling her what she wanted and didn't want to hear.

"So," she said finally. "Are they happy?"

"Mom, do we really have to do this?"

"I'm just asking. Not that I care. Just making conversation."

I took another bite, making sure my mouth was too full to answer. But then an image popped into my mind. I giggled through the toast. "She calls him honeylambshank."

"A what?"

"A honeylambshank."

Mom plunked down the cup, spilling coffee everywhere. We both knew how absolutely my father was not a honeylambshank. "Oh, Oksana. Really?"

"Yeah. And . . . and you know what he calls her back?"

"I'm afraid to find out."

"His little sparrow."

She slapped both palms on the table, her face tomato-red. We laughed until my sides ached.

COFFEE BEAN

Every morning in our little apartment, I woke up to the comforting aroma of strong coffee.

Mom drank it in a tiny espresso cup, always black and barely sweetened, a cigarette poised in one hand. It was one of the most prevalent customs of Armenian life; a young girl's ability to make a good cup of coffee increased her chances of catching a husband.

After she'd finished and the grounds had settled thickly at the bottom of the cup, Mom would turn it over on the saucer to allow the remnants to run down the sides and dry. When the dried grains had transformed into intricate designs, the fun part began: the telling of one's fortune.

Usually Mom read only her own cup or those of other adults. But sometimes I convinced her to let me have a drink so that she could glimpse my future, too. "My dear," she'd say, "you are destined to marry a prince and have so many diamonds you could use them for backgammon pieces."

Unlike Olga's fortune-telling services, my mother's coffee reading was a hobby, one shared by plenty of Armenian women who regularly gathered at one another's houses. Aunt Siranoosh claimed that this interest in divination might've come from the time when Romani travelers first camped out on Armenian land, sometime in the eleventh century. When Romani made their way from India to Europe (a journey that took hundreds of years to complete), it was the first country to allow the travelers to settle on its land. They stayed for so long that even today many Romani dialects contain Armenian words.

Mom reminded me of Agrefina. She was remarkably accurate in her predictions without the use of incantations or the need to stage a "spiritual place" to get people in the mood.

Rosa marveled at Mom's ability to see things in the black grounds, and I found our landlady's fascination with fortune-telling puzzling. Was Olga onto something with her predictions that she could make money in this city?

Inside a week, the neighbors came knocking on our door, each with an apologetic smile and a strong premonition about their mother, their job, their sex life, their dog's eating habits.

"This is good!" Rosa said as she paced our kitchen one morning, strategizing. "Susan from B12 asked about her son. He's in the military and he has gas problems. She hope is no cancer."

"Why is good?" Mom said. "I no hev much coffee."

"I tell you why, Nora. Because I tole her to pay you ten dollars and she said yes."

At first Mom was adamant about not taking money for readings; in Moscow, a priest at our family's church, who was also a close friend, had cautioned against reading for monetary gain, warning that it'd bring terrible luck. *Dvoeverie* was as Christian as it was pagan. The priest was a well-known oracle, or, to use proper churchspeak, he had the "gift of discernment"—a new term to coat an ancient concept. But no one dared call *him* a fortune-teller because his sight came directly from God. Years later, a number of his predictions in regard to our family came true.

He'd predicted my parents' divorce, an estrangement from family, and even the gambling addiction my mother would struggle with in the future.

But Rosa argued a good point. "Everybody here charge. Even kids who bring newspapers," she said. "Ju run out of money. How will bills get paid?" When Mom didn't answer, Rosa nodded with renewed conviction. "Nothing wrong with ten dollars. Later, we charge twenty."

Truth was, Mom and I had recently discussed the increasing money deficit. She'd come back one afternoon from a job interview at the Russian Market, ten minutes from our place. Imagine my mother, all made up, wearing her best turquoise silk dress and sleek pumps, strolling into a business whose only purpose is to produce the same greasy foods sold in stores back in the old country. And now picture the indignity on her face when the manager tells her she'd have to chop, marinade, and bake in the back of the store for ten hours along with three other Russian ladies (who all used to be somebody, by the way—one of them an engineer). All this for twenty dollars a day, cash. "In America our titles abandon us," he'd said with a smirk when she questioned his sanity.

"An engineer?" I said when she tossed her pumps aside and reclined on the couch later that afternoon.

"Plus a kindergarten teacher *and* a general's wife."

"Well, it's better than no job." My version of encouragement.

"For someone your age, but not for distinguished women like us."

"Why can't you ask Grandpa Andrei for help?" I said. Roxy and I hadn't spoken to Dad's parents since we'd moved. I thought it was too expensive to call but, judging by the shadows mobilizing on my mother's face, I'd been mistaken.

"Grandpa isn't talking to us."

"That's not true," I said.

"I don't know what your father told him, but our lines are cut. Forget about them."

"But it doesn't make sense."

"Not everything has to," she snapped.

I should've been used to cutting lines by now. After all, I had felt the snip of Aunt Varvara's scissors.

I crouched down and rested my elbows on Mom's knees. The fragrance of her French perfume clung to her dress. The bottle was long empty, but she still rubbed its lid over her clothes to get every last bit of the vapors.

"He's their son, honey. Who else would they side with?" She tucked a wisp of hair behind my ear and kissed me on the forehead.

"Would you take their money if they offered to help?"

"No," she said, and I believed her.

An idea came to me then. "What about Grandma Rose? Aunt Siranoosh? You know they would send us money."

"They mustn't know," she said. "Not yet. Not before I fix everything."

I was devastated by my grandparents' choice, but not as surprised as I should've been. Was I becoming unbreakable?

The coffee readings took place inside our kitchen in the evenings, after most kids were sound asleep and the only light outside swam from the bottom of the pool like a smoky blue phantom.

I stayed up, on account of my new job as the fortune-teller's interpreter. Well, it was more like an apprenticeship, considering I worked for free and with substantial help from my Russian-English dictionary. But at least it forced me to practice my language skills on real people instead of mirrors.

I can imagine how uncomfortable it must've been for the

clients to open up in front of a sixteen-year-old girl, especially one listening with fascination. But their worries always overcame that small inconvenience.

The readings reminded me of the game of telephone. First, the clients explained their trouble. Second, I completely misinterpreted everything they said. Third, Mom, suspecting difficulty in communication, simply told them what she saw. Good thing she got it right nearly every time.

"Ms. Nora, my wife is acting strange. Is she having an affair?"

"Mr. Kipfer says his wife is crazy."

"She's not. Tell him she's just pregnant."

"How will I know which man to marry? They have both asked, but I can't decide."

"Celia wants to get married twice."

"I see only one man in her cup, with a number seven below him. She should only marry the one seven years younger than her."

"I want to buy a bakery. Can you tell me if that's a good idea?"

"He wants to buy a bakery." Sometimes I did get it right.

"He should."

How many conversations I botched during those sessions, I'll never know, but the readings acted as some kind of psychotherapy. People left happier, more focused on hope instead of worry.

As per Rosa's predictions, the money helped, and we now had enough for a little more than the absolute necessities. I knew that our situation was all wrong, that my father never should've let it get this bad. But I was too fond of the fragile peace between my parents to confront either of them about it. That's why I went back to Dad's house on the weekends, per my parents' arrangement. Even while Olga and I kept snapping at each other like crabs, I wanted Mom to think all was well so as not to give her a reason to forbid contact. Also, I didn't trust my stepmother with

Roxy. Although Mom never once asked for a thing, Dad assured Roxy and me that he would help out as soon as the business took off, and we passed on the message, thinking it'd make Mom feel less depressed. It didn't.

We got home from one of our weekends at Dad's, and Roxy immediately stuck her wrist in front of Mom's face. "Dad got me this bracelet at the Venice Beach boardwalk. It's magic."

One glance at the bracelet made of thin beaded leather strips, and Mom looked fit to burst.

"I make sure you have something to eat every day! That you have clean sheets to sleep on! But, oh, thank goodness you have a father who can afford to buy you a magic bracelet!"

Even though Mom apologized later, Roxy began to hide her trinkets in her backpack.

Mom was having a difficult time accepting the fact that we had officially joined the ranks of the underprivileged. I knew how she felt. The disparity between Dad's lifestyle and our own pointed to only one thing: we were poor. The idea didn't fit into anything I'd ever experienced. There was a time when money held no value for me.

One day when I was ten, Zhanna and I were walking down busy Arbat Street in Moscow. January had frozen the ground into sheets of ice. Our breath clouded and our fingers froze. I'd jammed my hands into the jacket pockets and one of them ripped, sending a scattering of change over the sidewalk.

"Oh God, I can't even feel my knees to bend down," I pouted.

"What's the big deal? Leave it," my cousin said. We moved on, but as I glanced back, I saw an old woman crouched down on all fours as she carefully picked up the money we had discarded.

And now Rosa was driving us to the Hollywood welfare office, maintaining that one really could receive money without having to work.

Mom refused to accept this. "How anybody give you money? For what?"

"Ju are a single mom in need of help."

"How will we pay it back?" I asked.

"Don't have to, *mija*. Thas why is called public assistance."

It sounded too simple and not quite right to take money for doing nothing. But the first check came, and it covered rent, bills, and the groceries, leaving eighty-five dollars for the rest of the month.

Since we hadn't been able to celebrate my sixteenth birthday in our usual style, or Mom's birthday in November, or even New Year's, we split thirty dollars and bought one another one present each. Roxy got a play makeup kit, Mom got a sterling silver ring Roxy and I found at the DollarDream, and I got a pair of gloves.

Mom had never needed to manage money before. Growing up, I'd never heard my parents say, "We have no money." Whenever we needed something, like a new car, or a monthlong vacation to the Black Sea, they found a way. Often Grandma Rose helped, or my parents just played extra gigs.

In America, it seemed there wasn't enough money *to* manage, so like in the old times Mom splurged, baking a giant turkey she bought on sale the day we received the first check, and preparing her famous scallion mashed potatoes with two sticks of butter.

We had meat, vegetables, and bread that night, Roxy's fiancé serenading us with "Careless Whisper" from a mini tape player we had recently bought. Now all we needed were more people to share our joy. We invited some of our neighbors, and as I watched the people around me dancing, and eating, and joking, for that evening I forgot that the next day we'd be poor once again.

WHAT DO YOU SEE?

Many people upon hearing the term "Romani" or "Gypsy" promptly conjure up tarot cards, nomadic caravans, uneducated children, and dirt-poor families who are either too lazy to work or too care-free to give a damn. In Europe, the words "thief" and "swindler" are synonymous with "Romani," and the conflicts between cultures often end in violence. The roots of this animosity span centuries, and trying to make sense of them would take up an entire book on its own. Ask ten different people to explain it and you'll get ten different answers.

While living in Italy many years later, I met Milosh, a student of the Romani who tried to clarify some of it for me. The original Roma nomads, those who didn't settle in the Middle East and the Caucasus regions, eventually reached medieval Europe. For a while they shared the land with their neighbors and hosts, living in accord. But that didn't mean that either side wanted to change their way of life to accommodate the other. Paying taxes was a foreign concept to the self-contained Roma; so was submitting to a king they'd never met, considering how they had their own royalty chosen by the Romani and their councils of elders. Like

Europeans, Romani considered their race pure. This was reinforced when they, like the Native Americans, began to encounter mysterious illnesses that sometimes wiped out entire caravans. They were convinced that the Europeans were plagued by evil and therefore avoided dealing with outsiders.

In some countries the rich made a sport of hunting Romani for money. "Gypsy hunts" were lawful as a means to drive the nomads out and became so popular that even commoners were encouraged to participate. You got an especially large prize if your kill happened to be a Gypsy clan leader. And if you had trouble telling a Gypsy from the normal folk, the identifying brands on their chests, enforced by most feudal lords and the Church, came in handy. The Romani of medieval Europe were in the wrong place at the wrong time, one of the unlucky groups caught in the war between Church and monarchy. Many a Gypsy was burned at the stake during the Inquisition, along with the mentally ill, those unfortunate enough to anger a neighbor or a city official, or simply because somebody wanted their cow.

One of my friends once asked, "Why didn't the Gypsies just go back to India?" But that would've been difficult to accomplish; after wandering for centuries they didn't have a country to go back to.

On this side of the Atlantic, a Romani is given the famous Hollywood makeover, and suddenly "Gypsy" means a free-spirited hippie or a bohemian; it's not seen as a stigma or even a race but as an exotic lifestyle choice. Perhaps this view has to do with the beginnings of modern America, which are to me, like the big bang theory, violent and wondrous. No one was safe from hatred and betrayal. *Everyone* was fighting to survive. It seemed the American Gypsies weren't immune to the neck-breaking race for what became the American Dream. Like so many others, they were more than willing to cut their roots in order to stake their claim on prosperity. Could that be the reason the American Gypsies largely escaped the more malevolent prejudices their European counterparts suffered?

One day Dad and I stumbled upon a novelty store in the heart of Hollywood. Olga and Roxy had gone straight to the nearest mall to avoid being embarrassed by Dad. Walking down Hollywood Boulevard was one of Dad's favorite activities, and he had a habit of stopping in front of his favorite stars with his feet planted on either side, disregarding the foot-traffic jams he created.

"*Nu shto B.B. King. Zakourim* (Well, B.B. King. Shall we light up)?" he'd say, and flick out his lighter and cigarette.

"Dad. People are looking."

"Genius must draw attention. It can't be helped."

After I dragged Dad away from the lengthy worship of King's star, we took one of the smaller streets winding up the hill and passed a store called Gypsy Lair, which my father indignantly translated into "Gypsy Liar" until I corrected him.

"It might be someone I know, from the old country," he said.

But the clerk turned out to be a teenager with rosy cheeks.

"I'm, like, from San Fernando originally, but, like, I'm not at all like my parents." The girl tossed her blond cornrows out of her face and leaned on the counter littered with "Gypsy" hair clips and gargantuan roses in a variety of the season's trendiest colors next to a bucket of mood rings. She wore a billowy top and a long skirt with tiny bells that jingled whenever she moved.

"So you not own this?" Dad motioned around the store. It was smaller than our living room and crammed with Halloween merchandise that consisted mostly of varieties of Gypsy costumes. Sexy Gypsy and Vampire Gypsy hung next to long-haired wigs and fake-coin necklaces. There were baskets full of scarves like the ones Stevie Nicks wore and Steven Tyler wrapped around his mike stands, and a table stacked with palm-reading books and tarot cards.

"I wish. That's how come I love working here, 'cause I'm, like, free-spirited, you know. My parents, they're Republican, but I'm like a Gypsy. I like to travel. And, like, experience life."

"You Gypsy?" Dad asked, drumming his fingers on the rustic counter. He was smiling.

"I'm hungry," I said in hopes of saving the poor girl from what was to come.

"I'm so totally Gypsy. I even belly dance."

"Belly dance is Arab. You know, yes?"

She squinted.

"You know Gypsy is, how you say?" He looked at me. "*Natsyonalnost.*"

I had no choice. "It's a nationality."

The girl bit her lower lip and stood up straight for the first time. She scratched her eyebrow and I noticed a tuft of blond hair peeking out of her underarm.

"From two hundred of years back," my father continued. "In imperial Russia, Russian Roma has permission to citizen rights. They to train and sell horses. They pay *nalog*, which mean tax, and any business they want, they can do. *Vot tak* (That's right)."

"That's awesome," she said in a voice that had lost some of its free-spiritedness.

Dad turned to me yet again. "*Shto takoe* awesome?"

My translation produced a clearing of the throat that usually indicated displeasure.

"And this store," he said, "is no awesome. Is shame. In old Russia we has Gypsy counts and rich families. Gypsy has freedom but also they build big houses to live."

I knew that if I let him, Dad would go on with the history lesson until the store closed or the girl broke into sobs. I didn't understand this urge he had to lecture or correct strangers on the subject. But as I grew older I found myself doing exactly that, because the conversation never ended at "I am Gypsy."

Grandpa Andrei once warned Dad that if he thought in America everyone would accept him as he was, he might as well find himself a remote island to live out the rest of his life on.

"Remember," Grandpa told Dad during our very last Russian New Year's, "only your homeland will bring you happiness, especially in your old age."

Mom had joined two long tables and then covered them with a white tablecloth to accommodate several dozen guests. The Christmas-tree lights, along with the candles and the garland lights strung from the ceiling, bounced off the crystal wineglasses and the silverware. The living room looked like it floated inside a burst of fireworks.

Earlier Dad had gone to the butcher to pick up the suckling pig he'd ordered weeks in advance. By the time it arrived at our party it had been seasoned and roasted in the fire pit of a local restaurant. Mom made her famous *tort-salat*. There was also salted herring with raw onion rings and massive mounds of mashed potatoes next to piles of boiled dill potatoes next to stuffed potatoes and potatoes au gratin. Bowls full of garlicky yogurt sauce nestled next to grape leaves stuffed with ground beef and rice. Armenian *basturma* (wind-cured beef), Astrakhanskaya caviar made with eggplant, and regular black and red caviar were all present and ready to be devoured by our increasingly intoxicated guests. There was so much liquor, you had to lean around the bottles to speak with the person across the table.

All through the night more food and vodka appeared as if my parents had come into the possession of the fabled tablecloth straight out of a Russian fairy tale that granted your wish for any food or drink you wanted.

According to the Chinese horoscope, 1990 was to be the year of the metal horse, and since every bit of luck counted in our household, everyone was to hold something metal when the TV hosts rang the midnight bell. To increase the New Year's good fortune, our candles burned inside silver votives, people rested their cigarettes in iron ashtrays, and a neighbor named Timor brought a box of nails in case one of us found ourselves metal-less at the last minute.

"You're young," Grandpa said close to Dad's ear so as to be heard, "so you chase a perfect life. But do you really think there are no labels in America?"

"This land has brought us nothing but bad luck," Dad said. "For every good thing, five bad ones happen."

"Not that again. This damn curse will travel wherever you take it." Grandpa tapped his temple. "Up in that mulish head of yours."

The TV hosts were announcing that we had a minute left until midnight, and the voices shifted from scattered-loud to deafening. We counted down the year along with the TV, with our lucky charms raised high in our hands. I was holding a fork, Roxy a teaspoon, and Zhanna a pair of tweezers she'd found in the bathroom.

Dad smacked his knees, his face now animated with daydreams. "No matter," he said. "I don't want to end up eighty, playing chess on the bench outside my house with a bunch of drunks I've known since nursery school. I don't want to pretend to have nothing so that the *Kommunisti* don't show up at my door and confiscate my life away from me. I should to be able to enjoy the money I make, even if I'm Rom."

"What's this nonsense?" Grandpa said. "I enjoy my money, I do. But why flaunt it?"

"All I'm saying is that everyone wants to live there. Why? Because everyone is allowed to do as they please. In America you won't have to hide your wealth under the living-room floorboards."

But even then Grandpa's words felt more real than my father's. He seemed to know things others didn't. Very different from Dad, who acted like he knew things people just didn't get.

After his conversation with the salesgirl inside the Gypsy Lair, Dad stayed in a sour mood for days. How a young girl could possibly be familiar with the particulars of the class system of imperial Russia was a mystery to me, but the logistics mattered little to my father, who had found the first flaws in the country he had worshipped for so very long.

CHER AND I HAVE THINGS
IN COMMON

Communicating with strangers is death to an introvert, and even more so to a teenage introvert. How about a teenage immigrant introvert sporting a pair of acid-washed jeans with leg warmers pulled over the bottoms? As soon as I stepped on the campus grounds of Hollywood High on my first day of school, I recognized my folly. My Lioness did not fit in, either—not with the half-shaved skulls nor the locks streaked with blue.

In Russia, schools encompassed all grades. Seven-year-olds played hide-and-seek alongside the ninth-graders. Older kids took care of the younger ones. There, you were part of one community, whether you liked it or not, and all of us shared responsibilities according to our age. Teenagers helped out in the kitchens and on the playgrounds. Kids old enough to mop the floors of their classrooms or wipe the windows mopped and wiped, no matter what kind of a car their folks owned.

At Hollywood High, school was an empire divided, dictated by geography as much as by identity. On one end of the campus, the one closer to Hollywood Boulevard, you'd find the black-trench-coat territory, the Performing Arts Magnet School. Girls with purple hair, guys in dresses, and other artistic types with pierced noses and studded tongues lurked in the cavernous hallways of the auditorium, with its underbelly of music classrooms. It also housed the cafeteria—the only common ground for all students, regardless of their fashion sense, ethnicity, or level of weird.

Everybody on this end aimed to be a superstar someday. Hollywood High had given the world Judy Garland, Carol Burnett, and even Cher, who is adored as much as soccer by half of Europe. Using a prepaid international calling card (an essential in an immigrant neighborhood), I called Zhanna to tell her I'd be attending the same school that Cher once did. She screamed into the phone. According to Zhanna and Romani tradition, it couldn't be simple coincidence—it was a sign of great things to come. I hoped so. After all, I was in America now. Great things were as common here as Twinkies.

Only a few hundred yards away, on the side of the school bordering Sunset Boulevard, the buzz of foreign tongues filled the hallways, spilling outside through massive windows: Spanish, Romanian, Mandarin, and Arabic. Sprinkled in between endured a small number of American kids who happened to live in the neighborhood but did not aspire to superstardom. My first bouts of English tutelage took place on this side of the campus.

By this time in my life I spoke three languages: Russian, Armenian, and Rromanes. The Romani side of the family slipped into Rromanes only when they wanted to say something they didn't want anyone else to understand. After Mom left Armenia she preferred to speak Russian, said it made for a more sophisticated first impression. I had to ask Aunt Siranoosh to teach me Armenian. Every town had its own dialect. If two Armenians met on the moon, they'd know, after a few words, to which earthly city the other belonged. Armenian is livelier than Russian but not as rowdy as Rromanes. It has ties to Greek but is strongly influenced by ancient Iranian tongues. In fact, when I spoke it outside Armenia, people often assumed I was from the Middle East. It had come in handy only when I visited Grandma Rose in the summer, but I loved to practice speaking it.

And here I was, the bubble of foreignness keeping me prisoner up to that moment, about to be popped. Closer than ever to finally discovering the America of bootlegged movies that my parents collected like holy relics.

I wandered through the crowd, watching the entire population of the world milling about me. There were so many variations here that everyone fit in by not fitting in.

I was astonished to hear my counselor—the baldheaded and bespectacled Mr. Bedrosian—explain in Armenian how an American high school operated.

As far as Mr. Bedrosian knew, I had a Ukrainian father and an Armenian mother. He had no inkling of my "other" nationality, and I preferred it that way. I had long ago discovered that it was best to reveal my Roma side only to those I'd known for a while and to really anticipate how that piece of information would affect them.

A friend had called it the "Beauty and the Beast" syndrome. I was once waiting to meet up with Zhanna inside a coffee shop in Moscow, sipping my hot chocolate at the counter near a window overlooking a busy square, when a woman next to me started up a conversation. "How old are you?" "Fourteen." "Are those music books in your sack?" "I play the piano." "How wonderful! I've always wanted to try." Then she asked if I could watch her grocery bags while she used the pay phone. "Sure," I said, and she had made to leave with a grateful smile when her eyes fell on my cousin who'd come in through the door. Zhanna's long sparkly skirt (the way she dressed only when the laundry hadn't been done) and her long loose hair made the woman's step falter. The stranger watched Zhanna's progress across the room with a stifled breath. When it became obvious that the Gypsy was approaching us, she sat back down and muttered, "I'll call later." Only a few sips into our hot chocolate, the owner asked us to leave.

My Beast would remain safely veiled from Mr. Bedrosian.

The top of Mr. Bedrosian's head barely came up to my chin as he marched ahead of me down the hallway.

"First, homeroom," he said, pushing the office glass door inward. "Read the list. It has all the room numbers and teachers' names."

"Homeroom?" I asked, hastening after him.

He stopped to face me, eyebrows huddled above thick lenses. "Homeroom. Third floor. Last building on the left."

"What do we learn in homeroom?"

"Nothing. You sit and you don't ask useless questions."

As promised, homeroom proved quite uneventful. When I found the second class on the list, I thought I had made a mistake. I didn't know what ESL stood for, so I had expected a room full of American kids.

But the people in my ESL (English as a second language) class, chattering at fifty words per second, were like me: foreigners. The din inside the room rose in waves. No one was speaking English. As I picked a desk at the back, I even heard Russian. I stiffened, ordering my fingers to relax their hold on the notebook I had been strangling.

Growing up, I was never one of those girls with an inexhaustible appetite for socializing. I preferred my easel and paints to playground politics. Even before the kids at my school turned on

me after hearing my grandmother sing on the radio, I was already
solitary, memorizing epic poems with help from Aunt Siranoosh.

The singer Vysotsky once wrote:

Amidst molten candles and sundown prayers,
Amidst war trophies and fires of peace,
Lived book children who knew no battles,
Suffering their minor catastrophes.

Children always complain
of their age and their lot.
And we fought until slain,
And schemed mortal plots.

And our clothes were patched
By our mothers with haste.
We then swallowed books,
Getting drunk on the taste.

That's exactly the kind of thirst that plunged me headlong
into one book after another. Every package that arrived from
Aunt Siranoosh at our doorstep in Moscow sent me deep into a
waking dream. Visions of Sherlock Holmes's foggy London spun
behind my lids with the clatter of carriage wheels, and I scouted
with the last of the Mohicans. Mom complained that her well-
meaning sister was encouraging me to become a recluse and so-
cially inept, but Aunt Siranoosh maintained that the first step to
success is to learn human nature and that the surest way to do
that is through works of great men and women. She lived by
Plato's dictum: "And what, Socrates, is the food of the soul?
Surely, I said, knowledge is the food of the soul."

The ESL teacher, Mrs. Maxim, asked me to introduce myself.

My heart beat against the roof of my mouth.

"Tell us your name and where you are from. Don't be nervous. In this class, we are learning to speak English together," the teacher said slowly, clasping her hands and grinning. Her hair was almost as bad as mine, if a little shorter and frizzier.

I cleared my throat and scanned the room without seeing a single face clearly. "My name is Oksana. I was burned in Latvia."

"Burned?" Mrs. Maxim said.

"Yes. In the city of Riga. In October."

"Oh, you mean born. You were born in Riga, Latvia. Wow. Can you tell us a little about your hometown?"

My memories of Riga were the haphazard images of a child too young to remember the details—we had moved to Moscow by the time I turned nine—but they were filled with sunlight, the Old Town's cobblestone streets anchored by Gothic cathedrals, and the summer rains during which some Rigans danced outside in their swimsuits (a legacy of their pagan past). Back then, my parents and I had lived at Grandpa Andrei's house, where the backyard looked like a forest, abundant in gooseberry and loganberry bushes, studded with apple and cherry trees. Every spring Grandma Ksenia filled several giant buckets to the rim with ripe cherries, simmering the fruit with sugar until the entire house smelled like a candy factory. We kept some of the preserves and sold the rest to Scandinavian tourists.

To me, Latvia had always remained a land of enchantment straight out of a Hans Christian Andersen fairy tale, and I would have loved to share this with the class that day. But who had these words?

At the end of the day exhaustion threatened to knock me off my feet. Sitting at a bus stop, I realized that only seven months ago

Zhanna and I were making plans to get out of Moscow if my parents botched the American interview. We'd go to Armenia and get work at the city hall where Grandma Rose's best friend was a chief secretary. Or we'd head to the resort towns on the Black Sea. Zhanna's voice had blossomed in her last year at the music school. She'd sing pop tunes in the clubs and I'd be happy waiting tables as long as we had our own place.

And now I was here, in this dreamlike limbo where the past and the present ran parallel. Zhanna's excitement never diminished during our phone conversations. But I wasn't telling her everything. Not about the way Roxy jumped up and down whenever Mom dragged in a black garbage bag filled with used clothes she had bought at a garage sale or found on the curb, nor about the change we now counted with care. She also didn't know that I was thinking up ways to keep my Gypsiness incognito for now, that even being in America didn't stop me from replaying the events leading to Ruslan's death. My cousin, who never shied away from her heritage, would not approve. So every morning after that first day of school, I'd chant into my bathroom mirror, "If anyone asks what you are, you must tell the entire truth." My reflection seemed determined to comply, chin lifted and eyes sparkly, but every time the question came up she scurried into hiding.

THE MISS

Encouraged by the scores I was receiving from Mrs. Maxim, I decided to venture farther into the world of Los Angeles than I'd ever had the nerve to go before.

I peered timidly through the window of a secondhand shop off Highland Avenue. The girl I was staring at barely smiled, her pencil-sketched form ghost-still, but she was beautiful and regal to me. I pressed my forehead to the glass and sounded out the words on the book jacket: DJ-E-IN AI-RR.

My pulse jumped. I knew the name; sometimes I believed I loved Rochester better than Jane did. I'd read *Jane Eyre* in Russian several times but had always dreamed of reading it in the original language. Without hesitation I purchased the tattered copy with a few dollars I'd been saving. Home, I flopped on the bed, ignoring Roxy and the three open bottles of nail polish beside her on the floor.

Her only reason for going to school at that point was to show off her affluent sense of fashion. The girls in her clique were quickly becoming the sought-out experts on headbands and color-coordinated outfits. Many a morning Roxy scrunched up her face at my outfit and endeavored to secure a lock of my hair with a Hello Kitty clip. Apparently everything hot pink was in, but black T-shirts with grimacing rockers: so not.

"What are you doing?" she demanded, grabbing her left foot and blowing on her toenails: two red, two black, and one pink. "Can't you read in the living room? Maria's coming. We're gonna play the Oscars."

"This is my room, too."

"I'm telling Mom." Roxy scrambled up and left in a huff.

I ignored her, opening the text to a random page:

The old crone "nichered" a laugh under her bonnet and bandage; she then drew out a short black pipe, and lighting it began to smoke. Having indulged a while in this sedative, she raised her bent body, took the pipe from her lips, and while gazing steadily at the fire, said very deliberately—"You are cold; you are sick; and you are silly."

"Prove it," I rejoined.

"I will, in few words. You are cold, because you are alone: no contact strikes the fire from you that is in you. You are sick; because the best of feelings, the highest and the sweetest given to man, keeps far away from you. You are silly, because, suffer as you may, you will not beckon it to approach, nor will you stir one step to meet it where it waits you."

I'd been sure I would recognize the contents no matter which passage fate led me to, but I didn't. With help from my dictionary it took me an hour to learn that the section was one of my favorites. Rochester, disguised as an old Gypsy woman, was reading Jane's fortune.

I threw down the book and paced the narrow room. Seven months in America, and what did I have to show for it? I could tell you that I was born in Riga but nothing about the city's Gothic beauty. I could name my favorite movie and not be able to explain why I avoided watching it. Perhaps I wasn't studying hard enough, or maybe the material we used in the classroom wasn't challenging enough.

First, I dialed Aunt Siranoosh. Mom didn't call home as often as when we first moved. When she did, it was to report how well we were doing. And though everyone thought Nora was crazy-busy making American dollars with no time for mothballing (Roxy and I were practically the next Hollywood starlets), I knew Mom's ever-growing stockpile of lies had gotten so shaky that she was afraid to let the wrong things slip in conversation and make the whole thing tumble. And because Mom was aware of her sister's skills in the area of stealthy information retrieval, I was instructed not to call unless Mom was present. But the situation demanded immediate attention, and so I sneaked the phone into the bedroom. Aunt would have the answer. "Darling," she said. "I don't have the answer. Talk to a teacher. Teachers always know what to do."

Mrs. Maxim was the next logical choice.

But when I walked into the classroom the next morning, I lost my resolve, intimidated not by Mrs. Maxim but by an unfamiliar face.

The rain outside pounded so hard, it seemed likely to drown the world. Soaked through, I had run shivering into the classroom and right into his stare. He reclined behind his desk as if he owned it: long legs extended, arms crossed, a self-satisfied smile creasing the corners of his eyes. His dirty-blond hair reached past his shoulders and down tanned arms accentuated by a plain black T-shirt. I had never noticed plain black T-shirts before. A pair of black jeans made for a nice finish (I had always noticed black jeans). A leather jacket was slung over the back of his chair.

"Check out the new guy. Isn't he gorgeous?" Natasha, one of the Russian students, whispered as I sat behind her. "I bet that jacket is real leather, and look, his eyes are so green I can see them all the way from here."

At the teacher's prompting he sauntered up to the front of the class.

"Hello," he said. "My name is Cruz Marchi. I am from Manaus, Brazil."

You'd think his words might lurch, considering this was an ESL class. Mine had. You might expect him, like the rest of us, to scuttle back to his desk, cowering in embarrassment. I did. But his English sounded surprisingly smooth, so what was he doing here?

"Do you like music?" Mrs. Maxim asked, folding her hands into the pockets of a furry brown cardigan. She was always looking for ways to keep us talking, and as soon as Cruz nodded she inquired what kind.

"All music."

Clearly the guy was a liar, I mused. Nobody likes all music. I should know. I'd been playing piano since the age of six because my mother insisted I get a formal education in a music school where neither rock nor jazz made it into our music-history textbooks.

My father didn't participate much in my piano education; playing instruments had been largely a man's job, and most Roma women danced or sang. In the old days a woman holding an instrument was a perverse sight, and maybe some of those sensibilities carried across the ages. If it had been up to Dad, I wouldn't have gone to a music school. I was too young to understand that he simply didn't believe I, a girl, could be a good musician. But I wanted to be good.

Especially at jazz.

My interest most likely came from Zhanna's older brother, my cousin Misha, who adored everything American. The walls of his apartment were covered with posters of Wynton Marsalis, Thelonious Monk, Miles Davis, and *Penthouse* models; he claimed that real musicians dated the most beautiful women, and that you found those women only in *Penthouse*. He was a full-time musician himself, and whenever he toured, Zhanna and their mom, my aunt Laura, would apartment-sit. Sometimes they invited me to stay with them, but I hated using Misha's bathroom, where spread-eagled naked women pouted from every direction, even the door. Aunt Laura taped paper flowers over the more offensive spots. "These girls are too young to see what a *manda* looks like," she told Misha.

On many occasions, Zhanna warned her stoner brother that God would someday punish him for his vulgar tastes, to which Misha replied that he was already being punished by having a Soviet passport and a black man's soul.

At the end of the class period I got my chance to talk to Mrs. Maxim as she sat at her desk making notes in her student record book.

"I have a question," I said.

"Let's see if I can answer it."

"This book. I read it before. Seven times."

She took the copy, leafing through the yellowed pages. "It's a great story. Wow! Seven times?"

"In Russian."

"Wonderful!"

I accepted the book back, holding it to my chest like a shield. "When will my accent go away?" I didn't mean to ask precisely that.

Maybe she sensed my discomfort, because her face remained politely amiable. "It might never go away. Why?"

"I should know English now. I should be able to read *Jane Eyre*; I should speak without thinking words first; should be thinking in English also, not only Russian; should—"

"Slow down. You're upset because you think your English isn't good enough?"

"I'm still a foreigner."

She stood, hands on my shoulders. "There is nothing wrong with that. Our heritage is what makes us unique. As for the language, it takes time, and you are doing very well, considering it hasn't even been a year. Give yourself a break. Recognize your accomplishments."

A rush of despair made its way up my body. I didn't want to be comforted just now. "Is not enough. I must learn faster. Show me how."

"It'll come to you eventually. Why are you in such a hurry?" When I didn't answer, Mrs. Maxim studied me. She squeezed her fingers for a second, and then let go. "I don't have the answers, Oksana. I can't give you a magic formula so that you wake up tomorrow ready for *Jeopardy!* I didn't say I can't help, though, so don't look at me like you're ready to bawl. Let's think about this. You're doing great in this class, right?"

"Perhaps."

She frowned, waiting.

"Yes. I'm doing good."

"Classics isn't where you start. The text is too complex; there are too many analogies, metaphors, double meanings, which may only be caught when one thinks in the language one reads. Think baby steps." She went around the desk and, from the bottom drawer, produced a thin paperback. "Try this."

"*The Miss and the Maverick*," I read aloud. The girl on the cover wore a man's hat and a defiant expression. In the bottom right corner, there was another image of her. Here she pretended to sleep in the grass, hair in disarray, shirt unbuttoned. A blond man hovered over her with a ravenous expression on his unnaturally chiseled face. The maverick, no doubt—whatever that meant.

"It's a romance novel," Mrs. Maxim said, to my perplexity. "About love. Not the most educational read, but much easier *to* read. You might still have problems understanding everything, but it's less complicated than Brontë or Dumas."

Thus began my education in the language of swoons and sighs. For the longest time, I called an umbrella a parasol, and my ideas of the American West came straight out of Linda Lael Miller's frontier novels such as *Caroline and the Raider*. I even joined the Harlequin book club and squealed every time the mailman delivered the package containing four brand-new romances. Suddenly I had a goal. The soundest, the most brilliant goal: like my mother (when she first came to Russia and re-created herself), I would master English, shed the old me, and become a brand-new, all-American Oksana.

BLATNYAK

Mom passed the next couple of months adding homey touches to our place and answering the ads that promised riches for stuffing envelopes and sewing handkerchiefs. She was still on the prowl for bachelor doctors, but they were rare in our neighborhood. Ex-convicts and ex–gang members, on the other hand? You couldn't get away even if you tried, their gallant whistles of admiration an ever present accompaniment to every trip down the sidewalk. Mulishly she held on to the big ideas concerning our future, but her drinking was starting to interfere with those. Again.

Mom's dark secret had been years in the making, but I'd begun to notice its impact only in the months before we left Moscow. When Dad drank, it didn't seem to make much difference in our lives. He was a man and an artist, which afforded him some kind of license to take that customary swig or ten before going onstage. Mom had always been the strong one, and when she crumbled, we crumbled, too.

One day, Mom came to my school bearing gifts of homemade dolma—stuffed grape leaves—for Mrs. Maxim. She appeared in the middle of the class, dressed up, her eyes shiny after a few cans of beer. She waved at me, grinning, as my surprised teacher ushered Mom to a chair. Mom was in that stage of drunk where she loved the world and all its fuzzy creatures. While the students worked on an assignment, she and Mrs. Maxim sat at the teacher's desk whispering, but I could tell by my teacher's strained smiles that she was uncomfortable.

Once at home, I confronted my mother.

She swayed into the kitchen, and my heart twisted when she pulled out a bottle of Keystone beer. As soon as Roxy saw that, she was out the door. I didn't blame her.

"I wish I had a video camera to record how you act when you're drunk," I said.

"You've always been jealous of me," Mom slurred. She unscrewed the beer cap and tossed it to the floor. Her eyes roamed the counter, searching for something that wasn't there. "You all are. Nobody has accomplished as much, and now you all want me to fail."

I was scared of my mother when she got to this stage, the one where her skin paled, her cheeks hollowed, her eyes sputtered rage. Slowly I moved from the kitchen doorway to the counter's edge where she'd left her wallet. She poured beer into a plastic tumbler and tilted her head back for a long swig. I snatched her wallet, hiding it in the waistband of my jeans. But I wasn't fast enough.

Mom slammed the cup down.

"Because of you, we divorced," she said, grappling behind me for her wallet. I fought her off, but what I really wanted to do was to bawl. "Your father hated your guts and I was the only one to defend you. We had more fights over you than anything else."

"Stop it, Mom."

"No, *you* stop it, Gypsy slime. You know what I see when I look at you?"

"If you need more, I can get it for you, okay? Just don't go out like this."

I smelled her breath on my face. It isn't Mom, I kept reminding myself. She thrust me against the wall. "You'll never thwart my spirit. I won't let you."

By the time I saw her fist coming, it was too late to duck. She punched me in the nose.

"I see your bastard father in that fucking mug of yours."

I shoved my mother back and she fell. There was a moment of shock when neither of us spoke or moved. Blood trickled from my nose.

I raced out of the apartment, leaping over the last few stairs.

"Oksana, wait!" she called after me, but I was through the front gates and around the back of the building.

Sitting on a rock covered with dried weeds, I leaned back on the wall and held my nostrils together. Mom's favorite threat during an argument was that she'd leave and never come back. And now my legs screamed to run. But if everyone got their wishes, my parents and I would be galloping off to the opposite ends of the world, leaving Roxy alone and confused. Seemed we were stuck.

Esmeralda had told me that people were both God and Devil, and I wanted to believe her. The rational part of me waited for hours until Mom slept off the booze. The God in her always returned then, and she remembered so little of what had transpired and apologized so ardently that I'd forget the Devil.

Not long after, I dragged her to see a substance-abuse counselor. It took guts for her to humor her sixteen-year-old daughter, take the city bus to Burbank, and get off in front of the building branded with a Something-or-other Rehab Counseling Services sign, but Mom was never short on mettle. That was something I'd aspired to even as we'd drifted apart.

"Ms. Polak. I no *alkogolic* because I can stop anytime," Mom said to the woman, who in my opinion looked too young to have the knowledge to tell bluff from truth.

She had on a blouse with frilly sleeves and a pleated blue skirt that matched the low-heeled pumps little girls show off at piano recitals. And could one really place any trust in the hands of a woman wearing a flowered headband? But even more discouraging than Ms. Polak's appearance was the way she conducted herself, like a kid playing doctor.

"It's okay," she said. "Now I will start a folder for you." She reached from her chair to the top shelf above the desk—"Here they are"—and pulled down a beige folder, which she then opened like it was the priciest item in the office. "I will ask you some, hmm, questions. Let me see." Her fingers plucked the blue Bic from a cup of pens. "Let me write down your name." As she wrote, she repeated Mom's name aloud. In fact, everything she wrote from that point on was recited aloud, even "Four bottles of Keystone a day."

By the end of the interview, Ms. Polak had deemed my mother "Not requiring treatment."

"Too bad you didn't believe me." Mom bumped me with her shoulder, kissing the top of my head as we waited for our bus.

But with each new betrayal, it was becoming harder to trust her.

Alcohol was killing what was left of my family. I began to hide the bottles and tried to waylay my mother before her now daily trips to the DollarDream. But whoever said "Where there is a will, there is a way" knew something I didn't.

Roxy's Spanish and Rromanes had begun to improve more than her English, in large part because she preferred to spend most of her days at either Maria's or Dad's. Out by the pool, she held language lessons with her best friend. Through the windows of our living room I often heard them practice.

My sister would slowly say, *"Ja. Po. Carr,"* which loosely translates to "Go fuck yourself" in Rromanes.

"Ja po carr," Maria would repeat, and add *"baboso,"* meaning "stupid" in Spanish.

I sometimes tried to get out of spending my weekends at Dad's house, still uncomfortable with a stepmother who called me a hussy for wearing pants—unacceptable to the Roma—but Roxy loved the visits. She and Olga would go to the mall and shop until their legs shook. Olga believed that the way to a child's heart was through new dresses and lip gloss. At home, Roxy had to fight Mom for every cheap trinket, but Olga never said no.

My father's house was always loud with people. Dad and Olga's fortune-telling business had taken off despite my misgivings. On some days Olga's clients literally lined up at the door to see her, and Dad used some of her earnings to buy new equipment. He'd started rehearsing again, and some of his new musician friends, who were mostly illegal Russians, practically lived on his couch. Soon the house began to resemble the backstage of a theater, and in many ways its busy energy reminded me of our Moscow house.

When my parents first decided to move from Riga to Moscow, Mom wanted to buy a condo, but Dad insisted on a house that would provide space and privacy for nightly rock-band rehearsals. They blasted Rolling Stones and Eagles out of their speakers night after night, shaking our beds as if an earthquake were rolling beneath us. I loved falling asleep to the riffs of electric guitars.

Every time one of my parents' acquaintances or relatives came to the city, they ended up sleeping on our couches. Once, a couple of circus animal trainers stayed with us along with their seven poodles. At another time, we welcomed an acrobat family with two of the most fascinating teenage boys I'd ever seen. They crossed the entire length of our house on their hands alone, and wrapped their legs around their necks, resting their chins on their butts. The only kind of sport I excelled at was shooting targets with retired army rifles that our PE teacher used for the Russian version of ROTC.

The house was often cramped, but I loved listening to conversations inside our smoke-filled kitchen, finding surprises in little details revealed by the guests coming briefly into my life. That's how I found out I had a half sister.

A girl of about sixteen came to visit once. I was twelve. She was cool. She had black spiky hair and a mouth that never slept.

The first time I saw her, she was in the living room with Dad, and they were exchanging chords on their guitars. Instantly I felt jealous of this strange girl who had Dad joking, treating her like family.

"So what's your name?" I asked when I caught her alone, smoking out on the veranda.

She flicked the cigarette and hopped on top of the squat stone partition that separated the veranda from the backyard. "I'm your half sister. Katia."

"You're shitting me."

"Nope. Dig your watch."

I held out my wrist, forgetting for a moment the hostility I'd meant to sic on her. "It's from America."

"*Ni huya sebe* (Well, I'll be goddamned)!" She grabbed my hand and tapped the plastic Mickey Mouse dial. "Hey. You know how to moonwalk?"

Katia stayed with us for two weeks, and I spent the entire time as her shadow. She was a full-blooded Romani—her mom had been a dancer in Grandpa's band before my parents met—but she acted like no Gypsy girl I'd ever met: supermodern with her views and completely disregarding her roots. Her guitar repertoire consisted of *blatnyak*, a genre of crime-themed music you'd hear at an illegal poker game or in jail. The songs were very popular in the USSR, but *not* something a decent Roma girl should like to sing.

> *Eh, dengi, denzhata*
> *Ya znayu s vami ray*
> *Eh, dengi, denzhata*
> *Bez vas hot pomiray*
> *Vy dlya menya kak deti*
> *Dorozhe vseh na svete*
> *Ey slysh bratok poday*
> *Day-day-day-day.*

> *Eh, money, money*
> *With you I am in paradise*
> *Eh, money, money*
> *Without you I could just die*
> *To me you are like kids*
> *Most precious thing there is.*
> *Eh, listen, spare some change*
> *Oh, give, hey, give, just give.*

She refused to cook, an art most of our girls perfected at her age in hopes of attracting the best mate. She could break-dance like she was born twirling her legs in a windmill, but that style would never make it to Grandpa's stage. She wore black leather pants and studded boots, and hung out with kids who got high to Black Flag and the Germs. There was freedom in her eyes and in the way she spoke about the world, which I had not thought a Roma girl could express.

Mom made delicious meals and asked Katia a throng of questions about her family and future plans now that she was out of school. I never detected a drop of jealousy. "Your mother must be beautiful," she said, "to have such a daughter." Dad seemed satisfied that Katia wasn't asking for money and had come only to reconnect with the father she hadn't seen in years. This elevated her in his eyes from a child of one night of passion to a respectful daughter. Had she been a boy, he probably would've worked her into our lives, but he all but forgot her once she was gone.

I tried to keep in touch, but I never could find where she stayed because she moved all over the USSR, crashing with friends instead of her strict Roma family. We never saw each other again, but every time I felt uncertain about making my voice heard, I thought of her.

I missed those days, and I might've enjoyed Dad's new house if it weren't a reminder of everything that had gone wrong in mine. Living with Mom was like holding a sputtering firecracker. Not a glorious sparkly one, but the kind that blows up in your hands unprovoked. I couldn't seem to stop her from self-destructing. Now she was the one hiding the wallet from me.

THE MAVERICK

The thing I remember with most clarity about that April is the rain: the raindrops on the backs of my legs as I ran the three blocks from the bus stop to the school, the misty air opening my lungs with restoring breaths, the way it transformed Hollywood into a fairy-tale kingdom of fog, sunlight, and bobbing umbrellas.

On one of these magnificent days Cruz cornered me in the hallway between ELS and choir.

"For you," he said, holding out a red rose. I instantly forgot my squishy shoes and the fact that, yet again, he'd caught me fresh from the downpour outside.

"Why?" I said.

"Do I need to have a reason?"

I shrugged.

He took one step closer, hair dripping from the rain, the bottoms of his jeans soaked. "A late Valentine's Day present. How about that?"

"Surely you jest." I must've picked that one up from *King's Man*, my latest Harlequin.

"You offend me," he said with one hand over his heart.

Now we both sounded like transplants from a romance novel.

He had the most expressive face, but I'd always been wary of people who seemed like they had nothing to hide. "Never trust anyone" was the motto my Roma family lived by.

I can't count the times I had to endure my father's lectures on the myth of sincerity. Every time I made a new friend, or raved about a teacher, he'd sigh and shake his head. "Most people will betray you the first chance they get." Mom would say loud enough for him to hear, "Distrust, Oksana, is as much a part of Roma character as stubbornness. Smart people utilize both in moderation." This usually produced an argument that was broadcast to the entire neighborhood.

"Sorry," I said to Cruz. "In my country we don't celebrate Valentine's Day."

"I'm very loud when I cry, and I tend to get down on my knees and beg if that doesn't work. Come on. Be nice."

Everything he said frustrated me because he didn't react in the logical way. Anybody else would've been offended by my hostility. Instead, he looked amused. I was dumbfounded by his behavior. You didn't just walk up to somebody and say, "Hey. I know you might mash my self-esteem into a pulp, but I have to tell you that I really, really, I mean REALLY like you. What about you? Here's a mallet in case you say no."

I glanced around, then back to him. "Why? We don't even talk."

"Maybe we would if you didn't act like a blowfish every time I came near you."

What was the harm?

"It's just a rose. I'm not asking for your soul."

Really? "Fine. I'll take it."

"Good." He handed me the flower, ignoring my bad manners, and shrugged out of his jacket. "Because I have one more thing for you."

"Two gifts?"

He draped it around my shoulders. "Not a gift. I definitely want it back, but you can't run around like that. I can see through your shirt."

I jerked the jacket tighter around me. Could he see my bra this entire time?

"Maybe I'll get you an umbrella for Easter."

"I shall not accept it, thank you very much."

The more romance novels I read, the faster my English vocabulary expanded. They didn't disappoint; quite the opposite. Something about the predictability of the happy endings brought me comfort and, as silly as it seems, hope. But there were still gaps in my comprehension, and I wasn't shy about asking for help. Usually it came from strangers; neither Mom nor Dad took advantage of the free English classes offered by the Russian Immigrant Outreach Program. They had more pressing things on their minds.

Meadow, the horn-rimmed salesgirl at the bookshop off Highland Avenue, kept a stack of fresh historical novels for me to salivate over. Once a week I pleaded with Mom or Dad, depending on my coordinates, for five dollars. Funds acquired, I stopped after school and stayed for hours, reading on the floor in the corner where other kids my age gave each other hickeys. I could buy only one book at a time, and it tormented me to have to pick. Covers, or rather the male models on them, played a key role in the selection process. On this particular day I faced a dilemma between two men so remarkable that my heart sang "Heaven" by Warrant just looking at their flowing locks. I flipped through the first one, decided that I fancied Highlanders over Vikings, and grabbed the other, turning to a random paragraph. I sensed that something incredible was occurring behind phrases such as "burning loins" and "aching bulge," and I hunted for an explanation in my dictionary. A literal translation produced "flaming pork chops" and "painful protuberance."

After she finished ringing up a Chinese couple who purchased multiple copies of maps to the stars' homes, Meadow explained this mysterious combination of words.

"This is juicy," she said, burgundy lips suspended in a wicked grin. "Nothing like the Harlequins you've been reading, right? X-rated stuff."

"I don't know what that means."

"Sex," she exclaimed. "In Harlequins they kiss, but here, oh man, this is like soft porn. Cool shit. But what's the problem? Didn't your parents talk to you about sex?"

Unimaginable. But I knew a little something about porn.

Adult films, yet another thing that's illegal in the USSR, couldn't be purchased in stores. But some people managed to set up clandestine bootlegged showings to satisfy the demand. After eavesdropping on a conversation between Zhanna and me about her crush on our neighbor's twenty-year-old son, Esmeralda, Zhanna's half sister, decided the time was ripe to teach us about sex.

"You're both thirteen," she told us. "At your age there are Romani girls who've already had their first kid. Not that I approve, but still. Men are not like us, and you need to know how they're different so they don't take advantage of you. This is especially important for you, Oksana, because in America, erotic education is a subject taught in schools. If you ever get there, you don't want those people to think we're primitive, do you?"

"I know about men." Speaking from experience. Ruslan and I had had a couple of secret dates by then. When we kissed, our mouths stayed shut like the portcullis of a castle, the same way they did in the love scenes of all the Russian movies. By Roma standards, Ruslan was too old to be a virgin at sixteen. The other band members teased him endlessly and sent prostitutes to his hotel rooms with notes of instruction tucked between their breasts. This irked me. I didn't know precisely the steps to losing one's virginity, but I was sure I didn't want Ruslan to take them without me. Stepan once joked, "After you get the hang of it, it'll be like dipping your finger in a rainbow." Ruslan's answer sent the rest of the men into a roaring fit. "A dip might be fine for an elderly goat like you, Stepan, but I won't do it until I can dive in headfirst."

Esmeralda came up with a proposal. We would either watch her with one of her boyfriends through a peephole in her closet or see an educational film. In our culture, parents don't talk about sex until the wedding night, and even then it's often just a reluctant instruction on how to lie down when your husband takes you. Esmeralda was determined that we be more prepared than she had been.

The makeshift movie theater was hidden in the basement of a seven-story apartment building down the street where two guys took money at the bottom of the stairs with urgency in their speedy fingers. We joined a slowly moving line of men and teenage boys whose nervous footwork gave them away.

The room was wide and had linoleum floors, disco-era wood paneling, and ceilings veined with coughing pipes. Several rows of folding metal chairs had been arranged in front of a large bedsheet hanging from a clothesline. In the back of the room, a man loaded a film reel onto the arm of a rusted projector.

Zhanna and I scuttled to the last row near the wall, our eyes everywhere but on the other people filing into the room. Esmeralda took her seat next to us and crossed one leg over the other under her stylish black skirt, her shoulders shaking from laughter at our behavior. Her wavy hair hung past her waist, shiny and soft: once a week she soaked it in olive oil. Her complexion was dewy, eyes coquettish and bright. A few men tried to get her attention with winks and nods. I remember unfolding myself in my seat and trying to mimic Esmeralda's effortless poise. Might as well learn something.

The film was poorly dubbed and not easy to follow, but from what I gathered, the two main characters really liked each other and took off their clothes to prove it. Their only hindrance was the lack of suitable places to get naked.

"Now pay attention to the missionary position," Esmeralda whispered. "As a rule this is the best one for the first time."

Zhanna leaned over to me. "They have rules for this stuff?"

I stared in fascination at the man on the couch, the bedsheet screen sending ripples through the image. His white dress shirt was unbuttoned to his waist, one shirttail carelessly slung over the top of his black dress pants. His eyes were at half-mast, and his fingers drummed a slow rhythm on his glass of bourbon.

"Hike up your skirt," he orders the woman perched on the edge of the ottoman with her legs spread wide.

"Yes." She complies. Centimeter by centimeter. The higher the hem travels, the closer to her he tips, as if an invisible string attached from her skirt to his head pulls him onward. She halts only when her thighs and the shadows between are exposed. The man exhales and rubs a shaking hand across his lips. He points at the shadows accusingly. "That, right there, is what rules the world."

"Wasn't that great?" Esmeralda asked as we walked home that night. "Kind of artsy, and didn't feel the least bit amateur. And the acting! Usually these types of movies don't have good stories, but this one really surprised me."

"I bet it's against the law to get naked in public," Zhanna said.

"Half the things they were doing are against the law," I said.

"Why do you think we had to sneak into a basement to watch them?"

"Please," Esmeralda said. "That means every Soviet over the age of sixteen is a criminal. This is natural and beautiful. Especially between a husband and wife."

"But you're not married," I said.

"Well, no. One can only wait so long."

Zhanna and I were still getting over the fact that we'd left our innocence back in the room fitted with disco paneling.

The next time I mentioned the neighbor's son, Zhanna threw her hands up in the air. "So over him."

"But why?"

"I'm not ready for the natural and the beautiful."

AT THE DELI

Months after I last saw Uncle Arsen and my cousins, Mom came home very late one night. I was waiting for her outside by the mailboxes, but knowing I'd get in trouble for snooping, I had hunkered down in a spot shy of the security lights. This way I could sneak back inside unnoticed.

She wasn't alone as she stumbled out of a car—my uncle's car. I didn't know why she'd gone to see him; perhaps to make up? Or not. Walking together toward the building, they looked as irritated with each other as the last time. Mom swayed and Uncle caught her by the elbow and shoved her through the gate. They began to argue. I was too far away to discern their words, but knowing Mom, she was probably insulting him. Then she swung at him and lost her balance, nearly falling onto the metal gate's decorative spear points. She caught herself in time, but when she straightened I saw a dark splotch on her left cheek. I forgot all about hiding, and when Uncle saw me shuffling toward them down the concrete walkway in my slippers, he jumped into his car and took off.

Back at our place I helped Mom onto her cot, fully dressed

minus her pumps, and pulled a tissue from a box nearby. Next to us my sister lay sprawled over her blankets, mouth open over a round spot of drool on her pillow. I covered Mom with a sheet. The smell of vodka and blood invaded my nostrils. I'd never be able to forget this combination.

Mom's lids shuddered. "You're so strong. I never worry about you."

"That's great, Mom." I wanted to clean off the blood, but I was too scared to see it spread to the edges of the tissue like a living thing, to have the scent cling to me.

"Not worried about Roxy, either," she mumbled heavily. "I wish I was her. Too young to understand anything."

But I think she was wrong about that.

When we first got kicked out of Uncle Arsen's house, I wrote a note on the back of the phone directory I found under the kitchen sink of our new apartment:

We are a broken bottle, jagged edges rising from what used to be whole.

I was not really sure why I didn't write those lines in my journal. After I finished, I ripped out the scrap of paper and flushed it down the toilet. When Roxy walked in on me hovering over the toilet bowl as if I held a grudge against the L.A. sewer system, she wrapped her fingers around my wrist. "Why are you always so sad?" she asked. "Makes me wanna be sad, too." I didn't answer, as had become my habit. I must've made her feel invisible countless times, so involved was I in my own world. An older me often thinks about the inaccuracy of that note. I still had a family to preserve: my sister. Instead, we started to ever so slowly drift apart.

Roxy practicing for stardom in one of Mom's altered costumes

In our apartment, life was a rotten potato lost between the fridge and the counter. No matter where you went, the stink followed. But at Dad's, too much excitement and novelty made our troubles invisible. Olga proved a riveting distraction, a mischievous sprite out to grab your soul. I understood why Roxy shot down the stairs like an arrow every time Dad came to pick us up, but I was still avoiding his house as much as possible.

"School is out for the summer and you have plenty of free time. Don't you want to spend it with your father?" Olga would say every time I tried to get out of visiting. A question that could be answered in only one way. It wasn't just Olga's presence; after that first channeling session, she'd been trying on "nice." Mostly my reluctance had to do with the habitual way Dad and Olga used me, like my mother had, as their interpreter. The ironic part was that they didn't really ask but embarrassed me until I volunteered.

At a doctor's office once, my father got down on the floor and started pumping push-ups to convince the man that he had the heart of a lion.

"Quit acting like an imbecile." Olga hunched over him, shouting.

The doctor clutched his file with both hands and retreated into the corner.

Dad jumped to his feet. "You call me names in front of the good doctor?"

"I'll call you whatever I want. We're married!"

"They're always this loud," I said, in case the poor guy wished to take notes. "Eastern Europeans always sound like they're arguing."

"So they're not?" he asked quietly.

"If you want to stay married, you'll get the hell out," Dad was saying.

Olga yanked open the door. Some of the nurses had gathered outside, pretending not to appear curious or worried. Dad and Olga hollered things about each other's mothers loud enough to make me want to hide in the cupboard under the sink until Olga stormed out.

Our first trip to Santa Monica, Dad drove up to a man on the corner of Highland and Sunset to ask for directions. He rolled down the window and said, "Excooze me, sir. You know vay to bitch?" At a drive-through, Roxy or I would beg to order, to stop Dad from saying things that could land him in jail. Things like "I hav six penises of change to that dollar."

Only one thing granted me the get-out-of-jail-free card: getting my period. As long as I blamed "female problems" for not coming over, Dad left me alone; he had great fears of anything concerning childbirth, menstrual blood, and especially tampons. In Romani culture, men don't usually participate in female matters. A woman on her period is unclean and to be avoided. Even in marriage, the wife is encouraged to keep her menstrual and childbirth issues to herself. Roxy and I would work out a story, and once there, she'd go into detail describing the cramps rendering me bed-bound.

One day Olga called and pleaded with me to come by. She wouldn't say why over the phone, but it sounded serious.

"Oh! You're in love," Olga said almost as soon as I'd stepped through the front door.

"What?" I said. "Don't be crazy."

I began to defend myself against her silliness when I noticed another person in her kitchen, and I went silent; I had too much dignity to discuss this in front of a stranger in a pink velour jumpsuit. Olga's guest was roundish, with short red spiky hair and a rat face.

"So what do you need?" I asked, crossing my arms and avoiding eye contact with my stepmother.

Hands on hips, Olga clucked her tongue. "Oksana. You know I'll find out one way or another. You can fool your father but not me. All I can say is that it better not be some pimple-faced *gadjo*."

"Stay out of my business."

Narrowing her eyes, Olga sat down beside the woman and

put an arm around her shoulders. "Svetlana's husband is cheating on her, so we need to go to the deli up on Highland."

No other explanation was offered; Olga often assumed that other people read minds, too.

As if on cue, Svetlana pressed a napkin to her forehead, mopping sweat from under a shock of red bangs. Normally Romani women wear their hair long, but Svetlana had reinvented herself after leaving her first husband, a drunk from Siberia, for a sober Russian Jewish accountant.

"Oh, my Igor, my sweet Igoriok," she moaned. "How could you do such a thing? Cheating! Damn your black soul. May your balls dry up into raisins, you bastard."

As Svetlana continued her lament, Olga tried to comfort her with Twinkies. I felt for Svetlana, but more so for Igor.

"Oksana, please. Can't you see how the poor woman suffers?"

"And how is this my fault?"

All of a sudden, Svetlana was on me, squeezing my hands. "Oksanochka, sweetheart, he must return to me," she wailed.

"And I'm supposed to make that happen how?"

"The witch works at Giuseppe's Deli," Olga said.

"Ashley," Svetlana said, looking like she'd tasted a rotten egg. "American."

Olga patted her client on the shoulder. "Oksanochka, we need you to go inside and get one of her hairs."

I pried my hands from Svetlana's, slowly, so as not to disturb a woman who was clearly insane. "You want me to steal a hair."

"Yes," they said in unison.

"From a deli. With customers and meat and stuff."

"Yes, yes, what's the matter with you?" Olga said. "I need one of her hairs for my spell. That's all I ask. I'm not an evil stepmother. I don't make you scrub floors. This one simple thing is all I need from you."

"If it's so simple, why don't you do it, then?"

Svetlana grabbed me again before I could protect myself. "Sweetie, she'll suspect something if one of us goes. She probably knows what I look like. He's my husband," she moaned. "Please, I beg of you. Go in, buy a pound of roast beef, and on your way out, pluck one of the bitch's hairs."

I couldn't stand the idea of assisting Olga in any way, but as Svetlana bawled, her makeup running, she looked at me with so much desperation that I could almost feel it wrap around me like cellophane.

We drove to the deli. As I swung out of the car, Svetlana squeezed my hand and kissed it. I turned around and walked to the store with downcast eyes.

Delis are cheerful. You come in and you're instantly enveloped by bright lights and the aroma of cold cuts and fresh bread. Not the atmosphere in which to reach over the counter and snatch a handful of the clerk's hair.

"What can I get you?" my unsuspecting victim asked. She was so thin, probably four of her could've fit into Svetlana's velour pants.

And of course she wore a hairnet.

My brain scrambled for a solution, and I was beginning to lose feeling in my tongue. "I am supposed to buy roast beef," I finally managed.

"How much?"

"Can you show it to me?"

Ashley blinked a set of fake eyelashes before leaning over the glass case and pointing. "That one right there."

"The one on the left?"

"No, over there."

I shook my head in embarrassment, which, at that point, was

genuine. "Very sorry. Can you show me from here? If I buy the wrong one, my mother will beat me."

It was a long shot, but it worked. The woman looked at me strangely, then walked around the counter and stood next to me jabbing her finger at the glass. "The one that says 'roast beef,' right here," she said.

"I see it. Yes. So sorry. My reading is not so good."

A thin blond hair beckoned from her upper sleeve. I played my "creepy foreigner without a sense of personal space" card and gave her arm a grateful squeeze. "You a good deli person." And came away with my prize, closing my hand around it.

Ashley eyeballed me while she cut the roast beef and wrapped it. I left the deli, memorizing the location to make certain I'd never shop there again.

I jumped into the backseat of Olga's car. The interior was a nebula of smoke and I coughed, rolling down the window.

"How did it go?" my stepmother asked.

I handed her the hair along with the roast beef, a little disgusted and ashamed at the same time.

"Did she see you?" She dropped the hair into a sandwich bag and handed it to Svetlana, who rolled it up carefully.

"Well, yes, she saw me. I was buying roast beef," I said.

"Did she see you take the hair?"

"No. At least I don't think so."

"Good girl," she said, and started the car.

Only, I didn't feel so good, not just about violating that poor woman's privacy and subjecting her to a bout of witchery but also because Olga was driving.

Her approach was generally to go straight and turn only when absolutely necessary. Red lights were meaningless blinks in the distance. She rarely paid attention, flying through intersections, dismissing the traffic as I screamed for her to watch out, our car passing others seconds before impact.

In the midst of this madness, Svetlana turned to me.

"Wasn't she the scraggliest thing you've ever seen?" she said, giving me her best sour-candy face.

"I'd rather not talk right now," I said, wrapping my fingers around the door handle.

Olga tossed me an annoyed glance, and then patted the other woman on the shoulder. "Svetlana, don't bother my stepchild. She's left her sense of humor at home."

I was holding on to the door with one hand and gripping the seat belt in the other. Another red light, another heart palpitation.

Svetlana shrugged. "What did I say?"

It wasn't what she had said but my feeling of helplessness in the face of Olga's triumph. She gloated over how she'd gotten me to help her.

"Okay. I did what you guys asked, now let me out."

"Why?" Svetlana said. "Because your stepmother has such a big heart? Because she'll do anything to help people in need, people like me?"

"She didn't do this, I did. What if I got caught?"

"Doing what?" Olga said, driving with one set of tires on Melrose Drive and the other on the curb. "If we were in Russia you'd never complain like this. Such disrespect for your father."

"Jesus, can you watch the road, please."

"So true," Svetlana said. "Kids here are so spoiled."

Olga agreed. "It's because of Nora. Armenians dote on their children. Had she grown up in a real Romani household, she'd learn obedience, quick."

I was used to Olga blaming the Armenian side for my every flaw, but I always believed my big mouth was a result of my

Romani blood. I told her as much, at which point she stopped the car and let me out.

"I'm not done with you yet," she said, leaning over Svetlana to glare at me.

"You should drive a flying carpet," I said. "It'd be safer for everybody."

She sped off, cursing the land I was born on, and I mumbled a little prayer for all of L.A.'s unsuspecting motorists and one skinny deli clerk.

WHAT'S IN THE BAG?

A few days later Cruz asked me out, as he had been doing ever since he'd given me the rose, but my big American future didn't include a broken heart.

In a ten-dollar phone conversation with Zhanna, when I guiltily admitted that I spent hours daydreaming about a boy with green eyes, she berated me again for burying my scarf with Ruslan.

"So foolish," she said. "It's been almost two years, but as I suspected, he's still holding on to you. You're not free."

"Of course I am!"

"Then why haven't you gone after your green-eyed Spaniard? Why? You're pining for him in secret but sharpening your fangs every time he makes a move. Confusing the poor *gadjo*."

But the scarf was exactly where it belonged. Ruslan would never deny me happiness, even if my cousin thought otherwise. The guilt of my feelings for another, I decided, was written in me and by me. Only I could erase such nonsense, and all I needed was to figure out how.

Meanwhile, I continued to reject Cruz, difficult as it was. And yet nearly every day, he managed to find my lunch table or sneak a note during homeroom, a missive written halfway between an earnest request and a joke.

Let's go to Pizza Place after school.
I promise, I'll have you home by five.
Scout's honor.

I'd write back, "Sorry, allergic to Scouts."

If you listened to Esmeralda, flirting was a cracked window in a house besieged by a blizzard—nothing but trouble. She would know. Men tumbled back into boyhood around her, a transformation that provided hours of amusement for me and Zhanna. Not so cute were the fistfights if one date happened to cross paths with another on the stairs of Esmeralda's building. One of her wisdoms dictated that if a woman accepts a gift from a man, she allows him to brand her. She gives him hope for something more intimate.

I badly regretted having taken Cruz's offering, the rose that was now drying between the pages of *Jane Eyre*.

The only taste my parents had of Brazil was from the first soap opera ever aired on Soviet television, a telenovella about a slave girl struggling to survive in the cruel streets of nineteenth-century Rio de Janeiro. They prided themselves on their modern-day attitudes toward interracial relationships, as long as it was a step up, not down, the social class ladder.

I knew our relationship would be doomed from the start; Mom would never let me date Cruz because he wasn't an American doctor, and Dad because he wasn't Rom with a prestigious family name and at least a few gold teeth.

———

A week after the deli trip, Olga made it known that I was to join her yet on another excursion, this time to a nearby cemetery. "*Ny pryamo* (Yeah, right)," I said.

The Chinese sundry market might not have been the best place for this discussion, but Olga cared little for privacy, hers or others'. In the dried-seafood section she thrust a fish in my face. "Your father said you're going."

"You better not point that thing at me again," I said, and called out to Dad, whose voice boomed across the store. He was telling the Chinese salesclerk about the time a Mongolian medicine man taught him the miraculous uses of black moss to cure colon-related ailments. When I called him again, Dad vaulted into our aisle, the flaps on his leather chaps beating around his thighs like bat wings.

"Can you two never leave me in peace?" he said.

A couple of ladies quickly disappeared around the corner.

"She wants me to go to the cemetery with her."

"*Ny e shto* (So what)?" he said. "To translate in case she needs to speak English."

"With whom? They're all dead."

Olga shook her head with a triumphant snort. "You're going, you hear? Your father said so."

"I won't."

At half past midnight Olga, Svetlana, and I parked on the curve of the sidewalk leading to the cemetery. Recent vandalism in the area had left some of the gravestones festively spray-painted with local gang signs. A guard booth had been installed at the gate, and a single light illuminated the security guard who sat on its threshold, smoking.

Olga whispered, "You have the bags and the flashlights?" Svetlana nodded. "Good. Soon as you spot a grave with the name Ashley on it, you fill the bag quick as you can."

To finish the separation spell that would break up Svetlana's wayward husband and Ashley, Olga needed dirt from a grave of Ashley's namesake in addition to the hair I'd stolen.

Svetlana unfastened her seat belt and shifted her bulk forward. "What about the guard?"

"I'll talk to him," Olga said, watching him closely. "But what's this? He's not alone."

I squinted, and when my eyes focused enough to pick out the details of the other person's shape, I exclaimed, "*Huyovo* (This is bad)!" before I could stop myself.

"You recognize him?" Olga said.

"We go to school together."

"No matter. He'll never know what we're doing." She got out of the car and approached the booth.

"*Dai em deneg* (Give them some money)," Svetlana mouthed.

When Olga came back, she looked cross. Apparently the guard had resisted the bribe. She and Svetlana went back and forth with ideas: climb the wall, wait until the man fell asleep or went to pee, find another cemetery that was not so heavily guarded. I made the mistake of suggesting we go home. As soon as I spoke, Olga snapped her fingers. "You go. Your friend will let us in."

"Not a chance."

"If you do, I'll never ask you for help again."

I snorted and she crossed herself. "*Nu shtob ya sdokhla* (May I die if I break it)."

The security guard, clearly uncomfortable, yanked his cap off his head as I drew near. Already he was waving, telling me in broken English to leave. He held, between his thumb and forefinger, a fat joint that he laid on the ground. I looked past him at the figure now occupying the chair hidden from view from the street behind the booth.

"Hey," I said, and he jerked out of the shadows.

"What are you doing here?" I'd never seen Cruz shocked before, but even in that reaction there was a hint of pleasure, and it warmed me.

"Can you tell your friend to let us in? It's my stepmother's grandfather's death anniversary." I had to tell him something.

The joint in his hand sent wings unfurling into the air.

"Why should I?"

Not what I expected. "It's very important."

After a moment of consideration, he turned to the other man, who immediately began gesturing wildly at his badge and speaking in a language that sounded like a love child of Spanish and Italian.

"*Não, não, não.*"

"*Dá um desconto, primo.*"

The man gestured to all of me at once with a salacious whistle. "*Você esta louco por ela, então você é estúpido o suficiente para acreditar em qualquer coisa que ela diga.*"

Cruz whacked him on the back of the head. "*Eu vou trazer para você um* twenty-sac. *Apenas faça isso por mim.*"

They shook on it and Cruz swept an arm at the cemetery entrance. "Cousin Roberto says you're free to enter as long as you go to Pizza Place with me tomorrow."

The only thing I understood in their exchange was "twenty-sac," a term used regularly by Dad's rock-band associates in Russia. It was considered hip among the Soviet rockers to butcher American terms with Russian accents, therefore it sounded more like *tovenysuck.* But the meaning remained the same: twenty dollars' worth of any drug delivered in a Baggie.

"Are you dealing?" I said.

"You got all that? Impressive, but all the same."

"That's blackmail."

"A favor for a favor, that's all." Another hit and he passed the joint to Roberto, his voice strangled. "Otherwise the gate stays closed."

As luck would have it, there were several dead Ashleys, and Olga picked the grave with a tiny statue of Jesus clutching a bleeding heart in his ceramic hands. She filled the bag, but Svetlana dropped only a handful of earth into hers before hiding it in her bra. When she saw the expression on my face, she pressed a fist to her chest. "If I keep that bitch close to my heart, my prayers will be answered faster."

On the drive home the two women chatted excitedly about the forthcoming ritual. My only consolation was in the knowledge that the living Ashley would be unharmed. She'd slowly begin to un-desire her lover until their attraction chipped like the rouge from the ceramic Jesus' cheeks. As always, Olga paid little attention to the road, speeding through a red signal.

When police lights flashed behind us, she pulled over in disbelief. The officer sauntered over and asked to see our documents, capturing the interior of the car with one expert glance.

"Sir," Olga said, digging in her purse, "I do no wrong. Yes? Just drive like all peoples drive. You know I can see you hav big arms like Hercules."

The man took Olga's ID and gestured at the console. "What's in the bag, ma'am?"

I sank into the seat, wishing I could disappear.

"Dirt," Olga said, smiling.

The officer didn't reciprocate. "Please step out of the car."

We did, just as another police cruiser drew near. There were moments of confusion, and I did get to translate, as Dad had said I would. The cops were convinced that no sane person would be driving around at two in the morning with a Ziploc bag full of dirt. They took us to the station, where a Russian-speaking officer gave us the "all bad cop, no good cop" routine.

"What's really in the bag?" scrawny Officer Popov said. The only thing of substance about him was his belly. He could have been a proud mama carrying twins.

"Zemlya," Olga said.

"You know, jail is no place for Russian women."

"But it's dirt, I swear. Taste it and you'll see."

With a grimace, Popov made a ceremony of taking the bag to get tested. Sometime later he came back.

"What were you doing with a bag of dirt at two in the morning?"

Olga told him everything except where the dirt came from, stating she had collected it in Griffith Park. Once the man heard the words "Gypsy" and "spell," he got this shriveled-up look on his face, the one people get when they hear someone say, "I've been to jail, but I'm a changed person now." Regardless, he had no choice but to let us go with nothing more than a speeding ticket and another for running a red light. Olga took the steps to the parking lot as if she wanted to trample something solid and breathing. She wasn't upset over the tickets; six hundred dollars to her was the change you find inside a kid's piggy bank. But before letting us go, the Russian had confiscated her bag of dirt, advising Olga to start doing something more useful with her time. I would've thought the loss of the most important ingredient to Svetlana's happiness would upset her, but she merely put her arms around Olga's shoulders and led her away in case Popov rearrested us out of spite.

It wasn't until we had lost the police station to miles of paved roads that Svetlana freed the stash from her bosom.

JUST HAVING TOUCHED

I was eight the first time I performed onstage. I remember being in the wings of a theater somewhere in Russia, the waxy scent of old makeup with a hint of powder, violets, and roses teasing my nostrils. Dancers had rushed by me into the golden spotlights of center stage in a flurry of bright, ruffled skirts, women shining with jingling coin necklaces, men beating a rhythm with their tap shoes. I was so nervous that I froze on the spot. Then I saw my mother onstage, beckoning me to join her. It was enough. My skirt was midnight blue with sequined yellow flowers all over, and the blouse with slit sleeves was the color of honey. I remember holding up the edges of my skirt with both hands, letting the material fan out at my sides, and dashing into the spotlight, an open-winged sparrow.

It had been almost a year since I left the old country, and I was starting to miss the Romani of my childhood more than my one-page list could fit. I longed to hear their songs again and to feel the pulse of their performance beneath my feet.

At the end of the school year I signed up for my first recital, which also served as a rehearsal for the big year-end talent show

Grandpa's famous dancers, St. Petersburg, 1974

that attracted talent scouts from all over L.A. I picked Mark Edwards's "Just Having Touched," your standard ballad heavy on cheesy heartbreak and sentimental lyrics.

> *More than anything you do, having touched my life with you,*
> *Just having touched your love will be enough for me.*

I did what my parents had done so many times: I replayed the tape over and over and scribbled down the words. I learned the melody by ear, practicing in the music room during lunchtime. The recital was coming up fast, and I knew I had very little time to get back into shape. In Russia I had finished the preparatory music school and, had we stayed, most likely would have applied to a conservatory. As it was, though, neither Mom nor I mentioned continuing formal training in America. We were too busy surviving.

But now that there was no pressure to play, I began to actually crave it. As my fingers warmed up after such a long period of inactivity, I started playing all the time, frequently skipping lunches and classes. School was the only place I *could* practice, because Dad wouldn't let me touch his keyboards. He'd set up a small home studio in the back of the house, but it was always locked. Inside, the walls were covered with posters. Bob Marley beamed from above the Roland synthesizers, next to Wynton Marsalis with his trumpet pressed to his heart in a shared secret. There was also a large cardboard image of an alien's head with a pointy chin and enormous almond-shaped eyes. As soon as I decided on my song I asked Dad to use the room, but he waved me off. "Those are costly instruments for serious playing." I'd heard this many times in the past, and, while frustrated, I wasn't offended. Not even I could deny the seriousness of Dad's instruments.

Maybe he'd have felt differently if I'd told him why I wanted to practice, but I didn't want to take that chance. It was something I wanted to do completely on my own. Plus, if I bombed, I wanted my humiliation to remain a secret.

On the day of the recital, the usual crowd gathered inside the room outfitted as a theater.

I braved the stage with shaky legs. My heart hammered against the silence. But at the piano my doubts settled, calmed by the silky feel of the keys beneath my fingers. I was home.

It's easy enough to forget hundreds of eyes probing you when your only worry is to keep your heavy Eastern European accent from making you sound like Count Dracula. I cringed on the inside every time I rolled my *r*'s and sang "hard" instead of "heart."

I don't remember finishing, only the applause. Pride burned my cheeks. Later, as students and teachers trickled out, I still didn't trust my legs to carry me to my algebra class.

"That was a great performance," an older man with a hearty smile said from the aisle next to me. His skin matched the dark chestnut of his suit. "I'm Mr. North, the school band leader." We shook hands. "Are you a new transfer?"

"No. An ESL student." I thought that explained everything, and expected him to nod politely and move on.

"Why aren't you in the magnet program?"

"My English is not good."

"Couldn't tell from where I was sitting," Mr. North said. He told me of the acceptance interviews for the next term, and that he expected to see me there.

I ran home after school to tell Mom. Coming up the stairs to our place, I could already hear her, and (lucky me) she sounded sober. Roxy was at the kitchen table, writing something on an envelope. Her lips and tongue pursed and curled, respectively, in concentration. Mom hovered over her shoulder, eyeing the slow progress of the pen. Her English was still so limited that she relied entirely on me and Roxy to communicate with anyone who wasn't Rosa.

"What's going on?" I said.

"Power bill." Mom's voice was as grave as that of a doctor who had announced a life-threatening diagnosis to a patient. Suddenly she smacked Roxy over the top of her head. "*Shto delaesh? Ny vsyo. Nesi novy konvert.* (What are you doing? That's it. Get a new envelope.)"

I read the address Roxy had scribbled in chunky print. "Apparently we live in Mos Angeles."

"It's one letter. I can fix it," Roxy said, pressing her pen over the typo.

"The mailman will think we don't know what we're doing," Mom said. "What if he throws it away?"

"Roxy's right, Mom. No one will notice."

Mom mumbled something dire about her luck and went to the counter, where she tied a bay leaf, a few twigs of dill and parsley, and some peppercorns in a cheesecloth pouch and dropped it into a pot of water bubbling on the stove. The aroma of *boeuf à la russe* promised a delicious dinner.

"Mom, I did something really great today."

After I recounted my conversation with Mr. North, Mom wiped her hands on the kitchen towel and embraced me tightly.

"This teacher wants you to be in his special school?"

"Magnet school."

"That's the best thing I've heard in months." She pressed me to her without asking why I hadn't invited her to the concert, for which I was grateful.

Lowering the heat under the pot, Mom hurried out of the kitchen to get her telephone card. She dialed Aunt Siranoosh's number in Kirovakan and shouted into the phone so loudly, her sister could've probably heard her voice across the ocean without the aid of modern technology.

"*Akchi, asem ches havata* (You won't believe what I have to tell you)!" Before long, half of Armenia and Russia had heard the news that I was invited to join a school for the most gifted kids in America. Mom was so happy, I didn't have the heart to correct her.

I told Dad, too, thrilled to share with him that I might soon be following in his footsteps.

"What is a performing school?" he said. "You're a Kopylenko. You already know how to perform."

"It's not like I'd be joining the Communist Party," I said.

"Same shit. A handful of cretins decide what's good for you, and then they own you for the rest of your life, telling you what kinds of songs to play. You don't need someone else's approval."

He was right, of course. But for someone who hadn't been approved of all that often, I chased the possibility like a dog after a soup bone.

MAMA LOLA

That summer my sister and I alternated between both households, even though I still protested whenever I had to spend time listening to Olga boast about the loads of cash she was making, or about her recently developed connections with Shashi Kapoor, the Indian movie mogul. Olga, obsessed with everything Indian, believed she'd spent her previous life as a male dancer at an Indian court and was meant to become a Bollywood movie star as soon as she returned to her homeland. Around this time she and Dad were contemplating a move to New Delhi, and I often wondered which of the three of us was the real teenager. When Mom found out, she called my father to inform him that he could move his ass to Madagascar for all she cared, but the kids were staying in the States with her.

During those days the hardest part for me was seeing how Mom and Dad began reinventing their individual selves, the ones they'd sacrificed for their noisy marriage. In the process of moving on, they were leaving me behind, and I was too proud to call after them.

A few weeks after the cemetery incident, I was going up the stairs leading to our apartment when my sister came barreling down.

"Roxy, what happened?"

She didn't slow down, her flip-flops slapping on the concrete. "Rosa is going out and she's gonna take us if we behave. Then Mom said we can go to McDonald's for my birthday." She was turning nine in a couple of days.

The front door was propped open with a rock. Mom's voice came from the bathroom, muffled by the sound of a hair dryer working full blast. She was saying something about Rosa's ex, and it had several "fuckers" attached to it.

Inside the kitchen, Rosa was wrapping something long and thin in a plastic grocery bag.

"Where are you guys going?" I asked.

"He not man. He goat, I tell you," Mom shouted from the bathroom.

Rosa got another bag from under the sink and carefully placed the package into it, wrapping it again. "I know," she shouted back. "He thought I no find out."

Mom came in, her hair poufy, her makeup fresh.

"What's going on?" I asked again.

"Ayee, *tu madre*." Rosa rushed the package to the sink, leaving a trail of crimson drops on the linoleum. "Is leaking."

"Two-bag it," Mom said. "Here." She took out a plastic container from one of the cabinets and set it on the table. "Put here. So you not get blood in car."

I joined the two women at the sink. They peeled off the squishy plastic from the package. I watched Rosa slowly unwrap the thing, and took a sharp step back when I saw what it was. "Ugh, it's a tongue!"

Mom glanced back at me with a laugh. "You act like you've never seen one before," she said in Russian. She ran cold water over it.

Unfortunately I *had* seen one of these, and on more than one occasion; my mother had prepared the vile delicacy every Christmas for as long as I could remember. She garnished it with parsley and crispy onion rings, as if that could mask the fact that she was *serving her guests a tongue*.

"Yeah," I said. "And it gets more disgusting each time."

Rosa wrapped it again, this time in fresh bags. The look on her face suggested she agreed with me. "Is not for eating, *mija*, is for my psychic. She tole me is needs to be fresh. My ex's woman has put a curse on *mi familia*. She gossip about me, say I sleep around. Last week Rachel from the hair salon tole me she no have openings. I know she was lying. And yesterday I lose fifty dollars from my purse. Gone. Bad luck follow me, and is all that *puta*'s doing."

I looked at Mom, who just shrugged. I couldn't believe we were having this conversation, especially after my cemetery trip a few weeks earlier. "How do you know it's a curse?"

"People talking. But how I really know is I found lumps of hair and broken teet under my bed," she said, pointing at her incisors.

That I understood. It is an ancient belief in many cultures that hair, teeth, and nails hold extraordinary mystical powers, and if handled by a malicious person they can aid in bringing harm to their owner. Back in Russia, rivals disguised as friends once left a clump of hair with nail clippings and teeth in the back of our shoe closet. It sounds like harmless superstition, but the malice is all too real when you're the one whose fingers discover the stuff. And whether you believe in black magic or not, there's always somebody out there who does.

When we drove up to Mama Lola's house, my palms were sweating. Between my mother's coffee readings and Olga's plans to rid Hollywood of its money, I'd had enough magic to last me a few reincarnation cycles. But the opportunity to take a peek into the life of an American who openly practiced witchcraft was something I couldn't miss. I wanted to see the difference between Olga, Dad, and this Mama Lola, who, according to Rosa, performed miracles on a regular basis.

Full of nervous energy, Rosa practically ran from the car to the front door, where a petite woman with burgundy lipstick and flawless olive skin waited. They disappeared inside. Mom and I followed, but Roxy and Maria had to stay in the car; the psychic had instructed that no small children should be present.

There was something admittedly regal about Mama Lola. At about five feet tall, she managed to appear bigger and somehow more intimidating than any tall person I knew. In her frilly black dress and delicate shawl, she carried herself with the grace of a flamenco dancer.

The two women exchanged a few phrases in Spanish, and Mama Lola tossed a sideways glance in my mother's direction. She lowered her head in greeting, then beckoned us down the hallway. A pair of thick curtains hung at its end, their velvety folds concealing the rest of the house.

"Please," Mama Lola said, pulling them aside and gesturing into the living room. Her voice was pure silk trimmed with a Spanish accent.

I caught my breath. Beautiful things filled the room. Enormous paintings of nudes adorned the walls, their gilded frames shimmering in the tiny spotlights arranged over them. Intricate figurines danced as if alive on top of pristine glass shelves.

Upon closer examination, though, something rather obvious dawned on me.

The things around us spoke of a wealthy collector, not a psychic. I saw no symbols of protection or balance, nothing to identify a practitioner. In my father's house, religious icons lined shelves built especially for that purpose, crosses hung above doorways, and special herbs burned every evening, making the house smell like a basket of dried flowers. He was an Orthodox Christian by upbringing, but influences of *dvoeverie* were evident in his use of charms, talismans, burning oils, and incense to combat the residue of clients' negative emotions. Except for Baba Varya's, he didn't read books on magic to learn the ways a practitioner should defend himself. He simply asked his three spirit guides: Avadata, Kevoidana, and Azhidana. Shortly after he and Olga made up their minds about opening a business in L.A., Dad had performed three preliminary sessions to find his spiritual guides. Avadata had come first. But it took some time before the other two appeared; Kevoidana the philosopher, and Azhidana, who possessed the most knowledge of their realm.

"What time do you have where you are?" Dad asked during one session.

"The concept of time does not exist here."

"By what means do you communicate with us?"

"Through your mind."

"How do I protect myself from evil?"

"Faith and purity of thought."

"Anything more substantial?"

"Ancient symbols of protection and black clothes deflect harmful energies and entities. Yet again, if your thought is corrupted, you are doomed."

I remember Olga muttering, "What a lively bunch," and Dad gesturing at her to shut it. His main complaint during the years they conducted their psychic business was that she never paid the spirits proper respect.

As Mama Lola spoke to Rosa, I tried to get Mom's attention. She was watching the other two with a thoughtful expression. Beneath a mask of amiability, I detected from her a rising current of distrust.

Mom and I remained silent as Mama Lola accepted from Rosa the tongue along with a wad of cash. Her lips moved as she counted the money. Once satisfied, she tucked it into her belt. "I will be right back."

As soon as she left, Mom turned to Rosa. "How much you give her?"

"Five hundred. Usually she charge thousands."

"Rosa. I think she mostovly lie to you."

"But she will help me." Rosa sounded like she was trying to convince herself.

"I hope," Mom said.

We waited. Rosa couldn't stop pacing, growing more anxious by the minute. We had pretty much accused her psychic of fraud. That didn't stop her from hoping, though. She wanted a miracle.

An hour later I was fidgeting, too, but just then Mama Lola reappeared with the tongue, now wrapped in colorful cloth.

"It is done," she said, handing it to Rosa and bowing slightly. "Now you must do as I had explained earlier."

In the car Rosa revealed the most important part of the curse-lifting ritual. "The tongue is soaked with that *putana*'s curses," she said. "Now all we must to do is bury it under the train, and everything she wish on me will go back to her."

"We?" I said.

———

We drove through the industrial parts of the city for hours to locate a section of the railroad where we could bury the tongue without getting arrested.

The abandoned train station we finally found was a graveyard littered with rusted cars and engines. Lofty elm trees whispered in the breeze, creating the only movement above metal carcasses. The ground was crisscrossed with tracks.

We parked at the end of a gravel path, the clouds of dust kicked up by our tires staining the late-afternoon sunlight and flooding through the open window of the car.

"This is crazy," I said in Russian. "Mom, why do we have to do this? Can't you tell her it's not going to work?"

"No. And don't you dare, either. She's my friend. Besides, we don't know for sure. If she believes enough, it might."

To Mom, magic absolutely existed, just not all on its own. It had to come from within as much as from without. She believed that every person had a bit of magic inside them—some had the ability to apply it; for others it stayed dormant forever. Mom didn't arrive at this point of view all on her own, but adopted it from a clairvoyant friend from Tadzhikistan who used to visit us in Moscow every summer. Her name was Paywand, meaning "connection." A fitting choice: one day, her parents found Paywand playing by the river, conversing with an imaginary friend who turned out to be her grandfather's ghost. The spirit advised them to buy a certain neighbor's plot of land. Paywand's father—landless, moneyless, but superstitious—bought it with help from equally superstitious friends and relatives. Within several years the land blossomed into a pomegranate farm with the sweetest and juiciest fruits in town, and the poor man became a well-respected merchant.

I first met Paywand when I was six. Her almond-shaped eyes looked like they'd been traced with care by a painter's brush. But it was her hair that fascinated me. She wore it in a multitude of intricate braids down to her knees, as was the Tadzhik custom. During her first visit, as everyone sat around discussing world-wide supernatural occurrences, Paywand braided my own hair in that fashion. For two weeks I pranced around the school in my sweet hairdo. The eventual unbraiding was a two-hour ordeal.

Paywand could walk into any dwelling and sense a supernatu-ral presence. Countless times she was called to haunted sites to discern the type of entity residing inside. Yet she recognized mys-ticism and spirituality not only with a clairvoyant's sensitivity to spirits or a seer's awareness of the future but also in Rembrandt's brushstrokes and Dostoyevsky's madness.

"Are you some kind of a magician?" I asked her once.

"No," she replied. "I'm a flashlight, like everyone else, like you. The only difference is that I'm on and you're not."

"So if I turn on the switch, I can be a magician, too?"

"There is no doubt in my mind that you can shine!"

One of the reasons Mom didn't confront Mama Lola with her suspicions was probably because she hoped that even if Mama Lola had faked it, Rosa might've believed in the spell so much that it would work on faith alone.

"We must support her by releasing our own positive energies," Mom said.

Roxy and Maria were playing poker in the backseat next to me. My sister looked up and grinned. "I'm releasing my energy right now, Mama."

"*Yolky-palki* (For crying out loud)," I said, covering my nose. "You're disgusting."

Mom turned around. "Girls. That's enough."

But Rosa wasn't paying attention to us. She squinted at the intersection. "Mama Lola said to bury it where two set of track cross. Ju think I'm crazy?" She suddenly turned, and even from the backseat I could see the anguish in her eyes. She got a garden trowel out of the glove compartment and hesitated as if its cool weight had momentarily pulled her to reality.

Mom opened the door and got out. "If you crazy, I more crazy."

"It has to work," Rosa said.

"Right there, okay?" Mom pointed ahead, and Rosa joined her on the tracks.

Roxy and Maria jumped out. They weren't allowed on the tracks, so they played in the gravel, gathering rocks to take home.

From inside the car, I watched Mom and Rosa stumble over the tracks to the spot Mom had picked and dig at the base of one iron rail. Each of them had a lit cigarette sticking out of her mouth. After the tongue was safely deposited, they milled around for a bit, chatting.

Eventually they came back, their cigarettes long gone.

"I'm hungry," my sister said as she got in the backseat. Maria nodded in agreement.

"We have to wait for train," Mom said.

Maria scooted up and wrapped her skinny arms around Rosa's neck. "But I don't wanna wait, Mama. Take us home and come back later. Please?"

"No, *mija*," said Rosa. "Mama Lola say I have to *see* the train. It will no be too long."

It came an hour later, rushing by in a cacophony of horn and metal. I'd never been so happy to see graffiti swish by, and even the girls cheered, jumping up and down on the seat.

"It will work. You'll see," Rosa said with conviction, looking my mother dead in the eye.

VIVA LAS VEGAS

But in Rosa's case, faith wasn't enough. As a result, Rosa and Mom spent days barricaded in Rosa's apartment, drinking tequila.

I began to worry about the kids. Due to our mothers' preoccupation and my failure as a cook, they'd eaten cereal and toast for two days straight.

On the third day, I determinedly rummaged around the cupboards and in the fridge. Roxy and Maria took turns sashaying down an imaginary catwalk extending from the living room into the kitchen, heads adorned with hair made from Mom's panty hose.

"I hate olives," Roxy said when I picked up a can.

"Too bad for you," I said.

I thumped the can down on the counter next to a bag of elbow pasta, a green pepper, and a braided loop of Armenian string cheese made of goat's milk. With the exception of smoked cold cuts, Mom seldom bought processed food. We had neither frozen dinners nor a microwave to heat them in, but we didn't need to. Mom could whip up a meal out of anything.

"I wanna help." My sister leaned her skinny elbows on the counter next to me.

"And me," Maria said. "You can make mac and cheese, no?"

The girls seemed excited about the prospect of cooking without an adult. Not me, but it was better that they thought I knew what I was doing, right?

"Grab a skillet."

Roxy dove into the bottom cabinet and dug out the largest one she could find. Meanwhile, Maria got the task of washing the pepper. We were *so* cooking.

The three of us sat on the floor in front of the twelve-inch TV borrowed from one of the neighbors who never asked for it back. *I Love Lucy* was on, the episode where Lucy and Ethel get a job in the chocolate factory. Steam rose in willowy threads from my invention, piled generously on our plates. We gulped down the mush of overcooked pasta dotted with olives and green-pepper slices and topped with melting string cheese. The girls giggled at Lucy, her mouth stuffed with chocolates.

"What's this?" Maria asked a few minutes into our dinner, pulling something small and black out of her mouth. I studied the fragment that didn't fit the description of any ingredients I had used.

Roxy turned her spoon around her plate. "Look. I have some, too."

I found several similar pieces in my food, my heart falling at the prospect of having just poisoned two little girls. "Don't eat that anymore."

Running back into the kitchen, I turned on all the lights, Roxy and Maria chattering at my back like chickens in a coop.

"Maybe they're worms," Roxy volunteered as I removed the lid off the skillet, hovering over its contents.

"Too hard," Maria said. "One time, Mom found mouse poop under the sink. It could be mouse poop."

"Shut up, you two."

I grabbed the garbage can, poking around in it with the stick Mom used to prop up the kitchen window when smoking. Nothing. Back to the skillet. I snatched the cooking spoon I'd used and dug it deep in the pasta. I picked out more bits and laid them on the counter. As I lifted the spoon for another go, my eyes jumped to its bowl.

"*Mat' tvoyu cherez sem'vorot s prisvistom* (Fuck your mother through seven gates while whistling)!" I said. The plastic edges had shrunk back in thick charred grooves, slicked with melted cheese.

"What? Let me see!" The girls attached themselves to my sides.

"I melted the damn spoon!"

I still sympathize with people who are taken in by the Mama Lolas of the world. Were it that easy, psychics would be in more demand than doctors and lawyers.

To me, mysticism isn't showy ceremony. Agrefina, the old seer, saw the fortunes of others through flashes of vision, not in full pictures, and that imperfection made her real. These natural psychics are the ones I always trusted; the ones who showed vulnerability without fear and admitted freely that the art of divination was unpredictable, as changing as the universe. In my experience only charlatans had all the answers.

After days of moaning and bitching about women whose fucking East L.A. houses should burn to the fucking ground, Rosa knew what to do to make everything okay for a while.

She'd been played, and only one thing would cure it: a trip to Vegas.

In Russia my parents would have had no problem leaving us alone for a couple of days, but L.A. was still an unpredictable beast.

We all knew that three straight days with Olga might end in casualties. But Mom had bigger things on her mind, though she wouldn't share them with me. I complained for a few hours before she shipped us off, disappearing into the sunset in Rosa's purple Buick.

That evening Olga made us eat with her and Dad's friends at the dining-room table. Everything in my father's house happened around that table. All the important decisions and arguments, and the socializing. Dad had plenty to say about Mom leaving in such a hurry, though nothing of the kind I'd want to repeat.

"*Kakova huya ona poekhala tuda* (Why the fuck did she go there)?"

"She cares nothing for the kids. That much is clear," Olga added.

Olga's beef Stroganoff tasted like cat food, but she insisted we girls needed nourishment. In front of several women she fretted over our skinny elbows and drawn cheeks.

"You poor girls," she said in Russian, ladling more slop into Roxy's bowl. "Your mother should pick up a skillet once in a while."

"Mom went to Vegas to start an American life, not sit here pretending we're still in Russia," I said. "And so you know, she's a great cook." Just not lately.

Dad noticed Olga's scowl and turned to me. "It's the recipes, not her skill, that made the meals so good."

I was about to say something more in Mom's defense when Roxy kicked me under the table. "Stop making trouble or she'll send us home," she said in English, trying to whisper but not really succeeding. "I'm tired of eating Cheerios."

"See?" Olga jumped in. "Nora doesn't have time for you girls with all that drinking to keep her busy. You'd be much better off with us in India."

I stood, dry of the anger I had felt at my mother. "We're fine, so why don't you shove off!"

My father's fist came down on the table. The thud reverberated inside my stomach.

"Leave this table—now."

I hoped Las Vegas would turn out to be the miraculous city so many Soviets claimed it to be. A place where impossible things happened to immigrants. I envisioned Mom coming back to L.A. in a shiny Rolls-Royce crammed with money. We'd buy a mansion, uptown from Olga. If she and Dad came to visit (as they would, to swim in our Olympic-size pool), Ken, our buff security guard, would refuse to let her past our Gucci wrought-iron gates.

CONVERTING SHERRI

Olga's company consisted of women who started off as clients. She read their palms and tarot cards, and performed occasional cleansing or binding rituals in the séance room. Since Olga was a social creature, eventually they all ended up gossiping in the kitchen. Soon these women came by at all hours to drink tea and sometimes ogle my father and his many long-haired musician buddies.

The women were loud in the way birds are during the early-morning hours. When they sat in that kitchen together, they seemed to manage several conversations at once.

One of these ever present characters was a Russian hairdresser named Sherri (Russian name Elizaveta), who made the *Real Housewives of Orange County* look like the Singing Nuns. Every time Sherri and Dad were in the same room, her boobs pointed in his direction like radar dishes. Having almost no chest to speak of, I secretly wanted to ask her how to make mine more noticeable.

I couldn't imagine Olga didn't notice Sherri's interest in my father; perhaps she chose to ignore it, appearing to be content as long as the clients, and their money, kept coming.

Sherri paid in hundred-dollar bills but only for tarot readings. She avoided all other types of divination until one night Olga finally convinced her to join us for a channeling session. If I didn't know better I'd say she had agreed only because my father would lead the séance. Roxy had gone to bed earlier, but I was allowed to participate. Though I was still afraid, that didn't mean I wasn't curious. Plus I trusted my father with the board.

Dad laid the board on the kitchen table and fetched his plate from the bedroom. Sherri sat next to me with an expression of boredom, one side of her mouth pinched up, the same look you get from people who think you're lying and want you to know they know. Dad began chanting, and in a few moments, we were ready to go.

"We have someone new with us tonight," he said into the air. "Her name is Elizaveta. Will you answer her questions?"

The plate slid to "Yes."

Sherri shook her head. "No, no, I'll pass."

"Why?" Olga said.

"They're dead. Dead people can't talk."

"You think we're faking," Dad said.

Sherri crossed her legs nervously, the heel of her left pump nearly touching my pant leg. Suddenly she grabbed my hand. "Fine. But let Oksana go first."

Dad chuckled, but Olga wasn't as pleasant.

"Next thing we know, you'll say Oksana is in on it. That we trained her to ask certain questions."

"If this is real she doesn't have to ask the question out loud, does she?" Sherri said triumphantly.

Lately I'd been skeptical myself, because Dad's connection with his guides appeared unbroken. Any time he called, they responded. Mama Lola was to blame for my misgivings, and I hated her for it. Dad wasn't like Agrefina; he had no visions of his own the way a seer does. If anything, he was more like Paywand; instead of predictions that focused on a specific individual's energies and thoughts, he connected with entities who delivered "knowledge" through him. But what if he was like Mama Lola and I'd been unwilling to notice the signs? Though I wasn't a big fan of Sherri's, she presented a unique opportunity to find out if Dad was indeed a true medium.

I concentrated on clearing my mind, and silently asked the vaguest question I could think up: What should I do with my life?

Immediately I pictured myself passing out drinks inside a large commercial airplane, my baby-blue uniform crisp. Flying wasn't a dream of mine, and I was surprised by the image.

The plate spelled out "fly." I could almost hear Azhidana, Kevoidana, and Avadata giggling.

"Well?" Sherri said.

I shared, and Sherri promptly went from skeptical to leaving. She snatched her purse and keys from the kitchen counter. "I just remembered I have to buy some wineglasses for a friend's bridal shower."

"What's wrong with you?" Olga said. "Come back. Let's ask if you'll ever get hitched again."

Sherri rummaged inside her purse as if she'd lost a city in there. "Sorry, guys. I still don't believe any of this."

Her departure left Olga scrubbing out ashtrays as if she were going to use them for serving plates.

Meanwhile Dad asked the guides one of his favorite questions: "Why is my life so fucked up?" By this time he'd visited several L.A. recording studios and management firms in search of work or representation, but was rejected every time even before he opened his guitar case on account of being too old and foreign.

"It is your father's fault," the plate spelled out slowly.

"See?" He clapped his hands on the table. "Baba Varya's curse is strong. But I will find a way—"

"I don't care," Olga snapped. I was still getting over the fact that a porcelain plate had told me to become a stewardess, when she flung herself back into her chair. "*Ya etoy suke pokazhu* (I'll show that bitch)."

"Relax," Dad said. "She's afraid, but she'll be back."

"Dear spirits, you saw the disrespect Elizaveta showed you. Will you let her get away with that?"

"Olga!" Dad reached for the plate, but she clawed her hands around his to keep him away.

Quickly, before he could escape her grip, Olga cried out, "Prove your power to Elizaveta!"

Dad jumped up and wrestled the board and the plate away from Olga.

"How dare you, woman. You say those words and you give them permission to harm. How fucking stupid can you be?"

At a little past midnight Sherri came back. She'd been crying for a while, and the sleeves of her blouse were smeared with the makeup she had wiped off. Dad led her toward the kitchen, but she refused to go in there, hiccuping uncontrollably. In the living room, Olga and I brought cool washcloths and wine while Dad guided her through a breathing meditation. It took Sherri a good amount of wine to collect herself, but even then her hands shook.

"I don't know if I've gone crazy," she said.

"*Gospodi,*" Dad said. "What happened?"

Olga didn't seem happy to see Sherri in such a distraught state. It brought the other woman in close proximity to Dad, allowing her to cling to his arm and heave a frail sigh at his reassuring words, safe from Olga's retribution unless she wished to come across as a callous harpy. Maybe I detected some guilt, a reaction so unusual for Olga that I must've imagined it.

Sherri lit a cigarette and began in a thin voice.

"After I left here I went to that shopping plaza off Cahuenga Boulevard, for the glasses, you know. I parked on the street and went inside. No more than twenty minutes and I was back." She picked up two cigarette lighters from the coffee table and lined them up. "The red lighter is my car," she said. "The green is the BMW parked behind me. I get in, turn on the ignition. And out of nowhere the car jerks like somebody rear-ended me. So I look back and sure enough, the Beamer is on my bumper. He backs up and drives slowly around me." She slid the green lighter out of the imaginary parking spot and parallel to the red one. "I'm livid, so I roll down my window, waiting for the fucker to roll down his window. When we're even, I'm already cussing the roof off his convertible."

She hesitated.

"What happened then?" I asked.

The cigarette between Sherri's lips had grown an ashen beard, but she let it age.

"Who was it?" Olga asked, perched on the arm of the couch.

"Nobody," Sherri said. "There was nobody at the wheel! So I try to drive away, but it sits there, idling. I'm fucking pounding the horn to get anybody's attention, and then it rolls some feet ahead and parks. Like nothing happened."

"You *are* crazy," Olga said after a few moments. "Some kids played a trick on you, *starushka* (old lady)."

"There was nobody in the car."

"You sure?" Dad said.

"After all the noise I made, a guy runs out of the store and he's waving his arm in the air. I roll down the passenger window, and he starts yelling, 'Who stole my car?' I point to the demon BMW and he just stands there with his mouth open. How do you explain that?"

After taking a few drops of valerian, she went into a coma-like sleep on the guest-room futon. Dad and Olga stayed up until four in the morning, Dad lecturing his wife on the etiquette of channeling and Olga looking like a kid caught stealing.

My question had been answered. But having a medium for a father didn't end our tribulations in the strange country we now called home.

BLACK MAGIC

Dad's gigs did not turn out as much cash as Olga's readings. He refused to read tarot cards or palms; those things are done primarily by women. Instead he started to get deeper into the occult. My grandfather called it *chornaya magia* (black magic), though not everything occult is black.

For the longest time I didn't understand his aversion to metaphysical practices, but one day I came across my grandparents' photo album, where I found a picture of a young girl laid out for a funeral viewing. When I asked about her, Grandpa got so upset he locked the album in his desk drawer. Years later, Mom told me the story behind the girl's image.

When Grandpa Andrei was thirteen, Baba Varya traveled to the southern outskirts of Kiev to see a local soothsayer named Fokla, a blind man of indeterminate age. He lived in a hut with a dirt floor, surviving on the townsfolk's charity.

Baba Varya had come to Fokla hoping for guidance in a difficult situation. After her husband had died, she was barely able to keep her family from the streets. Baba Varya practiced magic by then, but like the majority of practitioners, she lacked the capability to foretell her own future.

She brought her children with her to the hut: Andrei, Boris, and Anna, the oldest at eighteen. But when they stepped inside, Fokla ordered the eldest two to wait in the yard.

Grandpa Andrei wished he could wait outside with them. Some claimed that Fokla had made a pact with the Devil: his sight in exchange for precognition. Looking around a room that he said smelled like a raw grave, Grandpa Andrei couldn't help but believe those rumors.

The old man rested on a sagging cot, both hands on top of an intricately carved cane. Grandpa Andrei, who was already into wood carving, said the cane was unlike anything he'd ever seen, especially the knob, the head of a roaring bear.

After a respectful greeting, Baba Varya placed her offering—a sack of freshly picked beans—on the kitchen table and then lowered herself into a chair across from the soothsayer. She said nothing else. No one came to Fokla with a list of questions. Instead, like Agrefina's, his gift consisted of sporadic visions of the future, and the client had to wait quietly in order for the old man to "see."

Fokla raised his head as if coming out of deep slumber. "The two outside will die young," he told Baba Varya, unprovoked. His milky eyes settled on Grandpa Andrei. Pointing an arthritic finger at the boy, he added, "But this one will accomplish much, and be the one to bury you."

Within five years Boris and Anna were dead of pneumonia.

On the day of Anna's funeral, Andrei sneaked into the soothsayer's hut through the cracked window in the back, stole his cane, and burned it to ashes in the stove, along with as many of his mother's magic books as he could carry. When he went back for more, Baba Varya was waiting on the basement stairs.

She beat her son senseless and, from that day on, kept her books locked in a giant lacquered bookcase.

Baba Varya died in 1961, age ninety-seven, and Andrei did indeed bury her.

It wasn't until 1973 that he decided to destroy the boxes full of his mother's belongings. Mom was there that day. She told me that Grandma Ksenia sat at the kitchen table the entire time, cracking roasted sunflower seeds between her teeth, and it was Mom—belly full of me—who braved the steps down to the basement that morning to help her father-in-law erase his mother's frightening legacy.

"Ksenia is afraid," Grandpa told my mother. "But I don't blame her. It took my mother very long to die, you know. She writhed on her deathbed for days, covered in blisters and sores."

"What caused them?" Mom asked.

"Nobody knows. They spread and oozed pus over her skin one day. She carried the notion that the Devil kept her from dying because of all the horrible things she'd done, so she sent for a priest. To him she confessed every hex. Two days later she passed. And at her funeral not a person spoke, terrified that her restless spirit would shoot down their mouth and possess them."

Tossing book after book into the furnace, Mom told me she fought the urge to keep at least one—a curiosity that she reined in perhaps out of respect for the man who had accepted her as his daughter. Mom helped him empty each box while he told stories from his childhood of the mother whom he loved and feared. Only one book escaped their notice, and it was now in my father's possession.

Grandpa was never sure if Fokla had indeed predicted his siblings' death or cast an "evil eye" and somehow willed them to expire. He feared either truth. When he found out that Dad had Baba Varya's book, he offered to buy it back for two hundred rubles, just to burn it.

"I won't sell it," my father said.

"I tell you, son, the Devil never gives without expecting profit."

"Don't you think I know better than to deal in hexes and bloody rituals?" Dad said.

"What I know is that the more you practice, the less of yourself you keep."

"What if I can fix it? Did you think about that?"

"You're not a practitioner," Grandpa said.

"Not yet."

As always, my father had taken the path staked by his own father with "No Trespassing" signs.

I knew that Grandpa Andrei had been right. My father soon forgot that he started practicing to rid his family of Baba Varya's supposed evil, infatuated as he was with the idea of tapping into a parallel world, of linking with beings that had chosen him as a receptor of their graces. He didn't have as many clients as Olga, but those who came to see him cared little for entertaining tarot spreads. I was chilled every time one crossed the living room on the way to the séance room. Often they left an unsettling impression after they'd gone, an invisible but heavy residue that made you eager to step outside and gulp sweet air into your lungs.

LEAVING LEXINGTON

Mom came back from Las Vegas three days later, the bags under her eyes and the crumpled clothes suggesting she had slept little. We were still poor, but she smiled more than usual and kept hugging us tightly. I'd missed her more than I'd expected, despite the unceremonious dumping of us at Dad's. Our apartment, ratty as it was, felt somehow cleaner, and I breathed easier as soon as we walked inside.

Roxy and I had tons of questions about Mom's trip. In Russia people who saw Vegas held a unique status, as if they'd had tea with the queen of England. Sure enough, the things she told us about the buffets, the beautiful uniforms, the twenty-four-hour life, and the machines that could make a millionaire out of an ordinary person all sounded like pure fantasy.

"Did you win lots of money?" Roxy asked, breathless.

"Better. I decided that we will move there."

My sister and I exchanged surprised looks.

"We're gonna live in a casino?" Roxy asked. Having heard things about Vegas from travelers back in Russia, we knew that it was in the middle of a desert where nothing but cacti survived.

"Don't be dumb," I said. "They probably fly people in for work and take them back later."

"Girls. Nobody has to live in a casino, and we're definitely not flying."

"Why?" I said, resisting the answer I already suspected.

"I didn't immigrate to America to live off charity. In Vegas, I will finally get my chance to start a booziness!"

Before we were granted permission to leave Moscow, Mom had been scouting the city for a potential site of a nightclub she'd designed on sheets of graph paper she pinched from my school folder. "In case we end up stuck here," she said. So close to the fall of the USSR, smaller businesses called "cooperatives" started to pop up, though still heavily regulated by the government or the mafia. Mom's dream had always been to be a business owner. It had lain forgotten under the pall of divorce and welfare checks until Shubi, the Indian woman at the DollarDream, suggested Vegas as the place with high enough salaries to save up for a down payment on Mom's nightclub.

"But what about school?" I asked.

"You'll transfer." Mom's initial excitement ebbed a little. "What are you so worried about? I'm telling you, this will be great."

As soon as she mentioned the word "transfer," I panicked.

"You mean kids live there?" Roxy asked.

"Lots. And you know what else? You'll have all new clothes and toys, and loads of new friends. We'll have more money, too."

"Wow! Will we get to win a million dollars on one of those machines?"

"No, silly. I found a job. The manager at our motel was Russian, and her sister works at the Gold Coast Casino. She's in charge of *sluts* there—that's what you call those machines. I told her about our situation, you know, the real version. And she said, 'If you're good with money, I'll have my sister give you a job.'"

"But you're terrible with money," I said.

Her smile fell. "I thought you'd be happy. We'll be living in Las Vegas. *The* Las Vegas. Can you imagine how jealous everyone will be? Can you see their faces when they hear that Nora has opened her own booziness?"

"Business, Mom. It's called a business. And I won't go," I said. "I like my school."

"Look at you. First I have to force your ass back in school, and now you're suddenly Miss Devoted. We're going, Oksana. I've already decided."

"You can't do that. I'm sixteen."

"Watch me."

Mom had good reasons for wanting to get out of L.A., where hundreds of émigrés lived comfortably on their welfare checks. She was eager for something better. Nobody in Russia knew the truth about our circumstances. Where we came from, senior citizens and the disabled received pensions and veterans' benefits. The rest were considered capable of taking care of themselves.

"We could start fresh. Save money. In a bank," Mom said, pinching my cheek playfully.

"Why can't you find work here?"

"And make shit the Russians call 'pay' for baking bread in the backs of their markets all day?"

I tore into her optimism like an angry paper shredder. We talked long into the night, but nothing swayed me, which, to be honest, surprised us both.

As a kid I hadn't minded moving around. I grew up in train cars, watching Russian pine forests give way to the pebbled shores of the Black Sea where maples and spruces greened the countryside. I loved the stern Armenian mountains crested with the ancient observatories of Karahunj and Metsamor and riddled with the Christian monastery caves of Geghard, and I loved the villages of central Asia where people kept homemade wine in cellars beneath mud huts and marinated fish in barrels filled with sour milk. They all belonged to me, the entire fifteen republics with all their curiosities.

But now it seemed I was recalling someone else's life. Those places lay far away, and I'd begun to grow fond of my new surroundings. I liked the idea of belonging. In the past months, pride and a sense of accomplishment had filled me like water fills a well. Now all of it could evaporate. Did I have the strength to start over again?

The closer it got to the end of the summer, the more Mom and I argued. She had a month to relocate, and by God, nobody, not even her stubborn daughter, could stop her. I begged Dad to intercede, even though the idea of living in the same house with Olga gave me instant heartburn. More and more people were coming each day to have their fortunes read, and Olga was smugger than ever: "Not bad for a country girl, huh?"

When I started threatening to run away, Mom finally stopped pushing. Not that she gave up her mission; more like she changed her tactics. For days, we didn't exchange a word. Every time Dad called and asked to speak with Mom, she locked the bedroom door. Both my parents rock-climbed life, but instead of spotting each other as partners, each went solo to see who'd summit first. Dad took Mom's new plan as a direct challenge to his psychic business endeavor.

"Your mother has always tried to outdo me. In business, in our relationship, she always had to prove she did things better. But this time, this whole Vegas business is gonna be her downfall. This time she has reached too high," he said, also pointing out her inability to take on something that required commitment and less drinking. Dad and I both knew Mom tended to run from trouble instead of facing it. Always she was filled with blind hope that things would work out as long as she could start fresh.

But she refused to give up on Vegas.

Finally she conceded that I could stay with Dad until graduation, two years later, but only if I'd give Vegas a go for one year after that. Roxy, though, was going with her. I readily agreed, certain they would be back in L.A. by then.

For the next month, Mom packed continuously. Between the curbside sprees and the neighbors' donations, we'd accumulated a three-bedroom apartment's worth of stuff. Mom refused to give away anything, even the plastic flowers she'd found on our very first excursion to Beverly Hills.

On the morning of moving day Rosa went to pick up Mom's U-Haul. I helped pack the loads of sheets and skillets Mom wouldn't hear of leaving behind. My stomach clenched. When I walked into the bedroom, stripped of its George Michael posters, I did so with lowered eyes. I'd tried to spend more time with Roxy, knowing I'd miss her outlandish humor and the way she got excited over our trips to the DollarDream or when she swiped one of Mom's lipsticks. She was still at that age when love was an unconditional thing she passed out to people like balloons. She was the only good thing our family had left.

My sister had stuffed her Barbies and bottles of nail polish inside a hot-pink princess backpack Maria had given her as a parting gift. Going to Vegas constituted adventure, and she couldn't wait to get on the road.

Rosa walked in through the front door, her white sneakers beaming in contrast to a brown sweater and aquamarine sweatpants. "I parked the truck in back," she said, taking a seat on one of the two remaining chairs.

Mom came in from the kitchen with two steaming cups of

coffee, handing one to Rosa. She'd been washing the last of the dishes and still had the kitchen towel slung over one shoulder. "I so tired, so tired I cannot speak."

"Relax, *mija*. The drive will probably take seven hours."

"You okay to drive big truck? How you think?" Mom had gotten her license two months before, but still said no to the freeway.

Rosa accepted the coffee and waved a dismissive hand. "Easy. We get to Vegas tonight, rent a car tomorrow."

"Oh, *Slava Bogoo*! Thank God. How you drive on American freeway, I never know. Is scare me."

Mom and Rosa exchanged one of those meaningful looks people always assume go unnoticed by others.

"Ju should go, Oksana," Rosa said. "Is a great place for a teen-ager, no?"

"She can't leave her Brazilian boyfriend."

I had forgotten all about Roxy until she opened her big mouth.

"Oksana, is that what this is all about?" Mom asked in Russian.

"I want to graduate from a decent school where they know me. We agreed, remember?"

Mom nodded knowingly. "Very good. You finish school, then you live with me. If not, I'll send you back to Moscow." Then she added, with a no-nonsense wag of a finger, "And none of that boyfriend rubbish. I didn't suffer all those years in Russia and move our entire family here only to see you marry some rock-star wannabe."

"Why not? You married one."

I raced out of the apartment when Mom swiped at me with the kitchen towel. She chased me down the stairs, shouting at the top of her lungs, with Rosa and Roxy at her heels. We raced around the pool fence, one lap, another. My mother ordered me to stop so she could whip me with the towel. Her slippers kept falling off and Roxy kept picking them up and handing them back, laughing loud enough to attract an audience.

On the ride to Dad's house, Mom tried to make peace, but I was having none of it. If she wanted a battle, she'd get a war. As I got out of the car she tried to hug me, but I wriggled out of her embrace.

She and Roxy drove away with the Vegas lights bright in their eyes. I held my breath as anger was quickly replaced by something heavier. Our life on Lexington was really over. I'd never go back to the apartment or the people who had propped up our shaky beginning.

Just like that, we had moved on again.

THINGS UNSEEN

During my first months living at my father's, our conversations ran in shallow streams of dinner talk (helmed mostly by Olga), discussions of the supernatural, and music-related topics, where it was safe. We'd been strangers for so long, Dad and I. The reasons are sharp and at the same time fuzzy inside my head, like memories I might've stolen from the life of someone I used to know. What had made us like this?

According to my sources, aka relatives who get sloshed at parties, one reason might've been the fact that Mom became pregnant with me the first night my parents spent together. Perhaps Dad married her only because he had to.

The problem with beginning as my parents did is once the heat subsides and two people realize they'd rather join the Communist Party than spend a minute in each other's company, their child becomes a padlock that keeps them in that cold place.

Of course, growing up I had no inkling that I was the whisk that truly stirred my parents into chaos. Oftentimes Grandma Ksenia called me a "child of sinful passion" when I misbehaved, which naturally made me think she was alluding to my wicked temperament. As I matured, my father's tough love bared its roots. In our culture, a child conceived out of wedlock brings bad luck, as it belongs to the dark spirit that rules our darkest impulse: lust. Little good is expected from it, but evil is assigned naturally. To some, I might as well have stepped out of *The Omen*, as Damien's female doppelgänger, and once I knew that, my honorary title made sense. And never more so than on the day I revealed to my parents a terrible secret.

When I was seven, our next-door neighbor was a beautiful blond man with a beautiful blond family: his wife, Brigita, with a voice as fragile as the spring buds of a pussy willow; his daughter, Gala, who was my age; and a toddler boy who went by Ponchik ("Doughnut"). Peteris was in his mid-thirties. I remember watching him cook for his family in their tiny kitchen, peeling potatoes for a farmer's omelet and feeding all of us kids the raw slices before tossing the rest into a skillet that sizzled with butter. I never knew that you could eat raw potatoes, but he assured us that in the old days Slavs used to eat them this way. I loved playing with Gala, who kept a burlap sack full of her brother's old baby clothes for us to dress our dolls in. I'd bring my own bag of Roxy's cloth diapers and onesies. We'd swap outfits for hours. On the nights my parents were gone performing, Peteris and Brigita often stayed at our place to watch over us kids.

One night I woke up.

My parents' bedroom overlooked the backyard, where birds sang even at the latest of hours. We had so many trees, they probably assumed we were part of the forest that spread around our neighborhood like a mantle made of pine needles. I felt safest in that room, in my parents' oversize bed, curled in their sheets, surrounded by their scent. To my left eight-month-old Roxy slept in her crib. To my right the moon peeked through Mom's curtains. Above me the ceiling whirled between light and shadows cast by the trees outside. And below me was Peteris. He'd pulled me on top of him, and the fingers of his one hand were inside my underwear, the other tugging my shirt to my chin.

"What are you doing?"

"You're dreaming. Close your eyes."

"I'll tell Mom."

"No you won't. If you do she'll be mad, and you and Gala won't be friends anymore."

"I'll tell."

He rolled me off him, and I drifted back to sleep.

The next morning I sat on the kitchen floor dressing Sipsik, my favorite doll, while Mom swirled a whisk through a pan of farina on top of the stove. She was humming a song from *Ironiya Sudby* (*The Irony of Fate*), a famous Russian romantic comedy.

"Mom, Peteris woke me up last night."

She leaned an elbow on the counter and continued to stir with the other hand.

"Why, *sladkaya* (sweet)? Did he have the TV on too loud?"

"He touched me."

I felt my mother vault through the kitchen and crouch before me. The farina will be all ruined now, I thought, black clumps and everything. She lifted my chin, and as Peteris had predicted, she was angry.

"What are you talking about?"

I said no more. Sipsik needed a change. I made to get up, but Mom planted her hands on my shoulders.

"Where? Where did he touch you?"

With each place I showed her, her fingers ground me harder into the floor.

"He said it was a dream."

I told her even though I knew I'd get in trouble. But I wanted to prove Peteris wrong. He'd sounded so smug. By all accounts

I was a child who routinely defied orders. (Grandpa once told me I was lucky to be a girl, as I'd make a poor foot soldier.)

I was more scared of her reaction than of the actual incident. Why was she ripping the covers from around my sleeping father's body, exploding with threats of dismembering his good friend? Why was she dragging him half naked down the stairs and out the back door, and hollering for Peteris and Brigita to come out? Within five minutes the five of us stood in front of the wooden fence with our neighbors on the other side. Mom was shouting and cursing, Brigita crying. She asked me over and over, "Did he really touch you there?" And every time I said yes, her face cracked as if I'd put a hammer to it. I also wanted to cry, not for me but as an instinctive response to Brigita; her hysteria indicated something awful had happened. I wished I could understand what it was. In all this confusion and melodrama, Peteris and my father, who insisted that I dreamed the whole thing, were calm.

"I wasn't in the bedroom, Oksana." Peteris winked at me, and I lowered my head. Something made it difficult to meet his eyes.

"You were."

"She's a kid," my father said. "We don't need to make such a big deal of this. Why destroy a great friendship over a child's imagination?"

My mother's hands flew to her face. "What kind of a child imagines something like that?"

Dad looked down at me. *A wicked kind.*

Soon after, Peteris and his family moved away. Having nothing to compare the incident to, my mind quickly pushed it down the basement stairs and locked the door. For years I never thought of that night. Not until I saw Peteris again when I was fourteen.

A month after Ruslan's death, our doorbell rang at close to midnight. Mom wasn't home and I thought it was her. I peeked out of my room and saw a tall figure in a black wool coat embracing my

father. Even from behind I recognized him, and my breath grew
shallow like I was breathing through a thick layer of gauze. I hurriedly shut my bedroom door, blasted the TV, and sat in the corner on the plastic chair I never used. The voices outside that door
were cheerful, the way they usually were when we had company.
My fingers clawed the chair's hard edges, and I pressed my knees
together so tight it hurt. I had only two thoughts:

1. God, please don't let him come in here.
2. How could Dad allow him into our house again?

The door opened. My father ushered Peteris in and swept an
arm in my direction.

"And here's our Oksana. All grown up."

I wasn't mad at him for not smashing Peteris's face back at
that fence: I can imagine that the two of them being such good
friends made it impossible for Dad to believe in the other man's
betrayal. After all, it's not easy to see those we love or trust as vil-
lains. But I've never felt more humiliated than in that room, more
invisible to my father, and this made a bigger impact on me than
the incident in my parents' bedroom.

Dad's instincts sided with his friend, and some would say that
it made *him* a good friend and that there's nothing wrong with
that. Only there was. Peteris could've survived a punch in the
mug and a few Gypsy curses. I, on the other hand, didn't fare so
well. My father's instincts wedged themselves between us like a
drunk on a crowded subway.

He didn't believe me.

The very last time I saw Agrefina, she said something so bizarre that I didn't understand it for years. She and I were inside her
house, warming our hands on a bench near the stove. Mom had
gone to use the outhouse. This was one of the coldest winter days,

and before Mom and I took the taxi from Moscow, I'd bundled up in a yellow faux-fur coat that made me look like I carried a lion cub on my back. The coat hung on a hook near the door, crystalline snowflakes melting on the wooden floor below.

Agrefina gently tapped my hand with her index finger. "Your beautiful coat has a rip, *detochka* (little child)."

I looked over my shoulder.

"You won't see it now. It's been there for years, though it's still tiny. But when you do see it, remember that it will grow if not mended."

All I could do was frown, worried. In this weather a hole in a coat could mean an awful cold later.

She smoothed my hair out of my face. "I'm not worried. You have a very good coat. Warm and sturdy. I'm not worried at all."

Not once did she point to or look at the coat in question. Back home I shook it and turned it inside out, but found nothing. At fourteen I wasn't too fluent in metaphors, but now I know what she meant. I wish it hadn't taken so long.

TO MAGNET OR NOT TO MAGNET

My father was always difficult to love, but I was no marshmallow Peep myself. Now, in a new country where brand-new experiences were being taped over our old life, maybe we had a chance to finally bond. Why not? We hailed from a gutsy stock, after all. Personally I would've given my right eye for my father's affection, and since it's the eye that does the majority of seeing for me, I was pretty desperate.

If only my father's heart were so easily breached. I'd spent years waiting for the moment Dad would look up, see me, and be proud. And the only way to accomplish that was by proving that I was an artist of exceptional talent. The magnet school seemed like the perfect place to make that happen, even if it was part of an institution of "organized learning."

Traditionally, Romani prefer to teach their kids at home. Among them there is a commonly shared opinion, even today, that the public school system alienates kids from adults, churning out generations of disrespectful, lazy egomaniacs who go through life without purpose.

Dad knew school had a place, but he insisted that family had the ultimate responsibility to its children. Only blood could shape us into what we ultimately became, his thinking was. He abhorred people telling his kids what to do. Where did that leave broken families like ours? I never dared ask.

During a discussion with my eighth-grade home economics teacher, Valentina Semyonovna, he set out to prove his point on the subject of social education. "Let's not forget identity and self-worth. Two subjects school curriculum skirts."

"Comrade Kopylenko," she said, "those kinds of notions are not healthy for the children's mind." She had refused the Armenian *sourj* Mom had made in a *jesveh*, a brass pot with a long handle used to make this traditional coffee. Mom disregarded the unintentional insult for the sake of diplomacy.

I knew the exact reason behind the visit. This was only a few months after Ruslan's death, and already I felt as transparent as morning mist, fading from my school's bleach-smelling hallways. By this time, my parents were living mentally in America, and believed that a Soviet education wouldn't be of much use to me once we moved across the ocean. Perfect, since school always felt like a battleground to me. I was failing every subject except for music and gun club. But how to get kicked out?

I had shown up one day wearing a blue skirt and a sweater with fuzzy penguins on the front. The outfit looked better than the mandatory crap-brown parlor-maid uniforms.

As soon as she saw me, Valentina Semyonovna, who was short and plump like Winnie-the-Pooh, said, "Oksana Kopylenko. You go back home right now and put on your uniform."

"It's in the Dumpster."

Now Valentina Semyonovna was in my home trying to convince my parents to let her take me to Young Pioneers camp.

"People need to be led, to be shown the correct path. Herded, if I may be frank."

"Sheep need to be herded," my father said, "goats led. Do I have horns?" This last with a chuckle.

Leaning on the kitchen counter out of Valentina Semyonovna's line of vision, Mom waved her arms at Dad and mouthed, "Shut up already!"

My teacher's cheeks were two ripe tomatoes, her back a broomstick.

"You are intelligent people. Surely you must recognize the ingenuity of our leaders' approach."

"Let us perform an experiment," Dad said. "My cat, Michael Jackson, loves music." The cat in question—a cantankerous hodgepodge of various Russian breeds—had been napping on the phone stand nearby. He heard his name and lifted his head.

"I'll prove to you now that even animals, when given a choice, can make the right one."

Dad fetched his guitar from behind the table, turned to Michael, and eased into "Affirmation" by George Benson. Michael stretched his body before sitting up to watch Dad play. His upper lip shook ever so slightly and lifted in a soulful meow. After each passage, which my father emphasized by a pause, Michael came back with an answer.

Valentina Semyonovna's face was transfixed.

Dad laid the guitar on his lap. "Ah? What do you think about that?"

"Remarkable."

"That's right."

My teacher reached for the guitar. "May I?"

As her pudgy fingers strummed the strings in a quick warm-up,

Dad sat back in his chair, arms and legs crossed, a smile on his face. Then she began to sing.

Otzie o svobode e shastye metchtali,
Za eto srazhali ne raz.
V borbe sozdavali e Lenin, e Stalin
Otechesvo nashe dlia nas!

Our fathers have dreamed of freedom and happiness,
They've fought for those rights more than once.
In struggle did Lenin and Stalin create
This wonderful homeland for us!

Michael turned a couple of times before settling for another nap with his posterior facing my teacher.

Dad clapped, for the poor woman or the cat, I do not know. "My dear Valentina Semyonovna. You were right about one thing. He is a most remarkable cat!" Even Mom had covered her mouth, complimenting the sour-faced teacher through tight fingers. For the brief remainder of my Soviet public education, I wore civvies.

Ironically, Valentina Semyonovna adopted Michael when we left the country. I hope he has learned to enjoy her taste in music.

I said nothing to my father about wanting to join the Hollywood High magnet school, lest he bring up the Michael incident, the way he did whenever I felt the urge to join a herd. When I'm famous, I'll surprise him, I thought.

I called Mom instead, explaining that the interviews were about to take place. Despite her fear of freeways, she drove from

Vegas the very next morning and picked me up a few blocks from Dad's place. I had not expected her to drive two hundred miles; a few encouraging words would've sufficed. Not that I didn't appreciate her presence; more like I dreaded her trying to administer her charm on my behalf. In Armenian and Romani cultures alike, parents will mend your clothes and cook your food until you're using a walker.

I jumped inside the car and she wrapped her arms around me, weeks of loneliness packed in that embrace.

"Goodness, it's like I haven't seen you in ages," she said, and pulled away, arms still on my shoulders. "I'm so proud of you."

"I haven't done anything, Mom."

"But you are about to, no?"

"Not if we're late."

The main auditorium was nearly empty of applicants. A row of tables had been set up near the stage, where the counselors conducted interviews and checked in applications. There was only one counselor left, a heavyset woman with a high blond ponytail and wireless glasses. Mr. North, I saw with a sinking feeling, was nowhere to be seen. Two stacks of applications rose on either side of her, the one on the right dwarfed by the one on the left. She smiled with a mouthful of neon-white teeth, face shiny and fresh like a baby's, and motioned for me to come closer.

Mom and I crept toward the table, clinging like conjoined twins. I handed her my application, hiding my hands behind my back. I had bitten my nails the night before.

"I wish to join the program," I said.

She perused the pages. "I see here you're a junior. Good. Oksana? Mr. North told me about you."

I hoped that was a bonus, and she seemed pleased.

"My only concern is your English," she said, and my hands started to sweat. "How are your ESL classes going?"

"I'm top of my class."

"She good in school. *Ona ochen talantlivaya* (She's very talented)," Mom said. "Like her mama."

"Mom."

She stepped back with one hand on her hip. But she didn't argue, which was so out of character that I've never forgotten it.

"It's okay," the counselor said. "Don't be so nervous. If you feel uncomfortable, there's always next year."

"I don't have that much time."

"What do you mean?"

"I have a plan. If I take regular English, it will help me to learn it faster, which is part of that plan. So you see, I must be in this program. Also, I need to become great musician fast."

"*Pravilno* (That's right)," Mom said from somewhere behind me. For the time being we both chose to forget that most of this was to impress my father.

The counselor considered me over her nearly invisible glasses. I couldn't tell what she was thinking.

"What are the four basic types of sentences?"

I stuttered.

"So vat?" my mother said, back to her post at my side. "My daughter write books from small-child time. You play Mozart? Debussy? Gershwin?" Mom was folding a finger for each composer I had ever learned.

No; the counselor shook her head. "But I don't see the relevance."

"She learn one measure, two measure, for hours, until perfect. Because she have *disciplina* and good brains. You tink she can't do something, and she do it."

"Mom, please."

"Program for talent, yes? Say so on your paper. She talent. Like her mama. I come America wit no money, no English. I alone with two childrens, but we do good. Is hard, but we harder. So, you take her, yes? No problem."

Where was the charm? Where was the mother who could talk a king out of his crown?

Mrs. Dominguez regarded us for some time before her expression came into focus the way it does when someone makes up their mind about something they find wonderful.

"I can see how important this is for you both."

"I won't fail," I said.

She put my application on top of the stack to her right. "See me in my office after school for the new schedule."

I don't know if the process of getting into the magnet school was different for other students. Did they have to audition? Show good grades? To me it was a miracle, and I was afraid to pry into its workings lest it burst into smoke. Mom and I walked out of that auditorium with wings strapped to our shoes. It wasn't really that big a deal, now that I think back. In California, magnet schools are as plentiful as parking meters. But when Mom and I parted that day for her to make the long drive back to Vegas, all I could think was, I'm not a foreigner anymore.

Cruz caught up with me on the bus going home, though he was the last person I wanted to see. Earlier I had found out he'd been flirting with Natasha, the Russian girl from our last year's ESL class, who gloated while telling me about it in detail during lunch. It was no secret that she had a thing for him. I was crushed. But maybe it was my fault. When Cruz blackmailed me into that date at the Pizza Place in exchange for gaining entrance to the cemetery, I had brought Natasha with me.

Inconveniently, Cruz lived three blocks away from my father's house, so I couldn't tell him to get lost.

"Happy to see me?" he asked.

Instead of dwelling on Natasha, I told him about the magnet program. For some inexplicable reason, I wanted him to be proud of me.

He congratulated me in a crisp kind of a way.

"What's the matter?" I asked, disappointed.

"Nothing. It's great."

Our stop came up and he followed me off the bus. We walked for a while in silence.

"We won't have classes together," he finally said.

I hadn't given it much thought. For a good reason: I was too busy planning my next big step, the perestroika of Oksana Kopy-lenko. Finally I had found a way to begin to reconstruct myself.

We walked down the narrow sidewalk, our shoulders almost touching. Sunlight splashed the city with buttery heat, and I wanted to stay as carefree as the weather and to forget my petty jealousy.

The thing with Cruz was that he was the easiest person to have as a friend. A few minutes in his company could supply you with confidence enough to last a week. People gravitated to him because of his knack for making you feel like your troubles were more pressing than his, for he hardly talked about himself. I studied his way with people as if tracking an elusive animal in its natural habitat. Amid all that flirting, I started to accept that Cruz's amiability was a character trait I sorely lacked and one I desperately wanted to master.

Besides that, his face was handsome enough to quicken my pulse. Every time he tucked his hair behind his ear, I'd get tingly and have to look away.

"So we won't have classes together. What difference does it make? You have Natasha."

He stopped, staring at me as if I had spoken in Russian. "We're not together, are we? Why should it bother you?"

That he chose not to deny flirting with Natasha hurt more than her bragging about it. "Forget it," I said, hurrying across a neighbor's lawn.

"Okay, wait." He caught up to me. "Let me tell you why I did it."

"Throw me off a cliff, won't you?"

Before I reached our driveway, he grabbed my shoulder, forcing me to face him. "You wanna know or not?"

"Not."

"I wanted to make you jealous."

"Great job. First-class performance," I said, my eyes stinging.

He let go. "Why do you do that?"

"What?"

"Always try to pick a fight with me. Can't you unfreeze enough to admit that it worked?"

Biting back tears, I finally pushed past him toward the house. "You can have your Natasha. I don't give a shit."

"Whoa, Oksana. Stop. I didn't mean it to sound that way."

"Believe it or not, not everyone worships at your feet," I said. Every time I moved, he blocked my way again. "If you don't let me pass, I'll scream."

"First tell me you're not angry."

"Go away."

Two things happened at once. He rushed me, his hands holding my face, kissing me, his lips fantastically hot. At the same time, the front door burst open, making us jump apart. Our kiss must have lasted all of two seconds.

"What is going on here?" Olga called from the doorway. "Valerio, come. Look at what your daughter is doing on our front lawn."

"Go," I whispered to Cruz, willing the world to stop spinning.

"We didn't do anything wrong," he said. But we had. Hanging

out with guys who hadn't been "approved" by the family was a big no-no according to my father's rules. I still remember the fits Dad went into after catching Ruslan and me reading together. Ruslan was a Rom. Cruz, a Brazilian, stood no chance.

My father stepped outside his house with a guitar in one hand. He'd been practicing, as he had been every day since I could remember. His scales and arpeggios drove us all mad, but we dared not interrupt.

"What is this?" he asked, and his face hardened with disapproval. Despite wearing a pair of acid-washed denim overalls, he still managed to look intimidating.

"Just a friend from school. His name is Cruz—"

"This little hussy was hanging off him like a chimpanzee," Olga crowed. "Thank God I caught them or who knows what would've happened next."

I had never been more grateful that Cruz could not understand Russian. "We're on the front lawn, Olga. In bright daylight."

"I don't want you bringing *gadjen* to my house," my father said. He hadn't acknowledged Cruz, as was his habit with all sorts of nuisances. "Send him home."

"But he wants to take guitar lessons," I blurted out in English, throwing a meaningful glance over my shoulder.

"Really?" Hazel eyes scrutinized the potential victim standing at my back. Cruz went a little pale.

"You want play?" Dad asked in broken English.

Cruz cleared his throat. "Yes, sir. Absolutely."

Had I known a useful prayer, I'd have been praying. I could only hope that vanity had not abandoned the artistic egos of the world.

I widened my eyes at Cruz and he said, "Sir, that's the most amazing guitar I've ever seen. I would be honored to learn on such a remarkable instrument."

There you go, I thought, as my father's frown softened.

Dad nodded in approval. The guitar truly *was* a piece of art, though I guess I'd gotten used to seeing it every day. For one thing, it had two necks, the top having four strings and the bottom nine, and its maple-and-spruce soundboard created a lush resonance. It was made by Master Krasnoshekov in 1872, and was considered a national treasure, but Grandpa Andrei had purchased it at a black-market auction before it could be transported into a government-run storage facility for safekeeping until it could be matched with a museum. Grandpa had then commissioned a local master to restore it.

"Come inside. I let you hear," Dad said, then shook a finger. "But you no think you play it. You play *Squier*." Which, according to him, wasn't much of a guitar at all.

I gawked at him. Clearly an invisible barrier had been breached, and I had no idea how to feel about it.

Olga remained on the porch and watched them go in. As I passed by she muttered, "That boy can sweet-talk the Devil. You sure he's not Romani?"

EXOTIC

On the first day of my magnet classes, I came to school one hour early, excited to finally experience school the American way. I had plaited my hair into a neat French braid and put on a plain black sweater with a pair of jeans; there would be no fashion faux pas for me this time.

I took a seat in the very back, my stomach a tight ball, watching students come in laughing and joking with each other. No one paid attention to me, and I was grateful.

Cruz sauntered in, scanning the room until his eyes settled on me. He found a seat next to mine, dropped his backpack on the floor, and put an arm around my shoulders as if his presence there were a blessing from the Almighty.

"What are you doing here?" I said.

I was smiling, dammit.

Lately he had been spending several days a week at Dad's house. That first time, he walked into our living room and his eyes immediately flew to the mantel. Above it hung a poster-size image of Grandpa's entire troupe posing center stage for a publicity photo. Dad had framed it in cherrywood, which made it even more impressive.

*The Andrei Kopylenko Gypsy ensemble, 1980. Grandma Ksenia
is in the middle; Dad is to her right, holding the guitar; and
Mom is on the floor, to the right*

"Who's that?" Cruz asked.

"My family." I stared right back at him as he raised his eyebrows and crossed the room for a closer look.

"That looks like you, a few years older."

"That's my mom." Patiently I waited for him to ask about the origin of the costumes.

My father walked in with a pipe in one hand and a rolled-up newspaper in the other, meaning he was on his way either into or out of the bathroom.

"Eh," he exclaimed. "*Beelo vremya kogda mi bili ochen znamenitimi Tziganyami* (There was a time when we were very famous Gypsies)."

Cruz turned, eyebrows so high I thought they might fly right off his face any minute. "*Ciganos?* Gypsies?" he said, and when my father nodded, he turned back to the picture. "Awesome!"

My expectations of Cruz running at the first mention of anything Gypsy were kind of deflated. But that also got me thinking.

Perhaps it was time to stop hiding and follow through on the message I chanted in front of my mirror.

The way Cruz reacted to the picture made my father even more affable, but I still expected him to wake up and realize he had opened the doors of his studio to a *gadjo*. While waiting for that moment to arrive, though, I utterly enjoyed listening to Cruz pretend to be a good student. He'd been playing guitar for more than ten years when Dad started teaching him the names of all the guitar parts.

During the first lesson, my father whipped out the flash cards he'd made himself.

"This note G," he said, holding up the one with the appropriate sketch.

Cruz's fingers hovered over the strings, lips moving silently, eyes determined to find that G string, as if he'd never seen one before. He bullshitted through that hour and kept coming back for more.

For his instructor's sake, Cruz missed just the right number of chords and hand positions to appear in need of constant supervision. In essence, Cruz was making the lessons all about my father and his pride. Naturally he proved to be a quick learner, and Dad attributed this remarkable progress to his own brilliant teaching methods. I thought surely Dad would figure it out eventually, even if he missed the *gadjo* part. Or maybe Cruz would realize that he didn't actually have to take lessons, that he said what he had said on that lawn only to prevent a massacre. But they got along so splendidly that neither seemed in a hurry to change things.

Olga was surprised at Dad's behavior, but she had a ready explanation. "He treats that *gadjo* like an offspring," she once said. "It's just sad. Maybe I'll do him a favor and give him a real son or two."

In the ESL program, too afraid to reveal my Romani side, I had remained an Armenian, a face in a crowd of similar faces. But like Cruz, the American kids were different. The majority of them were uninformed of life outside their own country, and yet they seemed more accepting than any other group of kids I'd ever met. They didn't know enough to judge me, and their ignorance provided me with a road map to individuality; I could take any direction I wished. I was grateful to retire from my school-fighting career.

A classmate once asked me what part of South America I came from. "You don't look Mexican," she noted, studying my face with interest. We sat a desk apart, waiting for our Shakespeare teacher, Mrs. Peacock, to make a uniformly late appearance. I was the only foreigner in the class and must've been completely mad for assuming I could handle Shakespeare. Nevertheless, I mulishly trudged through his works that semester just to prove to myself that I could. All the while, the students stayed at a respectful distance from me, guarded yet curious. But once we began to write our own plays and work together to direct and perform, it was clear that we had many things in common, like a knack for over-the-top Shakespearean parody. When Donna asked me that question, I found I *wanted* to give her a real answer. It came like a well-lathered ring off a swollen finger. I told her about my home, about the Romani who coiled their skirts onstage while I sat eating my dinner—kielbasa and cucumber sandwiches—behind the curtains. Exotic, she said. That's what she called me. I had added that word to my list of favorites, and it had an entry of its own in my journal: exotic—strikingly, excitingly, or mysteriously unusual. Me.

Growing up, I had never felt striking, exciting, or mysterious—just weird.

In primary grades, before Nastya began to plot my annihilation, my classmates had nicknamed me "Rice," a term used for Asians. It didn't bother me. My own grandmother looked at me sideways, so how could I expect anything less from strangers?

Years passed and my growing resemblance to Grandma Ksenia finally put all paternity questions to rest. We had the same pronounced cheekbones, full lips, almond-shaped eyes. She accepted me into the fold, something Grandpa Andrei had done much earlier. Much later I found out that my father was one tenth Mongolian. It still did not make me exotic.

Back when I went by "Rice"

Dozens of nationalities lived in Russia, but unless you were actually from Russia, you were often treated like a lower life-form—a relic of an attitude we had inherited from that first generation of Soviets and the time when Lenin and his comrades lassoed fourteen countries to create a union governed by Russia. The USSR was like the modern European Union, only with one ruling nation, Russia. The new country prospered with thousands of jobs, new roads, and markets full of foods from every season, with schools for kids who'd never seen a book before. Not since the Roman Empire had the world witnessed such an undertaking. There remained two problems: (1) although the union comprised fifteen republics, fourteen were treated as slightly substandard; and (2) even as the most reluctant of Soviets had never had it better, there was the small matter of freedom. No republic had the choice to secede if things didn't work out.

Even if you pretended to be Russian, once someone checked your ID the truth came out. Soviet IDs segregated people according to their nationality. A Chukchi remained a Chukchi, uneducated and dim-witted, even if they spoke flawless Russian. An Ossetian was just the man to hire if you wished to have someone rubbed out. A Ukrainian was never quite as pure-blooded as a Russian, and so on. Even if you lived in Russia all your life, your nationality shaped people's perception of you.

No Romani in their right mind would put "Gypsy" in their documents, unless they particularly enjoyed the breeze from doors slamming in their faces. Like Romani, many Jews masqueraded as Russians, and if they could not be that, then Ukrainian, or at the very least Moldavian. We were all branded by our identities. Luckily for my family, our mix of nationalities made it easier to choose the most advantageous one. Grandma Ksenia and Dad were both Greek according to their IDs because Grandma Ksenia's father was a full-blooded Greek. And being a Greek in Russia was better than being a Roma.

The union created an amazing blend of backgrounds and some of the most beautiful people in the world. I once met a gorgeous blond-haired, blue-eyed Mongolian, and yet an American horse breeder my father once drank a toast with was considered more exotic in my country than this girl.

Who knew that people in America would think so differently?

I wondered for a long time. Wondered until something so simple yet powerful became clear to me. Since perceptions are ever changing, as was the case at hand, the only thing left to do was to trust your own opinions. If you think you are something, that's what you become.

THE HUNT

In Hollywood High, diversity was a requirement for ultimate coolness; anyone too bland faded into the background, a yearbook picture the only trace of their existence. For the first time in my life, I flaunted the Romani Oksana, the one I had been hiding in the basement all these years. Of course I still came across the occasional look of disgust, a tightening of an arm around a purse, or train-station stories of Gypsy assault maneuvers on innocent bystanders, as if they were top-secret special ops teams, highly trained, undetectable, and unbeatable. But those reactions didn't faze me as much anymore. They were not important enough. I remember jokingly telling Zhanna about my tolerant self. "Oh, a regular Mother Teresa you are," she joked back.

But to be completely honest, I still cared about one person's opinion very much, and having Cruz's acceptance felt like an unspoken blessing.

We were on our way home one day, face-to-face inside a packed bus, our hands gripping the railings for support. The bus lurched at every light, swinging the after-school crowd to and fro like bamboo stalks in gusts of wind.

"My father used to buy pottery from an old Gypsy man who owned a stand at the local market at Manaus," he said. "Sometimes twenty or thirty pieces at once."

For the first time since we'd met, Cruz was talking about his family.

"Why so much pottery?" I asked, praying he wouldn't clam up.

"My father is a river trader. He sells food and things like those pottery jugs down the Amazon. We used to work together, sailing the boat for months."

"I didn't realize people lived in the rain forest."

"Everywhere. The villages are built into the riverbanks over the water. The forest protects them against progress, but people seem happier and healthier. I don't know why."

"You liked working with your dad?"

"Yeah." He laughed quietly. "Except he's the most stubborn person I know. Once he's used to something, he never wants to change it. I say, 'Papai, let's get a boat with air-conditioning. *Benedita* isn't going to last much longer.' He shakes his finger at me. '*A grande nau, grande tormenta!*' With big ships come bigger storms. We lived more on the river than the land, but he refuses to improve *Benedita*, no matter how many boat magazines I shove into his hands."

"Does he still have it?"

He nodded. "Everyone in the Amazon knows when Papai is coming by the rattle of that damn motor."

I wanted to ask him why he was in America when clearly he wanted to sail the Amazon, but something told me to let it go. Once again he had surprised me, and almost unthinkingly, I began to accept Cruz as someone decidedly non-*gadjo*.

Olga picked up things about Cruz and me that even I was oblivious to, and she made sure to voice her suspicions. She recognized the "signs," she told me. "Too much laughing, eyes shiny like marbles, and he struts like a damn rooster every time you're around." Of course, she had no proof, but not for lack of snooping. One word from her, she promised, and Dad would lock me in my room until I was married.

The more conventional Romani parents think of unmarried girls as a commodity, especially if they are virgins. Once, Dad, Roxy, and I met a Roma family in one of the downtown swap meets, this one a multilevel warehouse of clothes wearable only until that first washing. Right away, I could tell that they were more traditional than we were. The females, even young girls, wore long flowery skirts and scarves around their heads. The men, in crisp white shirts, slacks, polished shoes, and fedoras, looked like door-to-door salesmen.

The eldest man exchanged a greeting with Dad in Rromanes. "You a Rom?" "Yes, my brother." After that the conversation picked up, and a few minutes later, the man nodded in Roxy's direction.

"I need a wife for my oldest. Are you looking?"

There was a good reason he had skipped me. At sixteen, I was practically a spinster. Roxy and I exchanged looks—mine framed by a wicked frown and Roxy's filled with alarm. At ten she had a reason to worry. But my father could navigate blindfolded among Romani. He bowed slightly. "Thank you, brother. I am honored. Your son looks like a strong young Rom. But she's too young."

"Sure, sure, I understand. I meant no offense, brother."

Olga had become a wife for the first time at the age of twelve. Granted, the groom had kidnapped her to make her his wife, and she ran away a few months later. When she started to question my own virtue, especially at my ripe old age, I didn't know how to react. My parents were never so traditional that they made it an issue. I always knew I wasn't supposed to have sex until marriage, but for the life of me I don't remember how I knew it, since we never actually talked about it. Up to that point I hadn't given my hymen much thought. Yet there was my stepmother, acting like my raging hormones were keeping her up all night. My marriage to a good Gypsy boy occupied her mind almost as much as finding a way to get rid of Cruz before he ruined me.

Olga invited Cruz to a dinner party one night without telling me. It was an interesting tactic along the lines of "Keep your friends close and your enemies closer."

Judging by the creased slacks, button-down shirt, and pulled-back hair, the poor guy probably assumed it would be a dating interview of sorts. He might have anticipated a quiet but firm chat with my father about his aspirations and future college choices; perhaps a perusal of Dad's own accomplishments in the form of trophies or pictures. But nothing in our family was ever that simple.

The kitchen table was piled high with food arranged on plates patterned with flowers and bees. But pretty plates couldn't disguise Olga's knack for making even the simplest dishes revolting. There was an imitation-crab salad, runny because she'd left the serving spoon in it for hours, and a wilted green salad drenched in blue-cheese dressing. The roast chicken's skinny legs inspired pity. Mercifully Olga had sneaked off to the Russian corner store earlier, coming back with homemade *kotleti*, mashed potatoes, and even a seventy-dollar jar of red caviar.

Our guests were seated per the hostess's instructions. Sherri tried to grab a chair next to Dad, but Olga directed Cruz to take it. Sherri pouted as she parked her bosom next to me.

Svetlana and her newly repentant husband had also been invited. Whatever Olga did with Igor's mistress's hair and the cemetery dirt seemed to have worked, because he was admiring his wife as if she were Sophia Loren. I held the honorary place next to their eighteen-year-old son. Alan was the size of his mother, minus the hair spray and the velour suit, and smelled like a spilled bottle of Brut. Freckles dusted his cheeks and the tip of his bulbous nose. A Hawaiian shirt held on for dear life around his shoulders, but his jeans looked two sizes too large—the latest fashion trend straight out of New York, Svetlana mentioned in passing.

From across the table Cruz made conversation with my father. A phantom of mischief flickered across his face every time our eyes met.

"So, Cruz. I hear you are Brazilian?" Svetlana asked him. Earlier that evening my father had stated that, in honor of his student, everyone would speak English.

"Yes."

Olga placed a dollop of potatoes on his plate next to a chicken leg that would make an anorexic weep with envy. "Cruz is Valerio's best student. He wery talented."

"Oh, I love Brazilian men," Sherri said. "They're so . . . Hispaniol."

Cruz accepted the plate, smiling. "Actually, Brazilians are Latin, not Hispanic."

"Even better," she gushed.

Alan bumped his chair closer to mine and I was treated to a generous waft of his cologne.

"They look good with each other, hey?" Olga said suddenly, nodding in our direction.

I cringed, Olga's plans finally hitting me full force.

"My Alan is rolling on honors in school. I'm so proud of my baby. He will go to computer college next fall."

Svetlana squeezed her son's cheek as he tried to pull away. Igor and she continued to praise their giant offspring for an hour.

I felt a sliver of envy at the way Alan's parents cooed over him.

Nobody at that table, besides Cruz, knew about my acceptance into the magnet school. That was something to be proud of, wasn't it? Yet here I was, hoping that he knew to keep quiet. I needed more time to find the right way to tell Dad, because I'd get only one chance to impress him. Some part of me resented feeling the need to do so.

"Your boy make good husband, Svetlana," Olga said.

"Is there a girl out there good enough for him? I know not."

"What of our Oksana? Cruz, how you tink, don't they look a couple?"

I turned to my father, begging him silently for help.

"Olga, she's too young to think about marriage," he said in Russian.

"There's no such thing as too young," Olga said, switching to Russian as well. "Wait too long and she'll be plucked."

Heat splashed my face and I studied the salad on my plate.

"Doesn't Oksana have a say in who she marries?" Cruz said, his voice coming from afar. He sounded determined.

"You *gadjee* and us Romani, we-e-e-ry different," Olga said. "Give girl choice and she run with first asshole *gadjo* who wag finger."

"That's too simplistic."

"Whad you say?" Olga tipped away from him, exchanging looks with her friends. Only my father continued to listen with a tinge of mirth on his lips.

"According to you, Roma girls always make wrong choices. Is every *gadjo* a wrong choice?" Cruz said.

"I no understand you."

Cruz shifted forward in his chair and pushed aside his plate, both elbows on the table. "I know people from back home who blame everything that goes wrong in our country on others. The rich point fingers at the poor from the shanties, saying all crime is their doing. The poor say they don't have money to afford real houses and that the rich should share their money instead of complaining."

"*Shto za chepukha* (What's this nonsense)?" Olga shrugged at all of us again, then back to Cruz. "I talk of girls. *Gadjee* make Roma girls *prostitutki*."

"It's an excuse to isolate yourself from the rest of the society." He caught me shaking my head ever so slightly and cleared his throat. But he didn't back down from Olga's flamethrower stare. "Does every Roma woman who marries a Roma man make a good match? Does no one in your culture separate or divorce?"

"What you know about real problem?" Olga said. "You no live our life. I live with house with dirt floor when small girl, and I get water from well outside. Boy steal me when I virgin. You men only think sex." Olga pointed at his crotch. Not much of an intellectual debater, my stepmother.

Dad lowered the glass of Georgian Balsam he was about to drain. "Enough, Olga."

"I'm right, and you know it."

They were back to Russian.

"What I know is that you're a disobedient wife. Perhaps it is so because you were married so young; you didn't have time to learn about taking care of your man." Had my father ever called Mom disobedient, she would've beaten him with her shoe, but with Olga he felt justified to act superior. Come to think of it, he was becoming more and more like the rest of her family: Roma who followed a more old-fashioned code, according to which Olga was supposed to be subservient but also be the breadwinner. Grandpa wouldn't have approved.

"And you're going to teach me?"

"Premium idea. Start by learning how to budget."

Olga stopped chewing.

Igor drummed his knuckles on the table and picked up the half-empty liquor bottle next to him. "Come on, brother, sister. Who's going to toast the meeting of our children with me?"

"Marriage is trust, yes?" Olga finally said in English, turning to Cruz. "How you trust someone from different peoples than yours? Our passports show nationality for reason—we Armenian, Uzbek, Russian, all different."

Sherri shifted in her seat. "They don't do that in America."

Olga glowered at her from across the table. Igor refilled his glass until some of the golden liquid spilled over the edges onto the white tablecloth.

Normally my stepmother would have a fit over the stain, but she was too engrossed in the conversation. There were too many lit fires in the room; I stayed quiet in the interest of self-preservation, hoping Cruz would, too.

Dad motioned for Igor to pour him another glass, drinking the liquor in one gulp. "Tell me this, dear wife," he said in Russian. "If trust is so important, why do I feel that you're hiding something from me?"

"It's you who should be answering that question. You and that *manda* (pussy) across the table." She pointed a finger at Sherri.

"Olga!" Sherri and Svetlana said in unison.

This was going somewhere I didn't want to follow. But as embarrassed as I was, I also felt relieved. My father had unintentionally deterred Olga from her matchmaking plans for me and Alan. Of course, there was something else to worry about: Cruz was the only person between Dad and Olga.

She leaned around him and shouted at my father, her arms flying in all directions. "Don't 'Olga!' me. I know everything about you two, everything."

Those of us familiar with my father and his wife knew not to get involved in a fight unless we desired to be flogged with curses.

Among my people these fights were never mere words but carried the menace of an arrow shot from a master archer's hand. One particular curse was so feared that it was barely used among the Roma themselves: "May I see you in a coffin." Olga and Dad passed it back and forth like a volleyball, in addition to "May you be shot in the forehead," "May you burn in the blue flames of Hell," and my favorite, "May your liver shrivel and fall out of your body while you're still alive."

The entire time they argued, Cruz wore a politely blank expression, his arms crossed over his chest in a relaxed manner. But I wouldn't put it past Olga to punch him instead of Dad simply because of their proximity. A couple of times I jerked my head at the front door, a hint for Cruz to make his escape, but he only narrowed his eyes at me as if to say "Stop worrying, everything's fine."

Dad hurled his shot glass at the wall and began to shout, accusing Olga of jealousy and stupidity and calling her a few choice names. It took both Igor and Cruz to calm him down. They dragged him outside before he broke something crunchier than glass, like Olga's ribs.

But I knew from experience, the madder Dad acted, the guiltier he usually was.

CITIZENS OF NO-LAND

In December 1991, a little more than a year after we'd left for good, the USSR collapsed. I was in Vegas visiting Mom and Roxy for the first time since they'd moved when the Russian cable channel we were watching made an abrupt switch from the Moscow Christmas special to the Moscow newsroom. The newscaster, a wiry man with a pink nose the size of a golf ball, announced with a startled expression that the Soviet Union was no more. Perestroika had swept the nation on waves of anxious excitement. But not everyone was celebrating. Gorbachev (the guy with the birthmark shaped like North America on his head) had planned to transform the country into a Russian version of the United States, but something went wrong and the system abruptly crumbled. The Soviets, who hated the idea to begin with, bitterly accused Reagan of filling Gorbachev's head with renegade ideas just to break up the union. In some religious groups rumors of the Western Devil tricking the unsuspecting Russian leader into a faulty contract circulated. The sales of *Faustus* spiked.

In Mom's one-bedroom apartment, Roxy and I sat on the floor with Mom poised on the edge of the couch, a soup ladle in one hand. Roxy used to ask to play with the Soviet passport Mom kept in a tiny metal safe. It was red with a golden Soviet State coat of arms in the middle. Not that Mom valued it, just figured it might come handy. "We are still USSR citizens," she'd say. That always made me nervous. Life in America was proving to be complicated, but everything from commercials to music playing on the radio came with just enough hope to keep us going. I wanted but one thing from Russia now—the rest of my family—but it had a claim on me.

In reality it was the one place we officially belonged until the American government approved our applications for green cards. This was how it worked for most immigrants I knew. First a resident visa sent by a citizen or a permanent resident; then, if you behaved, a green card; and only after having the card for five years could you apply for the ultimate prize, citizenship. Most of us give little thought to the importance or the meaning of a homeland. Not until we ourselves are foreigners fighting for acceptance, stripped of all ranks and titles and viewed as inferiors, do we miss that privilege. The process of becoming a citizen is daunting. Suddenly your character is questioned and what you were as a citizen of another place is erased and must be proved all over again, even if you are ninety and have been slowly forgetting important things such as your kids' names or an impressive military career. You have three choices: stay, live as an illegal alien, be deported. For the young, the choices are made by the adults, so the effects aren't felt as much. But for everyone else this process can be tricky and laden with temptation. Some years later Vova, Dad's drummer friend, was lucky enough to get a resident visa from an aunt. He messed up when he was caught in a scam that included sleeping with single rich women and then cleaning out their houses of everything but the door handles. He was sent back to Moscow and blacklisted, meaning he could never come back to the States. Unlike Vova, it seemed, we no longer had a place to go back to in case a life of crime appealed to us.

"What's going on?" Roxy asked, frowning at the TV, then at Mom.

"You know the place you were born?" I said.

"So?"

"It doesn't exist anymore."

Roxy jumped to her feet, following me into the kitchen, where I dumped our dishes in the sink. "Where did it go?"

"Oksana, shut up!" Mom cut in from the couch.

I leaned on the doorframe separating the kitchen and the dining-room area and crossed my arms, fingertips icy against my skin.

"So does this mean Roxy can have your passport now that we're citizens of no country?"

"What have they done?" Mom said.

The immigrants and those who stayed behind had seen change slowly chip away at the Communist ideologies as far back as the eighties. But it wasn't all good change. Food started to disappear off the shelves, paychecks shrank, and the crime rate increased. As naive as it sounds, the more enthusiastic folk believed the republics would enter into a state union, like the United States, and go on with nary a hiccup in their daily lives. These were probably the same people who thought communism should've worked in real life and not in theory alone.

I had heard my grandparents quarrel only once. It was over Grandma Ksenia's Bolshevik father, who maintained until the minute he died, in 1952, that the Soviet people would soon practice the goodness they held within them. There would be no crime, and anyone would be able to walk into a store and pick up groceries for free. Money would be used for toilet paper in a utopian society straight out of Milton's imagination.

"My father was a patriot," Grandma maintained.

"A fool, like the rest," Grandpa said. "Our country is no different from any other. All run by one master. Greed."

In Mom's Las Vegas living room I heard her whisper, "I guess we're staying for good." I was quite startled. Had she thought about returning to Russia? I never did, because no matter how complicated things were in America, to me they had seemed unbearable back home. This event tossed my family into a state of limbo for a little while, as if we were kids of parents caught up in a vicious divorce, which felt painfully familiar. I remember how awkward it felt telling people where we came from, and how my personal sense of identity, screwed up as it was already, became almost impossible to distinguish. Being a Soviet citizen was one thing I knew I was for sure. All of a sudden, even that was taken away. But it was also a cleansing of sorts. There was no going back, because the country we knew, like the family we knew, was no longer. The sole option now was to make a new home.

HOW MUCH FOR THE VIRGIN?

Over the next few weeks arguments between Dad and Olga escalated. Some of these had to do with the fact that she suspected him of cheating with clients, specifically Sherri; others with Dad trying to bring his parents over from Russia now that the country had fallen apart. As my Bolshevik great-grandfather once predicted, rubles now *could* be used for toilet paper. My grandparents had nothing left but their flat and Grandma's stage jewelry. Neither Roxy nor I had any contact with our grandparents, which really confused both of us, but I recall thinking that if only they moved to America, we'd come together again and rejoice. Olga had refused to even consider it.

The bulk of the problems between Dad and Olga sprouted from her inability to hold on to money. No one knew where it went, only that as soon as it appeared, it would promptly vanish. Olga claimed she was so busy guarding her husband from the female population of Los Angeles that she didn't have time to keep track of the finances.

Just as she couldn't prove my involvement with Cruz, she kept missing the opportunities to catch my father cheating. "How is it that you have so many female clients?" she would ask. "Because women are more prone to demonic influences," he'd answer. "Their mind is not as strong as a man's." Olga was also busy sneaking out of the house and behaving suspiciously herself: a trip to the bank, for example, at eight in the morning when Dad snored the loudest. (Much later I'd glimpsed the name of this "bank" on a crumpled-up receipt: Big Papa's Pawn.)

Equally bereft of evidence, they yelled at each other instead, both having something to hide and someone to blame. The "honeylambshank" and the "little sparrow" were replaced by *huesos* (cocksucker) and *padla* (whore).

On January 14, the day on which many Eastern Europeans celebrate the departure of the old year, pagan-style (another excuse to get drunk, some say), Dad and Olga laid down their weapons in a temporary cease-fire. Christmas trees remain decorated until this time, and on the evening of the fourteenth, a table is set, toasts are given, and people share memories of the previous year, which they hadn't given much thought to until that fifth or sixth drink.

"Oksana needs a husband," Olga had told Dad a few days before the Old New Year's celebration. She had decorated the Christmas tree herself a month back, and ever since then it had remained in the throes of a most festive death, choked with garlands and drowning in tinsel.

"No, I don't."

"Be quiet," Olga said. "Nobody's talking to you."

"Stop pestering me, woman. I still have three song arrangements to finish for the Bobrov wedding," Dad said.

"She won't stay a virgin forever."

"Shut up, Olga. I'm not marrying anyone to make you feel better."

Mom had always voiced her gripes with arranged marriages.

Had she stayed in Armenia, she told me, her own engagement probably would go something like this:

A boy in town fancies her. His parents pay a visit to her parents and they discuss the advantages of their offsprings' union while they drink coffee and eat Belgian chocolate. Mom's parents pry about the other family's financial stability, and in return the boy's mother inquires after the regularity of Mom's menses to assure favorable childbearing genes. All the while Mom makes, pours, and takes away coffee. Mom's parents ask for several days during which to consider the offer, and then they decide. Without Mom.

I never thought that could happen to me because my father, happy not to be in charge of much, agreed that an arranged marriage was out of vogue. Until Olga started to whisper her fiendishly outdated notions into his ear.

"Our reputation is all we have, Valerio," she said. "God only knows what Nora's doing in Vegas. Probably teaching Roxy about grubbing for tips and dressing in casino uniforms. If you ask me, Roxy's place is here, where we can raise her properly."

"Don't you think I know that?" Dad said. "But she won't budge. What am I supposed to do?"

"Do something for Oksana before it's too late. Make her obey me. I can teach her the trade. Then pick a family who can provide a large bride-price. Svetlana just bought a brand-new Nissan, you know. You could use new recording equipment."

That bitch, I thought. Diverting attention from herself by plotting my downfall, using the promise of a TASCAM multitrack recorder to reel my father in. My protests were ignored. Dad listened to her suggestions; his plan for fame involved a recording studio and major CD distribution of original music he liked to call "smooth Gypsy jazz" or "Gypsy fusion."

A few days later Dad asked me to set the New Year's table, telling me what an important night this would be. Then he disappeared into the back of the house again to practice, while I felt a cold dread settle deep into my bones.

Clearly January 14, 1992, was a poised guillotine. As I watched our guests arrive, the beginnings of a migraine thrust through my head. They took plates and exchanged jokes. I could well be married by the end of the month, hitched to a freckled Gypsy computer geek with strange body odor.

While everyone was catching up on the neighborhood gossip, I sneaked away and knocked on Dad's studio door. He opened it only far enough to see who it was and stood in the doorframe, one hand around the doorknob. Behind him a drum machine clipped away at a waltz.

"Tell Olga I'm almost done."

"Dad—"

"You need to learn to listen. Nobody says you have to marry the guy, but talk to him."

"I don't want to talk to him. He smells. And I don't want to be like Olga, telling fortunes for money."

"It might do some good, learning the craft. Not like you have so many options. What else are you going to do with your life?"

As kids Zhanna and I used to play at the abandoned church cemetery down the road from our house. The land was overgrown with stinging nettle, the graves grassy mounds we tripped over and then crossed ourselves so as not to anger the dead. Every time we came home, our arms and legs bloomed with hives. As if stung by nettles, my skin prickled once more with my father's words.

"If you and Mom were together this would never happen," I said.

He locked himself in again. Nothing new there. As long as he had his music, the world remained a pink-clouded festival.

He was still absent (incredibly rude by Roma standards of

hospitality) when Alan moved his chair closer to mine—too close—later that evening. Dad, please stop tinkering with your guitars, I thought. Would you really sell me for a recording machine? The C-sharp scale rang across the house, then arpeggios, then the latest arrangement of "I Will Survive," with salsa rhythms pulsating in the hardwood floor beneath our feet.

Igor, as the only adult male at the table, raised his glass. Four glasses joined his, one belonging to my potential husband. He didn't have sexy sideburns or long, beautiful fingers. He was Alan—a cologne-soaked, thin-haired, big-lipped, nail-chewing mess of adolescent hormones.

Since no one was openly discussing marriage thus far, I grudgingly entertained the notion that perhaps I had overreacted. Grandpa Andrei used to say that a teenager's emotional state resembles a busted compass with the needle spinning. Knowing Olga, the entire thing could've been a farce to make me squirm.

I took a pile of dishes into the kitchen, planning on staying for a while, maybe even washing a few plates.

"Hey," I heard from behind me.

I set my load on the counter, breathing deeply.

He stood too close, and so did his Brut.

"Crazy stuff, huh, this marriage business," he said.

Relieved to hear a sensible opinion, I turned around. "I know. Maybe we should tell them together."

"Tell 'em what?"

"That we don't want to do it."

"But I do . . . wanna." His eyebrows wiggled and he placed a hand lovingly over his crotch. "It'll be good for us, for both of us. I've got mad skills."

It wouldn't do to burst out laughing. I stared at his face, unblinking, ignoring the stuff happening below his waist, but the movement of his hand was unmistakable.

"What are you doing?" I said. "Stop it."

"I'm hung like a horse. That's why I don't wear briefs."

Was he trying to shock me? He didn't seem intelligent enough.

"Good to know," I said finally, turning back to the dishes.

He grabbed my arm. The bulbous part of his nose reddened. "You don't believe me."

"I'm not interested, Alan."

"I can prove it." He reached in the back pocket and took out a scrap of paper.

"What is it?" I said. There were names and numbers of three girls written in surprisingly neat handwriting.

"My exes. They can vouch for me."

Out in the living room the gossip had moved from local to international. "You remember so-and-so from Moscow? I heard they had one of those surgeries that make a penis out of a vagina." "Now I've heard it all." "Oh, you think so, do you? Listen to this one. My mother's neighbor Artem was walking down the street when an icicle broke off the roof of a nearby building and impaled him straight through the skull." "What a way to die." "He lived!"

The carefree banter continued even when Alan and I joined the table, though I didn't miss Svetlana's knowing nod and a pat on her son's shoulder as he sat down. I had a sudden urge to run for Vegas, get lost in it the way my mother had.

ENDINGS AND BEGINNINGS

Reprieve came from the most unexpected place. Grandpa Andrei died of kidney failure and my father became a beehive no one dared to disturb. He endured the loss in solitude, even his guitar mute. My own grief, two years after Ruslan's murder, was like an old cut seeping blood again.

For days, Dad talked about the past. The time he drove his father nuts when he gambled away the old man's gold cigarette case, and about having to steal it back or get kicked out of the band. Finally Olga put him on a plane to Moscow for the funeral. While he was gone, Olga and I didn't fight, too worried over Dad's state.

He came back with two waterfalls of silver down the outer edges of his beard: his own father's trademark.

Several weeks later, and without telling Olga, Dad bought a plane ticket for Grandma Ksenia. With Grandpa gone, it was up to my father, as per Romani tradition, to take care of his mother. When Dad informed Olga of his mother's arrival that very day, my stepmother hurled a nearby vase at his head (one of many airborne attacks to follow).

Grandpa Andrei, with Dad and Aunt Laura, 1953

Out of all my relatives, I would turn out most like Grandma Ksenia. Back in our days of rancor, of course, neither of us had expected such irony; although I was named after her, Oksana being a derivative of Ksenia, she'd been a stranger to me for all of our time in Russia, and I honestly didn't know the proper way to act around her now that she was coming to America. My childhood memories are vibrant with the faces of my grandfather, my parents, and the many band members. Grandma Ksenia is the only shadow, perhaps because we often seemed to clash—not only over my questionable lineage but also over silly things like the whereabouts of Grandma's favorite Pavlovoposadsky shawl or how her cold cream ended up smeared all over our cat's face. I admit there were times I was Dennis the Menace to her Mr. Wilson, but we did have our moments of truce.

I loved visiting her at Easter. Dad's family, like most Romani, was very religious. Even Baba Varya attended church services. Romani don't have a common religion, often adopting that of their country. Their original beliefs were similar to those of many tribal people: the land is the mother and all depends on her mercy. But the people I grew up with were Russian Orthodox, especially Grandma Ksenia.

Every Easter our visit followed the same course: we'd walk up the steps where Grandma already waited, having phoned earlier to make certain we were coming. "*Isus voskres* (Jesus has risen)," she'd say, and kiss us one by one on each cheek. We took turns replying, "*Vo istinnoh voskres* (In truth, he has risen)."

Inside the house, the aroma of citrus and vanilla led me to the pantry. I cracked the door and found my prize under the pristine white cloth: *paska*, a traditional Easter bread as tall as a ten-gallon hat. From its flushed russet crust a fragrant cloud of steam escaped. I wanted to break off a piece and taste the sticky-sweet raisins waiting on the inside. Last time I did that, I was grounded for two weeks, but it was worth it. Grandma was a fine baker.

Now Grandma walked through the door with Dad at her back, and I hardly knew her. She held herself as if making a stage entrance, an action so instinctive that she hardly noticed it. Two years had passed since I last saw her. She had aged twenty. Her short hair lay sparse and coarse, with a generous band of silver at the roots. Time had creased her face, rubbed the pride from her now sunken eyes, pinched once perfectly contoured cheekbones. The only sign of the well-known songstress was the crimson-red lipstick. When I was little, I thought she kissed pomegranates.

"My dear granddaughter," she said, and spread her arms. All my qualms forgotten, I went to her.

Olga came clinking out to greet her, dressed up in her finest. She must've worn all of her jewelry at once.

"Welcome to my home, Ksenia Fyodorovna."

She led Grandma away, as if showing the house and the furniture couldn't have waited for later. But Dad's shoulders visibly relaxed.

Several weeks went by in startling peace. It became a habit for

Grandma Ksenia could bring an entire theater to tears

my grandmother and me to listen to the morning radio program in Russian. The first part was a thirty-minute exercise routine accompanied by a crisp piano. It had been created especially for seniors, but I didn't mind that, so surprised was I at the old woman's determination to finish each day's routine. We'd follow the instructor's voice. "Turn at the waist from side to side! Now stride in place! Get those knees higher! One, two, three, four! Don't forget to breathe! Chest open! Chin lifted!" We also started taking the bus to the beach every time Dad and Olga forgot their truce and turned up the volume. "Adults have no time for the children or the old," Grandma would say on our way out the door. Santa Monica was her favorite beach, though she swore her preference had nothing to do with the sweaty guys playing volleyball in their Speedos. We'd sit on a bench and I'd tease her about it. "Grandma, I never knew you liked sports so much."

"Child, if I were twenty years younger I'd be out chasing that ball."

"With all those hairy guys?"

"What other kinds are there?" She chuckled at the shock on my face.

Later I found black-and-white pictures of my grandparents on the Black Sea coast where they vacationed every year. Grandma's legs are ballerina-slender and Grandpa's legs are not bad, either, quads and calves like rocks beneath a flowing river. She's propped up on a huge boulder near the water, holding one of those Chinese paper umbrellas with peacocks painted on it, looking like a wartime pinup girl. Next time we went to Santa Monica, I brought a camera. The only picture of us together was taken there, by a man who claimed to have once dated Marilyn Monroe.

On Santa Monica beach

Grandma Ksenia had spent years wading through the gossip and scandal of stage life, and she was an early riser. Both turned out to be bad news for Olga, whose pawnshop trips and disappearances were becoming habitual. When Grandma told Dad that she suspected something shady, an affair perhaps, he confronted his wife.

"Why doesn't your mother keep quiet and enjoy our hospitality?" she said.

I had just come from school. Grandma Ksenia stood in the living room between Dad and Olga.

"Is it true, Olga?" Dad demanded. "Are you sleeping with another man?"

Grandma implored him to sit. "Calm down."

Olga's face, her bulging eyes, spit hatred at the older woman. She stood in the kitchen doorway, her normally braided hair a thick black foam of curls down her back. She jabbed a finger at Grandma Ksenia.

"Buy her a ticket back to Moscow."

Over Grandma's shushing, the argument inflated until Olga stormed into the kitchen. I'd thought she went in search of her keys to get away, but she ran back with a ten-pound sack of oranges, which she heaved over her head and flung at the old woman. The sack sailed across the living room. I scrabbled to intercept it, and Dad shoved Grandma aside as it crashed into her shoulder.

"*Nou suchara, podozhdi! Ia seychas boshkou tebe otorvliu!* (Just wait, you bitch! I'll rip your head off!)" Dad lunged at Olga, with me and Grandma dragging him back.

"If she's not gone in a week, I swear, Valerio, I'll destroy all of you," Olga shouted.

She was gone for four days. My father found a home on the other side of town, owned by a bedridden Russian immigrant, where Grandma Ksenia was to live from now on. I couldn't understand why he hadn't stood up to Olga, and I am not sure I do now.

As soon as Mom had a couple days off from her nonstop overtime shifts, she and Roxy drove down to see Grandma Ksenia—the woman who'd hated her, who'd cut off all contact after the divorce.

While she and Mom talked in soft tones so as not to wake Grandma's landlord from his nap, I studied the grout between the tiles and the dull green curtains, the kind you'd see in motel rooms. The clinical-looking tile floors throughout and the smell of a dying man in the next room made my skin break out into goose bumps. I listened to the metallic moans ensuing from Grandma's bed every time she moved, and picked my nails with topmost dedication; anything to spare me the bedraggled sight of my once elegant grandmother.

My sister was saying things I tried to follow but failed.

"Oksana. Oksana. Oksaana!"

"What?" I turned to Roxy, oddly grateful.

"I was saying that my school looks like a flying saucer and the playground gets so hot that it burns the soles off my shoes. I hate it there."

"Nora. *Dochenka*," Grandma was saying. "Never in my life would I have imagined this. But perhaps it's my punishment for being so cruel to you. I regret every one of those days."

"Don't think about the past, Mother." Mom was leaning close, holding the old woman's hand. "This home looks lovely. Very quiet neighborhood."

"It is. It is." But giant tears spilled from her eyes.

"Mother. What is wrong?"

"I don't think I can do this."

"Do what?"

"*Oy, dochenka*. He's so heavy. It takes me an hour to get him out of the bed and to the toilet. Most of the time he doesn't even make it that long and soils himself right there in the hallway. Good thing it's all tile."

A cold weight was lodged inside my throat, and I looked at Roxy, who thankfully wasn't paying much attention, picking out an outfit for her Barbie instead.

Neither Mom nor I had known that Grandma Ksenia was the old man's live-in caretaker, that she woke up nearly every night to clean the excrement from his behind and change his filthy bed-sheets.

Mom did ask Grandma if she wanted to move in with her, but she said, "My place is here with my son." But soon after our visit, per Olga's demands, Grandma Ksenia went back to Russia. She would die there a few months later.

Olga had calmed down for a while. Did she feel guilty for send-ing the old woman away to a lousy end? I hoped so. I did, though there was nothing I could've done to improve the situation. The way you knew Olga's conscience was stirring was when she spent more time doing the dishes, a task she executed rather poorly. This meant that my father was also in the kitchen constantly re-washing them. He had more time on his hands now, since he barely saw his clients and had canceled most of his gigs. "The fibers in the rope of our family," he said once, "are splitting one by one."

During this time a man came to see my father, walking with shoulders hunched as if preparing for an air raid. Bob's new-born daughter was dying and he begged my father for help. He had heard about Dad from a friend who avoided knee surgery after a regimen Dad prescribed, involving a compress of dried horse sorrel and garlic. That same day the three of us, me as a translator, drove down to Huntington Hospital in Pasadena.

His wife, Kim, was crying when we came in. She clumsily wiped the wetness away with the edge of the sheet and smiled at us.

"I don't know if I can help," my father said, and I translated. "Something like this is in God's hands."

Kim sat up straighter and Bob immediately added another pillow at her back. He remained at her side, biting the nail of his index finger.

"The doctor wants me to just give up," Kim said. "If you were me, would you give up?"

As I repeated the words in Russian, Dad considered the couple with respect.

"We'll pay whatever you ask," Bob pleaded.

"I do what I can do," Dad said in English. "But I no take money."

Did I notice how quickly and earnestly my father was willing to help these strangers? Yes. Even if I was ashamed for the misplaced envy, I let it creep into my mind anyway. This was the first time I'd seen Dad interact with a client, and his kindness seemed limitless. He was a Zen master, breathing hope and tranquillity into the lungs of the lost. I envied that little girl whose life was slipping away, begrudged her my father's Zen. What was wrong with me? Was I really that desperate?

The doctor came in and did a double take. I would've laughed if the situation hadn't been so dire. Dad had on one of his black fedoras and a long leather trench coat beneath which he wore a black dress shirt, black leather pants, and steel-toed cowboy boots. His long hair trailed down his back. The doc eyed it before seeming to remember why he'd come in.

"Any change?" Kim's fingers twisted the sheet over her belly.

The doctor shook his head.

Dad asked the couple if he could talk to the doctor in private, and when they consented we stepped out into the hallway. Dad asked several questions about the baby.

"She has a metabolic disorder," the doctor said.

Perplexed, I admitted that I didn't know what that meant, but Dad wasn't discouraged.

"You tell me not like doctor but like patient," he suggested to the man, who clearly wasn't used to being questioned.

"If you wish, although I don't see the difference."

"Please."

"She's like a car that's running out of gas. Once it's gone, she'll stop working."

Back in the room Dad rubbed his hands together. "I no promise anything, but will pray. You must hold baby, never let her down, and feed her more. Take turn but keep her close to your body all time. She not make life energy, so you give her yours, keep her safe with yours."

The couple looked incredulous. I was doubtful myself, but I could tell that hope was the only thing left to them, and then I remembered Paywand and her theories on magic being all-encompassing and attainable by everyone. My father always tried to explain to his clients the logic behind every séance or healing process: All matter is energy. We are energy. God is energy. Devil is energy. It has neither form nor boundaries. It is what we make of it.

The couple followed my father's instructions, and though the staff objected at first, eventually they let the parents be. On the tenth day the doctors announced that although the metabolic problem had inexplicably disappeared, the little girl's kidneys were now failing. Three weeks later it was her heart. But the parents kept holding her.

Six years later Kim wrote an article about her daughter's miraculous recovery, which was published in a Russian magazine called *Panorama*. She spoke of the Gypsy man who spent days and nights at her daughter's side.

The funny thing is that my father's own mending took place during his visits to the hospital, on his vigils, while he prayed over the sleeping baby. Without her, who knows if he'd ever have snapped out of his grief.

Life has a funny way of sweeping you back into its current.

CHASING FRIENDSHIP

One night Svetlana and Alan paid us another visit, although no one dared to mention marriage in the presence of my father while he was still in mourning.

Half that night I spent twisting in my bed to stay awake until everyone else went to sleep so I could sneak to the kitchen phone and call Mom. Even after the guests had left—the whir of their car unzipping the tightness in my rib cage—I could hear the staccato of Olga's voice chased by Dad's powerful bass for hours. It's worse than living with vampires, I thought when their bedroom door closed at dawn. I slunk into the kitchen, where the wooden tick of the clock was the only sound on the planet. Then there was the shrill of the phone ringing, and I grabbed it before it woke anyone up.

"*Doch* (Daughter)?"

"Mom? Is that you?"

"Who else?" She chuckled. "My shift just ended. Got home a few minutes ago, but I'll wait to get Roxy from the neighbors until at least eight, you know. Everybody's probably sleeping still."

"Are you okay?"

Knots of silence marked by a swift gurgle going down the neck of a bottle.

"Mom? I was about to call you."

"Gotta tell you. I bought a brand-new fifty-four-inch RCA yesterday. Roxy helped me pick it."

"Mom."

"I swear, it's the size of a car."

"You can't watch the programs on a smaller TV?"

"Soon I'll get my raise, a dollar a year, you know, and then we'll get out of this one-bedroom matchbox and buy a house."

At this point Mom still thought that purchasing a house in the States was like purchasing one in the old country, where you paid it off all at once. The concept of credit cards and loans was foreign to her.

"I have to go. We'll talk later, okay?" When you're sober, I almost added.

"Talk about what?"

Everything rolled out of me in one hot whisper.

"You father wouldn't dare," she said.

I pressed the receiver closer to my chin. "This is serious, Mom. I'm not ten. I know what's going on."

"I'll talk to him, but I think you're overreacting." And she was gone.

It was my own fault, I knew. Had I not brought Cruz home, Olga's alarm never would've gone off. She'd have been too busy making money vanish to worry about me. The funny thing was that nothing was happening between us. Nothing tangible. Our connection was a rush, a flurry of wind out the car window. We soared in a perpetual state of foreplay. Caught in a trap of my own devising, I spent days thinking up ways to get Cruz out of our house. Not that I didn't enjoy watching him lean over his guitar, strumming those strings with his clever fingers. On the contrary, during lesson time the living room called to me in a siren voice. Before long I'd find an excuse to dust a shelf, polish a table, or do any other kind of housework in the area so I could enjoy the view.

But after Alan's whackathon, I was convinced the only way to stop Olga's husband-hunting was to pretend Cruz and I didn't associate. Surely then she could point her guns elsewhere.

It proved surprisingly difficult to feign indifference. Cruz's presence made me clumsy and absentminded. If I happened to glance at his hands, my face burned as if he'd touched me. My eyes followed, in slow motion, as he turned the pages of his sheet music. I could even tell his footsteps from everyone else's.

Meanwhile, my stepmother made a list of families with brand-new cars.

Cruz had to go.

I rehearsed my speech all the way to his cousin's house. I'd ask him to stay away for a while, not disappear completely. He was my best friend. And *that* I recognized as something to protect.

The person who opened the door took a large bite of a banana with lips painted tar black. "Hi, sweetie," he chirped. "You looking for Cruz?"

I nodded, taking in the black lacy dress and the makeup.

"In here," he said, crooking one purple-nailed finger. "I'm Brandon."

"Oksana."

"Oh, I know. You're only the most talented Gypsy in school." We went through a dimly lit hallway toward the sound of a booming TV and ended up in the living room. "Well, the only Gypsy I know."

Annie, Cruz's cousin and a fellow magnet student, sat up on the couch to say "Hi" before slumping back down. A cloud of

smoke lingered around her, unmoving, even as two albino ferrets
scurried off her chest and under the couch. I'd seen the little creatures before. Romeo and Juliet. Annie often brought them to
school, hidden in her backpack or coat.

Brandon waved one graceful hand at the couch. "Sit. Don't
be shy."

I didn't at first, too busy wondering why both of them were
eyeing me with such blatant interest.

Brandon finally spoke. "So, I don't mean to be rude, but I
have to ask. How long have you been practicing?"

"Practicing what?" I asked.

"Being a Gypsy."

I laughed a little until it became obvious that he wasn't joking.

"I'm sorry, sweetie," Brandon said, exchanging glances with
Annie, who stayed peculiarly mum. "I've always been fascinated
with the whole bohemian-lifestyle thing . . . and when I heard
about you, well, I couldn't wait to meet you." When I said nothing, he continued. "I know. I'm being totally rude, but I'd rather
ask someone who knows, you know?"

He had a point.

"It's okay," I said. "But I don't think I can be of much help if
you're looking for the bohemian version. I've never lived in a
caravan or anything like that."

"No?" Brandon cocked his head to one side, and it was his
turn to look puzzled.

"Ahhh, no," I said. "Most of us have become pretty domesti-
cated, you know, like cats." I was trying for a joke to keep the
mood light. "Listen, I really need to speak with Cruz. Is he here?"

"I'll go grab him," Brandon said, and disappeared into the
back of the house.

Annie offered me the skinny joint and, when I refused, took a
deep pull herself. "Come on," she said, blowing out the words

slowly between her lips, eyes half-closed. "Don't be a geek. I have something with less pollution if you're picky."

In my parents' line of work, almost everyone got high on something. I remember during one concert, Dad came out of the dressing room already late for his stage entrance.

"Dad, you have sugar on your mustache," I said. He wiped it and shambled past. Behind drawn curtains, the MC was announcing the song, trying to stretch his words until one of the guitar players signaled him that Dad had caught up. When the curtains opened, my father was sitting at the piano, pulling off his shoes and socks and draping them on the instrument, shouting into the microphone, "It's so fucking humid here in Odessa."

Central Asian opiates were the most popular substances because they came cheap and were not yet regulated by the government. Once, in Kyrgyzstan, while our tour bus was passing a field of crimson poppies, I'd unknowingly witnessed the harvesting of hashish. I remember someone on the bus exclaiming that now they could finally score some top-quality *anasha*, or maybe even *plan* (a derivative of opium). Outside, several men, wearing nothing but underwear, were running through the flowers, their bodies glistening in the sunlight. Before taking to the field they had been slathered with sunflower-seed oil so that the flower pollen would collect on their skin. Later the women would roll the pollen off with their fingertips, then either dry it to be smoked in a cigarette or shape it into squares small enough to fit into a pipe. I grew up around many addicts. I can't remember the number of times an ambulance screamed its sirens into my dreams, jolting me awake to see my parents running in and out of our hotel room because a band member had overdosed on coke or was doped up enough to crawl up the walls.

That said, I wasn't about to lecture Annie.

Moments later Cruz came into the living room, his white

T-shirt wet around the shoulders, snug above a pair of faded jeans. "Hey," he said, smiling.

Neither one of us spoke as he led me to the door at the end of the hallway. Nothing but a mattress and a small desk with a chair occupied his room, yet it invited me in. Pinned above the mattress hung a small photograph: a close-up of a young woman with pixie-cut blond hair and enormous green eyes.

A dark blanket covering the windows cast a shadow over the surroundings, but not so much that I didn't notice the stacks of cassette tapes and books piled about. Many of the books had yellow Post-its peeking out.

"Sorry for the mess." He shut the door and the room went black. The smell of him, something like falling leaves, drifted in the air. How was I going to do this? "Hold on," he said. A moment later a floor lamp went on. "Do you want to sit?"

"It's okay."

"What's the matter?" he said. He raised his hand to accept mine, but I took a step back.

"We have to talk."

"Yeah?" He crossed his arms and leaned against the wall. "Is that asshole still coming around? Someone should remind your parents they don't live in Transylvania anymore."

My fingers itched to touch his hair, dark at the ends where water dripped. "You have to stop the lessons," I said.

"Why?"

"Because we're lying, and when they find out we'll both be in deep shit."

"And?" He waved a hand, waiting for me to continue.

"And Olga's convinced something's going on between us. She's husband-hunting to save me from you."

He looked at the floor and laughed softly. His shoulders shook with it. "I don't believe this."

"You think I can do whatever I want, but I can't."

"Because I'm not a Gypsy? It's not like we're living in the twentieth century or anything. Did you ever think that your stepmother's doing all this to piss off your mom? What if it has nothing to do with you?"

When I didn't answer he went on, his voice louder, sharper, his accent thickening. "Maybe if we went out a couple of times you'd find something worth standing up to your family about. Why are you afraid of this?"

"You're the closest thing to a friend I have—"

"There's more than friendship between us. But you won't even give us a fucking chance without expecting the worst."

"I'm trying to be logical—"

"And how's that working out for you?"

My thoughts scattered out of reach. I couldn't bear to upset my father by choosing a boy with no past and no future, like I had done with Ruslan. Every mention of Cruz's family flashed in and out of our conversations like a streetlight passing by a car window.

"I can't," I finally said, and studied the tapes at our feet with utmost interest. He was staring too hard, as if to catch the thoughts spinning webs inside my head. "You're making me uncomfortable."

"*Merde!* Finally, a little honesty."

"My family will never agree to let me see you. Do you want to sneak around like criminals?"

"I don't mind," he said. "Why are you making such a big deal out of nothing?"

"Because it is to me." I moved to leave, but he barred the door.

"Okay. Let's try it," he said. "We'll be friends—fuck, it's not like we're anything more now—but on one condition. I'll prove that I'm right, that we should be dating, and the moment you admit it, all these bullshit rules are off the table. No matter what your family says."

As promised, the lessons stopped. Cruz told Dad that he was failing several classes and was required to attend after-school tutoring to get back on track. My father sulked for about two hours. But as he lived in a world most of us didn't occupy, he got over it. I couldn't read Olga as well, but having experienced her bloodthirsty nature firsthand, I kept myself on guard.

Meanwhile, to uphold my part of the bargain, I hung out with Cruz and his gang. Remaining friends with him proved tricky because I liked him even more now that I couldn't have him. I looked at him and imagined wrapping my arms around his neck like the monkey Olga compared me to. Only three things kept our friendship from spilling over into something more intimate: Olga; a friend of Annie's named Alison who tagged along after Cruz; and school, where I spent so much time I should've had my own cot in some corner.

The band teacher had taken me under his wing, becoming my mentor and champion. The music wing of the school auditorium building was never empty, not even hours after the last bell. And that was where I went to escape life. But I wasn't alone. The students who went hungry at home or came to school with bruises on their faces had also found their makeshift home on the carpeted steps of Mr. North's band-room stage, books and homework folders out, pencils scribbling. A kid with tribal body piercings once confessed that he slept in the band equipment room whenever he could sneak in unseen. "It's the only place my father can't yank my pants off," he joked once. Mr. North tripped over him one morning, all bundled up in the red-and-white marching-band uniforms of the Hollywood High Sheiks, but never reported him.

Sometimes after school, I sat in the chair closest to the teacher's desk, piled with dog-eared paperbacks, and listened to Mr. North quote the inspirational authors he loved. He'd balance on the edge of his desk, feet up on a chair.

"Paulo Coelho once wrote, 'Tell your heart that the fear of suffering is worse than the suffering itself. And no heart has ever suffered when it goes in search of its dream.'"

"But I have a dream. I am learning how to be a real American."

Mr. North slapped his khakied knees with amusement. "Slow down, Pinocchio. How about you be what you already are."

"Like what?"

"Figure it out. Pretend you're holding a block of clay yay big. Now make something out of it."

Music was the only clay I knew. I started to perform as much as possible: recitals, concerts, school band recordings. We even made an appearance on one of Dennis Miller's TV shows (I played cymbals, since my piano was too heavy to haul to the studio). My self-confidence soared, and before long, even my family's theatrics didn't faze me so much anymore.

Whenever someone looked at me as if to say "Are your parents for real?" I reminded myself that this was how *exotic* people lived, so suck it.

Cruz turned up at every performance, as a good friend might, sometimes with Alison tailing him to make sure we spent as little time alone as possible. The girl was Marilyn Monroe to my Carol Burnett. She knew it and I knew it. After a while I desperately wanted to ask Cruz if they were together. Friends asked questions like that, right? Annie and Brandon came, too, flanked by other Goths. They intrigued me; I liked the idea of their darkness in the face of color-coded normalcy.

Secretly I'd yearned for friendship all my life.

Mom had several best friends back in Russia, and the way

they brought over groceries or the latest perfumes freshly smuggled in from across the border, and assembled weekly inside our smoky kitchen, convinced me that friends *are* family. That was the kind of care these women put into their relationships: if you came over, my mother would have the tea brewing and the stew heating up and her ear open before you'd taken off your shoes. She got that quality from Grandma Rose, for sure.

There was this place in Kirovakan, up on a hill near the town's rim, where people gathered to collect mineral water from several elaborate drinking fountains built on a natural spring called Sour Water, or Tetoo Dzhoor in Armenian. Grandma and I took plastic jugs up that path several times a week during my summer visits. We usually went at night, when the air blossomed inside our lungs. People made their way to the spring from all over town, the tips of the men's cigars and pipes like a stream of lights in motion. "Just a quick trip," Grandma promised every time. But once at the fountains, old friends and neighbors accosted us and the conversations filled hours. You'd think Grandma was everyone's relative, not just mine. "Rosik *tota*. Let me help you carry the water home?" *Tota* in Armenian means "auntie," and younger generations will use it as a respectful address for elders. Men call each other *akhper* (brother), women *khirik* (sister). The Armenian language is designed for kinship. I sipped the mineral water straight from the fountain and let it flow down my throat like a cool fizzy firework, and I sat on one of the many benches and waited while Grandma made inquiries of Artem Petrosyan's legal woes, and Ani Ovsepyan's family troubles, and Florik Mahachetryan's ability to have that ninth kid without complications even if she was past fifty and should start thinking about herself instead of her husband's lustful nature. She never appeared bored or impatient, her face open, voice compassionate.

Grandma and Mom bickered over countless things, but maybe it was because they resembled each other so much.

My father, on the other hand? Well, most of Mom's friends avoided him. Something about his guarded manner.

Dad used to warn me regularly against trusting the *gadjen*. But despite his voice of vigilance ringing in my head now, I began to open up to my new friends and crave their company.

It turned out that the house Cruz lived in belonged to Annie's mother, Delma. She worked a night shift at a local hospital and slept most of the day, unseen until the weekends, when she'd grill steaks the size of Frisbees and sing catchy tunes in Portuguese along with Annie and sometimes even Cruz. Brandon and Alison practically lived at Annie's, and they had free run of the house.

I knew more about Annie's mother than I did about Cruz's parents, but every time I asked him about them, he changed the subject. How was that fair? He asked me to relax and let him in while he kept me out. It seemed that the details he'd shared about his dad and *Benedita* were as much as I'd hear of his past, as if he'd left himself unguarded for that one bus ride, then barred the doors before too much escaped. Annie had volunteered some information, but nothing specific, only that Cruz had often come to stay throughout his childhood and that I should refrain from asking him about his family. But Brandon let it slip that Cruz's mother left home when he was a little kid and that he'd been obsessed with finding her ever since.

I had plenty of time to figure out a way of making Cruz talk.

Thanks to Dad's preoccupation with his musical arrangements, and to Olga's disappearing acts, I finally had the freedom to come and go as I pleased. At seventeen I felt adult enough to act as irresponsibly as they did, and old enough to recognize that Dad had been wrong about friendship.

ON THE ROOF

On most days walking home from school I could hear Dad and Olga shouting, and if they caught me at the front door, they immediately pulled me into their fights. Soon I started to use my bedroom window instead of the door.

Back in Moscow when my parents fought, I became the reluctant spy. Roxy was too young, but both my parents knew that I was the right age to remember events in detail.

"Did someone clean the living-room rug while I was gone?" Mom was saying one day as we entered a public *banya* located inside a five-story neoclassical building.

"I don't think so."

This particular *banya*, with its mermaid-themed mosaics and gigantic windows, was my favorite. When I stood in the main bathing area the size of an Olympic swimming complex, I felt like a fish at the bottom of the ocean with sunlight streaming down over me through the water.

"Oh. It looked like it was moved."

"Dad probably used it under Vova's drums during rehearsal." A mistake, since Mom had forbidden my father to set up drums on the Persian rugs. We pushed our way through the busy lobby lined with kiosks selling cigarettes and newspapers, shoeshine booths, and hair salons where women with rosy cheeks were getting perms.

We found our lockers and undressed, hanging the clothes on the hooks and locking the valuables behind dented doors. The *banya* split into two wings, men's and women's; inside those areas modesty was as distant a Russian concept as pay-per-view. Naked, we found our bench—one of many dotting the tiled floor of the main bathhouse—and on it our buckets, along with eucalyptus branches tied in a bunch. As we bathed, Mom fumed over the fact that Dad's friends drank the three bottles of Armenian cognac she'd been saving to use as "gifts" for our case worker at the American embassy. I hadn't wanted to tell her those details, but between the steam flushing my cheeks pink and the soothing murmur of women's voices bouncing against the high ceilings, I was in a great mood, tongue unguarded.

"Just proves your father's head is stuffed with cotton," she said, upending a bucket of warm water she'd drawn from the raised pool nearby over the suds in my hair.

She picked up the eucalyptus branches and started to gently smack me with them, a traditional massage therapy. Combined with the steam, the minty smell of the plant was sharp inside my nostrils.

"What's the big deal, Mom?"

"You always take his side."

I had been so used to this kind of scenario that no way was I getting in the middle of Dad and Olga's battle royal.

Walking up the sidewalk to our house, I heard shouting. Behind the living-room curtains, a silhouette picked up a chair and smashed it on the floor. I heard Olga congratulate Dad on breaking yet another Thomasville, her tone climbing into a falsetto.

Their voices lashed across the front yard, up and down the empty street.

As I passed Sherri's Mercedes in the driveway, I slowed down. Earlier that day, I'd left her and Dad alone; Annie had invited me over to watch *Monty Python and the Holy Grail*.

The front door burst open and Sherri raced outside, a mixture of tears and mascara transforming her face into a Halloween mask. She was missing a shoe, and the straps of her dress hung off her shoulders like noodles. There were scratches on her arms and legs.

Olga stumbled into the doorway. "*Nu pizdets tebe, suka* (You're fucked, bitch)!"

My stepmother sprinted after Sherri. I'd never suspected such agility.

As Sherri limped to her car, Olga tossed a clump of frizzy orange hair on the lawn before jumping on Sherri from behind, making her stagger backward. "This is what you get for sleeping with my husband, *manda* (twat). Me!"

She pulled another fistful of the woman's hair. Sherri screamed, her hands flying to her head. "You crazy bitch!"

"I'll have you paralyzed. You'll be shitting in diapers when I'm done with you." Olga's threats slurred and stumbled.

"I'm a man," my father shouted over and over again. He was outside now, a bottle dangling from his fingertips. "Let her go, Olga! I order you."

As the struggle progressed, Dad circled around them, shouting things like "Girls, that's enough!" and "I demand you stop!" and "I'm a man, dammit. I can do as I please!"

But they ignored him, falling and rolling on the ground like kids in a wrestling match, flinging obscenities at each other.

The three of them were so drunk that I suspected somebody would end up in a hospital before the night was over. Acting on impulse, I picked up the garden hose and turned it on, covering the nozzle with my thumb and letting it rip. The women screamed and sputtered, and let go of each other to shield their faces. I didn't stop until the water had soaked them through.

Dad wiped at his shirt and sway-walked in my direction. "Hey, that's Oksana." He gave me a sloppy hug. "My daughter. Hello, daughter."

"Dad, someone's going to call the police if you don't get her out of here."

"I'll give them one of my CDs," he said.

"Great. Why don't we go inside and I'll make coffee. Okay?"

"Premium idea, daughter, premium idea." He ambled toward the house.

Sherri finally managed to make it to her car and left, the tires screeching with a startled yelp. Olga refused my help as she scrambled to her feet, muttering curses in liquor-tongue all the way to the bathroom.

I took a deep breath as I went inside, locking the front door behind me. The quiet was a good sign. No sirens, no cops. I made Armenian coffee and poured it into two espresso cups. That stuff is strong enough to make the dead dance, Grandpa Andrei used to say. Dad drank his while gazing at the cuckoo clock on the kitchen wall. Olga refused to come out of the bathroom. There was no point asking what had happened, not that I actually wanted to know; but judging by the worried expression on Dad's face, it was obvious that Olga had finally gotten proof of his unfaithfulness.

When Olga came into the kitchen, my father grinned at her.

"Don't even start." Olga shook a finger at him.

"But it was nothing, my sparrow. I did . . . she attacked me, you see. I didn't want to but—"

"You fell into her pussy, I know," she said. "Men are dogs, only dogs don't lie about being dogs. They don't screw the clients, expecting their wives to say nothing." Olga rummaged through every cabinet, huffing at all of Dad's awkward apologies, until she found a full bottle of vodka under the sink.

I reached for the bottle and tried to pry it from her hands. "Come on, Olga. It's late. Go to bed, okay?"

Olga spit on the floor. She then went outside with the bottle tucked under one arm, leaned the garden ladder against the back of the house, and climbed to the roof. "I'm not sleeping with that man tonight," she shouted from above. "Throw me a blanket, will you?"

I did.

A few minutes later Dad came outside and stood in the backyard, where the grass grew in bunches terrified of all the barren spots. I think he had sobered up a little after the coffee. He looked lost—an unfamiliar sight to me.

"Stop this nonsense, wife. It'll get cold up there," he said.

"No colder than down there," she said. "I'm not sleeping with you. Ever."

Then she started to sing.

I will flee o'er the mountains
Up the path my moon has painted . . .

The bottle quickly emptied, giving Olga's lungs more clout. She was a terrible singer. Multiply that by the 40 percent alcohol rushing through her system, and the result would shame a yowling cat. No matter how we tried to get Olga down, she remained unmoved. The threats, the pleas, even the bribes were cut down by ten verses and ten choruses.

Every time Dad spoke, Olga raised her voice. By three in the morning, vacillating between rage and the very real fear that I might see Olga fall, my body demanded a bed, but I settled for a lawn chair. I fell asleep to the sounds of Olga singing and cursing at the sky.

The doorbell rang at seven-thirty. It was our landlord. The neighbors had complained about the inebriated five-foot-three Gypsy woman hollering from the roof all night. Since he also owned the two houses on either side of ours, they were kind enough to call him instead of the police. The house on the right had a neat row of cannabis plants blooming on its patio, and the one on the left contained a large family of illegal immigrants.

"Mr. Roy," Olga said from the doorway. The landlord's name was Roy Shuck, but she always called him Mr. Roy. She had finally descended half an hour earlier. "Mr. Roy. I go on roof for count stars. Is my job. Come, I do chart for you. Only one hundred dollars. You take off rent, yes?"

Roy was a tall, sinewy man who lived in his bike shorts. I'd never seen men wear such tight outfits, except for the dancers in the Bolshoi Ballet productions, and even then they used codpieces for modesty. The first time I met Roy, I nearly lost my innocence; he showed up to collect rent in the most perversely crowded pair of animal-print Lycra shorts I hope never to see again. This time he had on a canary-yellow number.

Roy patiently explained about roofs and why tenants shouldn't go on them. "You're old enough to know that," he said jokingly.

Olga took that to heart. "I no old. I wery famous psychic. Clients need hep, so I hep. On roof, inside, everywhere."

Unfazed by Olga's indignation, our landlord insisted that from now on all stargazing and client support be done from inside the house. They finally agreed, but according to Olga, only because she'd needed to pee since four in the morning and no longer wished to talk to the idiot in yellow underwear.

KENTUCKY FRIED CHICKEN

As a child I remember reading an article in one of Moscow's trendier magazines about 7-Eleven stores. It was like peeking into a world in the distant future, created by Jules Verne himself. The glossy photos depicted grinning workers surrounded by brightly colored food and sodas and the kinds of gizmos one might expect to see in a sci-fi movie.

The article described the daily tasks the 7-Eleven employees performed, their lunches, their uniforms. If only I had the opportunity to work at such a marvelous establishment!

By the time I decided to search for my first job, I'd seen plenty of 7-Elevens, and I'd learned that not many people worked at convenience stores by choice; it was a transitional job reserved for those on the way up or down. But I so wanted to work. Mom and I talked a couple of times a week and our phone conversations were chock-full of praise for a steady paycheck. We both knew being a cash person in a casino wasn't a dream career, but Mom's friends were American, her regulars were American, her life was sprouting Americana like a Chia Pet.

She and Roxy drove down to see me one day. They picked me

up after school in a powder-blue 1971 Oldsmobile that Mom had bought for five hundred dollars. The body had rusted, the passenger-door handle keened in agony when used, and the plastic air-conditioning vents had breathed their last. Mom called the car her tank. "You'll see," she said as I got in the front. "If we're ever in an accident, there won't be even a dent, but the other car will fold like an accordion."

We ate lunch at the Pizza Place, in the same booth where Cruz, Natasha, and I had had our first date. Mom went on about the perfection that was Las Vegas.

"One of my regulars owns houses in Italy and France. She vacations there during summers because Vegas gets so hot, but I love the weather."

"I don't love it at all," Roxy complained.

Mom went on. "I have another client who buys everything with plastic and credit."

"I want plastic, too," Roxy said.

"It's for grown-ups only."

I bit into my pepperoni slice, cheese stretching like lace. Pizza was now my favorite food, though I'd never tasted it in Russia. I picked the cheese between my thumb and forefinger and stuffed it into my mouth. "Are you saving money, like you said you would?"

"What kind of a question is that?"

"You keep it in the bank, right? One of those special accounts?" Earlier that year Annie explained to me the workings of the American banking system, and I sent Mom the instructions in a letter.

Mom took a long sip of her soda. "It's like you're my mother instead of the other way around," she said. "I needed the car, and this trip is not free, you know. Plus, I've been winning at the slots. You won't believe it, but every time I spend, I end up getting it back. It's like I walk inside the casino and I can feel which machine's about to spill."

"Mom. Tell Oksana what we wanna get her. Tell her, please, please, if you don't I will." Roxy bounced in her seat. Grandpa Andrei used a special Ukrainian expression to describe this: *shilo v booley*, or awl in the ass.

Mom clasped her hands with a euphoric smile. "We're going to the mall."

Roxy took a gulp of air and opened her mouth, and Mom immediately covered it. "Don't you dare. It's a surprise."

Inside the mall, we dashed through the throng of shoppers. Patience was not one of Mom's virtues. If she had an idea, she lit up like a dynamite fuse. We finally stopped in front of Bob's Music World, where keyboards covered the sales floor.

"May I help you?" said the salesman. He wore ironed slacks, a starched white shirt, and a tie with piano keys on it.

"I like to buy my daughter keyboard."

"Really, Mom?" I was stuck to the floor. "But what about the money?"

"I make money now from a real job, not a room in the back of my house, so I can get credit."

What a feeling it was to test those keys, knowing I'd have one of my own. I was already picturing myself inside my room, composing until dawn.

Once I picked the instrument, I hugged my mother until I could force myself not to cry. Roxy hugged the startled salesclerk, who quickly ran Mom's name and gave her a two-thousand-dollar line of credit. My new keyboard was about five years old (ancient in technological terms), and it came with a metallic stand painted black but chipped, shaky like an old man's legs. My own tank.

Mom was making progress in this strange culture, and she inspired me. In Russia work for a girl my age would've consisted of learning to cook and sew ghastly dresses from ghastly Soviet pattern books, but Hollywood teemed with opportunities.

For a while I simply went door-to-door, asking if anyone was hiring; from an Allstate office, to a tattoo parlor, to a Chinese massage parlor, to a place that was called Pussy Parlor but wasn't a parlor at all.

I soon learned that most immigrants in L.A. worked in their families' businesses, and that those who didn't found something in their families' friends' businesses. Per Olga's nagging, Dad kept suggesting I learn tarot cards and channeling and set up shop with them. "This way you could take over when I retire and have something to fall back on in case you fail at everything else," he'd say.

Dad and Olga's business was booming, and they could spare a few clients if I wished to make a little money.

On several occasions Dad hinted that he'd give me his special porcelain divination plate, or even the photo album Grandpa Andrei had forbidden me to look at all those years ago. Some of the pictures in it were so old, they'd nearly faded into white. I knew how much these items meant to him, but I also knew that by accepting them I'd be agreeing to be the keeper of my family's legacy. And at the time, I believed myself unsuited for that job.

To complicate things, Olga continued to drill Dad about my unengaged status. I started seriously to consider life away from the pressure to follow such outdated traditions. Dad wasn't the staunchest of conservatives, but even he treated girls as if we were a part of the home decor. Were I a boy, I would've been encouraged to go out in the world and get into as much trouble as I could. Romani boys are pampered first by their grandmothers, then by their mothers, then sisters, wives, and eventually daughters. They're passed on from one to the other like a suckling pig on a golden tray.

Misha, I remember, was the cause of an explosive argument

between Grandma Ksenia and Grandpa Andrei. One day Aunt Laura sent her teenage son to the market for a tub of sour cream. After Misha sulked out of the house and down the street, Grandma flew to the open kitchen window, yanked aside the curtains, and yelled for him to come back. He was too far to hear, and when Grandma turned around, her cheeks puffed out in fury. When Grandma got really mad, she threw things at people. If livid, she would become theatrical, bawling and lamenting while down on her knees. At the counter Aunt Laura was rolling meat patties between her palms for Moldavian meatballs that would be simmered slowly in paprika and sour cream sauce.

"Mother, leave him be," she said.

"Why'd you have to send the poor boy out in this wind? I could've gone instead!"

"This is the first time I've asked him to do a chore in months. He'll be fine. The market is only around the block."

Grandma squeezed her fists to her chest and shouted, "Andrei! Andrei! Come here right now. Come see what your daughter has done."

Grandpa shuffled in from the living room, where he'd been reading the morning paper in his striped pajamas, sitting in his favorite armchair. He examined his wife and his daughter from above the rims of his glasses with the expression of a man perpetually harassed. Grandma pointed a finger at their daughter, who kept rolling those balls. "She forced my Misha to do woman's work. What if someone we know recognizes him? What will people think? That we use our firstborn for a working mule, that's what. Tell her to leave my Mishenka alone."

Grandpa continued to stand in the doorway with his paper rolled up in one huge hand.

"Tell her!" Grandma demanded again.

Suddenly Grandpa raised the newspaper and whacked it against the doorframe, making all of us jump. "Leave her alone, woman. Your Mishenka is eighteen. His pecker's been over this neighborhood like last year's cold. You know how many girls he's already knocked up?"

"My God, but you can be vicious," Grandma breathed.

"He's a man, so let him get sour cream for his mother once in a while. Let him show he's good for more than—"

"Stop accusing my boy."

"He's not yours, Ksenia, and he's not a boy anymore."

No one thought twice about how many trips for sour cream or anything else the girls in the family made inside a week. Grandma used to send me and Zhanna across the street to a neighbor who kept chickens in his backyard. The coop was stuffy and dark, with three rows of nesting boxes lined with straw shavings. It housed about twenty hens and smelled like farts and old grass. I minded going only when this neighbor, an ancient man with a beard that resembled upturned shrubbery, was in the process of wringing chicken necks, but Misha was never asked to carry out this task. Collecting eggs stained with chicken shit was definitely women's work. So was carrying the still-warm body of a freshly slaughtered and plucked chicken across the street.

When I finally found a job, Dad let me know exactly how he felt about it the day I brought home my new aquamarine uniform embroidered with the insignia of my first employer: Kentucky Fried Chicken. I'd found the job by sheer chance. After hitting every spot up and down the neighborhood streets, which included a doctor's office, some jewelry stores, and a copy center, I'd come to the conclusion that to be employed, I had to be either a nineteen-year-old with colossal boobs or a college graduate with ambitions of being underpaid.

Worn out, I spotted a fast-food restaurant and went inside to get a drink; the place was packed with chicken lovers of all ages. Dad had recently developed a taste for McDonald's, where he regularly attempted to bargain down the price of a cheeseburger. He'd argue amicably, in broken English, while cussing in Russian.

"I buy six cheeseburgers. Four dollars," Dad would say, smiling.

"I'm sorry, sir, but the prices are nonnegotiable."

"Come, come. *Nasral ya tebe na golovoo* (I shit on your head)." Still smiling. "Okay. I buy ten. Five dollars. End offer."

I don't know why the KFC manager hired me. Based on numerous interview books I've read since, the phrase "I really need a job" sounds way too desperate. But then and there, Mr. Dai gave me a chance without even seeing as much as an ID.

As I made my way to the kitchen back home, I distinguished Igor's baritone arguing with Dad about Russian politics, as well as a hubbub of other chatter. I sent up a silent prayer begging for Alan not to be one of the visitors, and once inside the doorway, I let out a thankful breath. As always, the people at the table were clients who had, with time, become good friends. My father was telling a joke about a man who'd used vodka to cure his insomnia. He was holding his guitar, strumming the strings as if the joke were meant to be accompanied by a musical score.

But he stopped when he saw me and, in my arms, the uniform.

"School ended three hours ago," he said.

"I should've called. But look . . . I found a job."

He placed the guitar next to him like it was a small child and gestured for the uniform, which I handed over with a nervous smile. "Look, everyone. My daughter found a job. Isn't that something? We're going to be rich." That produced a few chuckles. "How much will this job pay?"

I hesitated, feeling stupid because I'd forgotten to ask. "Well, Mr. Dai didn't say specifically."

"So. You refuse my offer to teach you what *I* know, but you're willing to bake chicken for this Mr. Dai without even knowing how much he'll pay you?"

I was stung by his callousness, especially in front of guests. "I thought you'd be proud," I said. After all, I'd done it all on my own.

"Sit down, Oksana."

I did, and he gave me back the uniform. Somewhere in the recesses of the house, Olga's voice rose and fell. She was with a client, and that meant that with luck Dad wouldn't throw any major fits. Then again, he'd been known to kick clients out for not taking their shoes off before walking into his living room.

"I ask you, my friends." He placed both elbows on the edge of the table, brought his hands together as if in prayer, and nodded at the silent faces around the table. "Is this why we come to this country? So our children can slave their youths away while making some asshole rich?"

"You're absolutely right," said Igor, considerably more opinionated in the absence of his wife. "They're exploiting our kids, like the Soviets exploited us. These two countries are twins separated at birth. Had I only known . . ." His voice trailed off.

"But this isn't forever," I said. "Lots of my friends work just to have a little pocket money."

Dad wagged his index finger at me and then pointed it straight up. "They make you believe that you have all the time in the world, that you can work a five-dollar job until the real thing comes along," he said. "It's bullshit. One day you're seventeen, the next, your teeth are floating in a glass of water."

I sighed, louder then I'd intended, and he narrowed his eyes at me.

"Perhaps you *are* turning into an American, my daughter, living halfway, like they do."

Grandpa Andrei often said that the Kopylenko clan didn't live halfway. This meant that we spent lifetimes learning our craft from each other, *not* trading it in for a safer occupation. No one I knew was an accountant/musician. You were either one or the other. But like many old-school Romani, my grandfather had his own idea of what the right choice for his family should be. When Grandma Ksenia was invited to sing at the Bolshoi, it was my grandfather who forbade it. Grandma was a coloratura soprano, her agile voice capable of rich ornamental elements, sought out by the opera scouts. No matter. No Roma wife went against her husband, especially in such a public matter.

Grandpa ruled, onstage and off

But times were different now. There was no stage, there were no Roma songs, there was no touring. And the only thing my father was interested in teaching me was the language of the dead. My family was in a limbo, suspended between two worlds, and I for once was in a hurry to leap into the new one.

If a job at a fast-food joint wasn't going to accomplish that, I was out of ideas.

"Dad, come on. Not everything's a conspiracy. What's wrong with working a regular job, anyway?"

"I forbid you," my father said.

I took the job regardless. He knew about it. The smell of fried chicken saturated my clothes, skin, and hair. I sneaked home after changing at work, and if Dad and I happened to bump into each other in the hallway before I showered, he'd utter, "*Znachit tak* (That's how it's gonna be)," with a bitter shake of the head.

I'd feign ignorance with the sincerity only a teenager is capable of, but he'd lumber toward the kitchen with long, meaningful sighs.

I was at work one day, in the back, making mashed potatoes from a powdered mix. It struck me as most innovative, to have prepackaged food that required only water to be transformed into something fluffy and moist. I remember begging Mom when I was a kid to buy chicken nuggets stored behind the frosty windows of our local market.

"*Eto poloofabrikat govno* (This processed crap)? I don't think so. If you're hungry we'll go home and you can have *kotleti* and barley." Now I could have all the *poloofabrikat govno* I could wish for, to make up for years of homemade meals.

I heard Dad before I saw him, his voice reaching out for me with chilly promises of doom. I'd expected a scene, but he didn't ask for me. Instead he called for Mr. Dai.

I gathered enough courage to peek around the wall separating the registers from the prep counter where Dad was demanding that my manager fire me.

"Is very good here." Dad gestured around the store. "Good

energy, good peoples. But is not for my daughter, you understand? You have childrens?"

Mr. Dai nodded. "I have three."

"Then you understand. You forbid my daughter to make
chicken, yes?"

"Perhaps you're being a little hard on her. It's good practice for
when they're adults."

"No good," Dad said. "We Roma make money for family, not
boss man." He got his wallet, pulled out a hundred-dollar bill,
and handed it to Mr. Dai. "You do this for me, okay?"

My manager didn't take the bribe but quickly made an excuse
to end the conversation, promising to think about it. Dad left
disappointed, unprepared for such a catastrophic bribe failure.
Soviet life thrived on bribery; that was how things got done.

I came home that night bearing gifts from my manager: a
bucket of fried chicken with mashed potatoes, gravy, coleslaw,
corn on the cob, and biscuits. "A peace offering," he'd said. Dad
took the bag, saying nothing to me as he chewed on a drumstick.
Olga was with a client but came in as soon as she was done, her
nose searching out the unfamiliar aroma. They both ate with
zeal, licking fingers and noting the smoothness of the potatoes
and the sweetness of the coleslaw. The corn dripped with butter.
The biscuits, when broken, released sinewy steam.

The next morning, when I opened the fridge to grab some
eggs, I found no leftovers from the feast the night before. It was a
good sign, and I made sure to thank Mr. Dai for his clever idea.
My family's obsession with Mr. Dai's chicken took root. Soon
Dad and Olga grew so addicted that they left me alone as long as
I kept the food coming. At the end of the night shift, Mr. Dai
would also take some of the unsold chicken to a homeless family
living in the bushes across the street, until the day we got a memo

from the corporate office stating that stores must dispose of all leftover food in the industrial-size Dumpsters provided.

"How did they know we were giving away the leftovers?" I asked, reading the note over my boss's shoulder.

"They have secret cameras all over the stores. Didn't you know?" one of the other workers said.

"Right. And they fly by night and fight evil with lasers shooting out of their eyes," I joked nervously, especially since Mr. Dai had refused to comment.

The free chicken dwindled. My father and Olga thought it strange that so much food should go to waste, but since I didn't understand it myself, how could I explain it to them? I still managed to sneak some out now and then, but most of the time I ended up giving my loot to the homeless family, who apparently did not get the memo.

WHERE OLGA'S SECRET IS REVEALED

I signed up for the year-end talent show the same week I got my job. Every time our school gathered in the auditorium for an assembly, I'd savor the theater's dusty grandeur and make plans for our future together. Here was my chance to mold that piece of clay Mr. North had shown me I held.

Brandon claimed the place was haunted by ghosts. About fifty years earlier, a girl student had an unfortunate accident with the overhead lights, and more recently, a boy hanged himself from the balcony. But to me it felt like home, and I navigated the theater's murky atmosphere with light in my heart.

At Dad's, things were getting out of control. Not only did Olga keep magically disappearing when she came into money; she now disappeared with it for days at a time. The longer she was gone, the more he practiced his guitar, playing scales and riffs until my eardrums felt blistered. To stay out of their way I did all of my own practicing at school. I composed an instrumental song for the concert as I held together the pieces of enthusiasm I'd started to feel weeks earlier.

Still, I couldn't become invisible. Dad revealed to me his theories about Olga's whereabouts, expecting me to pitch in on the investigation, until one night Olga got caught in the web of her own deception.

It was two in the morning and I was about to go to bed when the phone rang. Dad was eating lunch with the phone at his elbow (he usually got up at four or five in the evening, so this was typical for him). He answered promptly, his scrambled eggs momentarily forgotten. He must've said "What?" at least twenty times before he thrust the phone in my hand, ordering me to take down the address the person on the other end of the line would give. As I did, I watched him stuff the half-eaten eggs down the garbage disposal, cursing them to Hell. The call had come from a Chinese gambling hall where Olga apparently had had a scrap with one of the poker dealers. "Gambling," he shouted. "Can you fucking believe it? If she thinks I'm gonna stand by and watch her shit away all our hard work, she doesn't know me. I'll divorce her in a fucking wink."

In the old country, the trains we rode teemed with quick-fix gambling houses. No cops patrolled the locomotives, which made a train compartment the perfect place for setting up card or dice tables and picking wagers out of the crowded, smoke-filled cars. During the stops, a couple of guys kept watch and whistled a warning if a guard boarded. My father participated in his share of all-night betting. "But I was young and money was no problem," he rationalized. "Your stepmother doesn't realize that dollars are much harder to come by than rubles."

We drove through slumbering Los Angeles in the direction of Chinatown. My father never stopped talking about his nerves wearing thin. I almost laughed because he reminded me of Mom. In the past, it was she who rode countless taxis around Moscow, searching for Dad in the local bars or bailing him out of jail. Before Roxy was born, I remember riding through the bitter cold often, all the while dreaming of the cozy bed I'd been forced to leave. Once, we found Dad at a nightclub just as he was ambushed by several members of a notorious Ossetian gang. Dad, drunk enough to insult one of the men's mistresses, hadn't expected such a severe retaliation. When Mom and I showed up, one of them had my father in a chokehold, a curved blade at his throat. The place swarmed with patrons trying to flee a potential crime scene. My mother got on her knees, begging him to let go of her husband. She was seven months pregnant with my sister.

It turned out to be a long ride before Dad and I came to a stop in front of a peeling two-story building on the outskirts of Chinatown.

From the outside it looked abandoned. The shiny black windows gave no indication of activity.

"Check the address again," Dad said.

I looked at the napkin where I'd written it down. "It matches."

We parked and got out. Dad knocked on a glass door with dark curtains pulled tight, and for a few minutes nothing happened. I walked up and down the sidewalk. He knocked again. The curtains moved this time to reveal an eye.

"Oh," Dad said. "Hello. I here for Olga. What? No. O-l-g-a. Long-hairs Gypsy vooman."

The eye was joined by a finger, which pointed to an alley on our left.

The back door cracked only wide enough to let us pass. Inside, cigarette smoke substituted for air. I followed Dad down a narrow hallway, both of us behind a balding Asian man who said nothing but nodded in the direction of a door on the other side of the poker tables. The place was jam-packed. The color red prevailed here—red lights, red carpets—and walls with giant mirrors multiplied us by the dozen. The music was an unrecognizable jumble nearly drowned out by voices and chips clinking in chorus.

My stepmother slept on a maroon couch in the owner's office. The look on his bulgy-eyed face suggested horrified alarm as he begged my father to keep the lady away from his establishment. He didn't want police involvement on account of it being illegal.

"Your wife is a menace," he said. "She terrorizes my patrons and employees, demanding back money she lost, accusing everyone of cheating. I think it would be better for all of us if she come here no longer."

How could it be that one petite female had managed to bully a roomful of hardened gamblers? I'd imagined, based strictly on my cinematic experience, that the muscle at such a place could easily drop-kick a troublemaker. Yet here stood a man on the brink of a nervous breakdown because of my tiny stepmother.

Dad agreed to keep Olga away, and hauled his wife out to the van while I followed timidly behind. At one point she woke up long enough to demand he take her back so she could finish her hand. He promised her that if she ever stepped into that place again, he'd send her back to the cold, vermin-infested village of Konotop from which she came. Unfortunately he failed to forbid her from going to the dozens of other underground gaming halls in the Los Angeles area.

After this humiliating experience, Olga put her gambling on hiatus, concentrating instead on clients (good) and on my still unattached state (bad). She plotted or sabotaged, or found a way to sabotage while plotting. As losing money at the tables was no longer an option, she began to lose it to her second favorite vice: alcohol.

Alcohol consumption is woven into the very fiber of Eastern European culture. (In Russian, vodka means "little water.") People make peace while drinking, forge business deals, talk politics and philosophy. If you were a businessman and you didn't drink, you'd be the only one at the table not making progress. But wisdom held that if you drank alone, you had a serious problem.

Olga stashed her alcohol supply far away from wandering eyes. She'd be all right in the afternoon, but by midnight we'd have to drag her from the ladder before she started mewling on the roof again.

It seemed the one thing holding Dad and Olga together at this stage was their business. In the same way that Olga tried to give up gambling, Dad agreed to try to behave around women. Money still poured in, so they patched up the leaky roof of their relationship for the sake of luxury and status. Where I made five dollars an hour, they raked in anywhere from two to ten thousand a day. For a simple love spell, Olga charged at least five hundred dollars, but since most of my father's clients had bigger problems than a fizzled relationship, he accepted what a client could afford. Sometimes it was one hundred dollars, other times a fruitcake.

When not in deadlock with each other, Olga and Dad greatly enjoyed their new lifestyle. Olga purchased diamond rings for each finger. Soon she sparkled like a disco ball.

Dad booked more gigs, playing jazz, rock, and jazz-rock fusion. He had little desire to play only Gypsy music, maybe because he was finally free to choose. After the shows he sold his home-cooked CDs for five dollars apiece. "If only your grandfather could see me now," he'd often say. Even though he didn't make as much money as Olga, he was really starting to enjoy himself. His one regret was that stardom still eluded him, though he was convinced it would not be long before the Grammys called.

He made sure to remind me daily that I could live in the same exciting manner if I changed my conformist ways. The only problem was, his idea of following my dream involved performing an occasional channeling and, let's not forget, settling down with a nice Romani boy.

THE WEDDING

Not long after our two a.m. Olga roundup, we were invited to a wedding. It was going to last for two days: a grand affair, Romani-style. According to tradition, the first day of celebration takes place at the groom's house, while the second continues at the bride's.

I can't say I willingly put on the sequined peach monstrosity Olga called a dress, but she'd paid for it, and she was acting like this wedding was a really big deal to her, so I obliged. Afterward, she made me turn in front of her bedroom mirror, exclaiming that I resembled a budding rose. Some sparkly jewelry followed, except for a heavy, solid gold bracelet—a gift for the newlyweds—which she carefully placed inside her purse. To crown it all, Olga orchestrated a hair-tease that created a halo on my head reminiscent of the long-gone Lioness. My hair was now almost to my waist—not because I wanted the trademark Gypsy locks but out of superstition. I'd heard Esmeralda say that the longer you grow your hair, the more patient you become, and with Mom practicing her plastic powers in Vegas, and Dad and Olga doing everything they weren't supposed to, I needed all the patience I could get. Even Roxy was in on it with me, both of us growing our patience inch by inch.

We drove to the groom's house through the hills of Glendale, Dad and Olga up front and me budding in the backseat. The sun had long since gone down, and darkness gathered like a cape pinpricked by the streetlights. My stepmother prattled on about the bride, who supposedly had such an enormous nose that her parents, also Olga's good friends, had no choice but to come up with their own *kalim*. A *kalim* is an offering of gold customarily given by the groom's father to the bride's father after they have worked out the wedding details. I didn't believe a word of it. First, Olga liked to exaggerate. And second, we lived in the twentieth century, where no self-respecting girl would allow her parents to settle her future over a handful of precious metals. The family had come to the States recently, but surely the girl had speedily grasped the disadvantages of ancient customs the same way I had.

Before we even saw the house, we heard the music. My heart tightened at the familiar sounds of Romani melodies.

"We're late," Dad said. "I told you we should've gone to the service."

We parked two blocks away; cars already lined both sides of the street all the way up the hill.

"I don't think they've started yet," Olga said, pointing out a stream of guests winding up the street to the house. "See? Everybody's still outside."

We joined a crowd of people gathered on the front lawn, stark against a house so lit up with Christmas lights that it looked like the sun had taken residence.

"Isn't that dangerous, all the lights turned on together like that?"

"*Gospodi*, Oksana. Only you'd notice something so trivial on a night like this," Olga said.

And maybe she was right.

The air hinted of roasted meats. Men, including my father, had brought their guitars, fiddles, and accordions. Many likely never left the house without them.

I stood there, breathing in the crisp air and the music, thinking, How could anyone not be moved by this?

Some of the neighbors had come out, watching us as if we were a circus pitching tents. Meanwhile the guests made small talk in Rromanes, Russian, and even English. Some shook hands, others embraced. Even if many of these immigrants didn't live a traditional Romani life anymore, they happily returned to it for special occasions.

"Why is everyone standing out here?" I asked.

Olga took the pipe Dad had lit up. He had bought it off a Hindu man who'd promised that it improved health. She puffed, her eyes half-closed, the smell of cherry tobacco kissing my nose. "The newlyweds will sit at the head of the table first, before anyone's allowed in. Then"—she pulled out the golden bracelet from her purse—"the gifts, and *then* we celebrate."

Finally the doors opened and the father of the groom invited everyone in to begin the celebration.

Two sets of long tables ran parallel to each other, from the living room through the French doors and out to the backyard. Another table was set at the back of the garden, creating the shape of a Russian П. That was where the bride and groom were already receiving gifts.

We stood in a slowly moving procession as if to meet royalty. When it was our turn to congratulate the bride and groom, I couldn't stop staring at their faces, flushed and shiny-eyed. They radiated an inner dazzle that had nothing to do with the wedding. The evidence of their love was almost tangible, and I imagined wrapping myself in it, letting its bliss tingle against my skin.

Once people delivered their presents and felicitations, they sat according to gender and age: men took the right side, women the left; the oldest sat closer to the head of the table, the youngest at the ends. This was done so the young would always be ready to refill glasses or fetch a shawl. In Romani culture, the elder generations enjoy almost unlimited power, and it's a great offense to slight them in any way.

The din in the room fluttered out the windows, but I picked up snippets of conversation here and there. Most guests spoke Russian, and they did so with their hands as much as with their mouths. To a *gadjee* it might have appeared as though the wedding guests were ensnared in some mass disagreement, when in truth they were just having a friendly chat.

A little girl dashed across the floor and into the arms of a woman several seats to my right. The kid's curls bounced, gold earrings twinkling from her tiny earlobes as she jumped up and down to get her mother's attention away from the animated discussion the latter was having with her neighbor.

"Well, here's my Ninochka," the woman said, embracing her daughter. She caught the pink bow suspended from the tip of one dark curl and quickly reclasped it at Ninochka's temple. The other woman, hair in a loose bun, bejeweled and heavily shoulder-padded in a dress that could've been made out of Liberace's cape, clucked her tongue and said in a voice rough as sandpaper, "What a beauty, what a beauty. Watch out, Alla. Ten more years and you'll be beating away suitors with a broom." She reached out and squeezed the little girl's chin with plump fingers.

"Bless you, Natasha," Alla said. "But you don't think she's too dark? You know how even some of our Roma boys prefer a porcelain doll."

"*Devlo* (Goodness), Alla. It's common knowledge that dark-skinned *tziganochky* (Gypsy girls) are better in bed," Natasha said, her massive bosom shaking with laughter.

This was welcome news to me. Cousin Zhanna had pale skin, hair the color of melted caramel, and eyes like two ambers, and even when she was little, she was considered a jewel among the Roma. Next to her I blended into the background like a muddy snow mound in the banks of a city road. Maybe I had attractions I didn't realize. And yet, surveying the room, I noticed several women who could've passed for Zhanna's sister. The younger men, all suited up and shiny-tied, had gathered close to them, their bodies taut with unspoken rivalry. In a crowd, no one would think these girls to be Romani, but such is the diversity of our folk.

My neighbor at the table was a tawny young girl of around twelve; everything she said was harnessed to a wide grin. Lila was already engaged to a boy who kept waving at her from the other side of the room.

Marriage deals can take place when the kids are young, but they don't normally get married until years later. Many parents choose to do this to secure a prosperous future for their children. "After all," many a proud mother would argue, "who better to decide the person you'd be spending the rest of your life with than your own mama, right?" Divorce is a black dress of shame, and to a man a sign of failure. Also, having a fiancé keeps many teenagers from fooling around (even with the fiancé) and ruining their reputation. If rumors of indecent behavior reach either party's family, the engagement can be withdrawn, and nobody wants that kind of shame attached to their name.

It took hours for the toasts to make their way around the tables. But even as people raised glasses in blessings, the music continued. I loved the songs, even if I couldn't understand all the lyrics anymore. With time and little use, I was slowly forgetting my Rromanes—and it hurt my heart a little. This, I would learn, is similar to the experience of many Americans born into a multi-lingual family: even if they're taught the language of their parents, sooner or later English becomes their language of choice.

Lila's enthusiasm about the wedding, the food, the way the old people danced with their hands high up and rusty hips sway-ing drew tendrils of joy from inside me. In that moment, I was a Roma girl, no matter what I or others thought. The music espe-cially invoked that ancient feeling of belonging that makes us reach out for our mothers before we can see. The lilting melodies made me cry; they still do, as if the music reconnects a loose wire between my heart and my heritage. Next thing I knew, I was dancing.

And the dancing never stopped; not for hours. At some point, a wiry woman bumped into me. "You know, the Crimean Ro-mani are the best dancers in the world!" she bragged, and danced a *Chechotka*, a fast-paced tap dance, so fast I couldn't see her feet move. Entire families came out on the dance floor, babies bop-ping up and down in their parents' arms, men clapping their hands and women shaking their shoulders. We followed the cur-rent and the music carried us out to sea.

At around one in the morning the groom's father finally took mercy and shouted for the musicians to take a break, and every-one, breathless and sweating, found their places. That was when the grandmother announced it was time for the groom and bride to follow her out.

"What's going on?" I asked Lila.

"They have to pass the trial of the first matrimonial night. After that they'll officially be husband and wife."

"But I thought they were married at the church."

"Yeah, but they're still called bride and groom until they com-plete the trial."

I looked at the bride, whose face had lost some of its shine. "I don't think she likes that idea, whatever it is."

Lila giggled. "Yanko is going to stick his pole inside Madlena. I heard it's like being bitten by a swarm of bees."

"They have to do that now, in the middle of the party?"

"Oh yes, to prove the bride's innocence. You know. That she didn't let other boys do stuff to her. Then she'll turn into a true wife."

"Don't tell me someone's going to stand there and wait for her to turn," I said.

"You're funny," she said, and covered her mouth, but not enough to conceal the grin. "Grandma Polyakov will bring out the sheet, so we can all see the proof."

With the progression of the old woman's speech, the groom flushed like an overcooked beet. When he stood, she proceeded toward the door, expecting the newlyweds to follow.

Only they didn't.

"We've decided to skip that part," Yanko said. His fingers dug into the snow-white tablecloth. "It's our private business. No one else's."

Relatives and guests froze in their merriment. Both fathers scowled, something dangerous simmering beneath their furrowed brows. Mothers bit their lips and chewed their fingernails. "It's a tradition," one of them said. "I knew it," the other said. "Pass the vodka," someone else said.

The bride stood next, wrapping a hand around her husband's arm. To me, as she lifted her head up above the sea of disorderly Romani, she was the most beautiful girl in the room. "Please respect our decision," she said. The words could cut steel.

The house exploded with voices: arguments, jokes, threats. Yanko and his mother were trying to calm down his father. But the man bellowed, hands flying in gestures of stubbornness. The girl's father and mother elbowed their way in, and the parents began to thrust their faces at one another, their fingers jabbing like spears. Their rigid bodies left little space between them: mothers with hands on hips; fathers thin-lipped and ready to brawl.

Confusion reigned. I felt anxious as well, but I admired Yanko and Madlena so much that on the inside I was grinning. It took real courage to stand up to centuries of tradition. How did they do it, and in front of two hundred crazed Romani? I wasn't even brave enough to be honest with my own father, and there was only one of him.

When the newlyweds' brand-new Firebird—a gift from an overzealous uncle—screeched out of the driveway, the merriment fizzled out. The young couple made off with two suitcases and their dignity intact, while the guests continued to quarrel over the lost chance to witness a bloodstained sheet. Did that mean they would forever remain bride and groom, or were they truly married now?

From the car window Los Angeles flickered by in a post-midnight hush. I listened to Olga and Dad blame the parents for their offspring's disgraceful behavior, and listened to condemnation delivered through curses more appropriate for wartime deserters. This is what you leave behind when you dare to go forward, I thought: your name, in contempt for eternity. And on that night, I became aware of something I'd never given much thought before: oppression can come from within as easily as from without.

I thought about young Mr. and Mrs. Polyakov. Had they realized that their actions might have severed them from the rest of their family? I wanted to ask what they felt the moment they stood up and spoke their convictions.

What would it take to be as brave?

STEVART HOPELAND

The day of the talent show rushed at me with the speed of a comet, and all I could do was to hold myself back from telling Cruz that he'd won our bet. He had claimed we could never be just friends, and I was trying to prove him wrong, but to no avail. None of the excuses I'd made up to stop pining for him worked anymore because my heart yearned for his affections. Against all logic, I loved him.

I'd just finished playing my composition in the practice room. It was an instrumental piece steeped in months of writing love poetry. When Annie heard it later, she said, "It sounds like something from *The Umbrellas of Cherbourg.*" This was a great compliment. When Aunt Siranoosh first took me to see the French musical, I was eleven. The heartbreaking love between Geneviève and Guy had such an impact on me that I planned to one day run away to Normandy and find employment at the umbrella boutique Geneviève ran with her mother. Aunt Siranoosh knew the songs by heart:

> *If it takes forever I will wait for you*
> *For a thousand summers I will wait for you*

The movie burst with colors, and the music, like first love, was effortless. Annie's comparison inspired me to be a film composer and write sweeping scores that made people weep.

Cruz sat cross-legged on the floor.

"I want to kiss you," he said when I finished.

My head swam. "Did you like it? I wrote it for you."

"Can I?"

I closed the lid and sat down next to him, reached out, took his face in my hands, and kissed him.

He froze as if expecting me to realize what I was doing and draw back. Then his fingers curled in my hair and the ground took off from under me.

"Does this mean you lost?" he said against my lips.

"Maybe. But I don't want to have to sneak around. Sometimes I can't even remember which lie I'm supposed to tell on what day, and I don't want to have to lie about us."

"I never asked you to."

"Do you know nothing about my culture?"

"I'm not a coward."

He got to his feet, pulling me after him. He wrapped his arms around me and playfully rubbed his face in my hair. The heat of him filled my senses, lulling me into contentment, and I felt his heartbeat, quick and reassuring beneath my cheek. "I'll wait," he said.

Somehow tireless Mr. North had met Stewart Copeland, the ex-drummer for the Police, who had become a music producer, and convinced him to speak to the school band. There he was, with his signature spiky blond hair and the cool suit: the man who'd spent years making music history with one of the greatest bands in rock, only a few feet away from me.

At the end of the class Mr. North asked me to stay behind.

"Stewart, I'd like you to meet one of my most talented students," he said.

Copeland shook my hand. "Great. Can't wait to hear your music." I was too terrified to remember anything more except the astonishing end to our one-sided conversation, when he handed me his business card and said, "When you graduate, give me a call. Perhaps we can set up an internship."

Mr. North let me use his office phone to call Mom in Vegas, and I described to her how good Stewart Copeland smelled and how white his smile was. I also shared with her my plan to dazzle Dad by telling him about Copeland's offer.

After a moment of hesitation she said, "Why do you have this need to please him?"

"What are you talking about? This is a great thing, meeting Stewart Copeland."

"At your age I was already on the train out of Armenia. I was independent and strong, a free spirit. Do you think I gave a damn about what my family or the neighbors thought?"

"You made Grandma Rose cry," I said.

"That's what she told you? She was happy to be rid of the disobedient daughter. Aunt Siranoosh was her angel."

I wanted desperately to say that when she left for Vegas, I, too, cried.

"Mom—"

"I'm only telling you this because you can learn from my experience. Who cares what your father thinks? The only person he's ever been satisfied with is himself."

But I didn't understand. It had been months since I started the magnet program, and Dad still thought I was an ESL student. In my mind, the appearance of Stewart Copeland gave the program real legitimacy. It was a sign to tell my father the truth and make him see the potential in what I was doing. He'd forget his silly notions about it being an equivalent of the structured Soviet-era arts unions where creativity was restricted and indoctrinated by a select group of "experts." And that's when I'd mention Cruz, in passing, and everything would fall into place. Dad would be so happy and so proud of my mingling with Hollywood stars, he wouldn't mind a boyfriend (who was *also* a magnet student). Silly, but at the time this line of thinking made complete sense to me.

I came into the kitchen with a purpose in my heart. No fear.

Dad was talking on the phone long-distance with Olga's distant cousin Pavel, who planned to visit from Russia. When he hung up, he chuckled and said something about how he couldn't believe the guy had become a priest after chasing skirts half his life.

"Dad," I said in Russian, "do you remember the Police?"

"Police? Why, what happened? Where's your stepmother?"

"No, Dad. The band. Remember? With Sting?"

"Oh." He looked relieved. "Yeah, yeah. Good stuff."

"I met Stewart Copeland today."

"Who the hell is Stewart Hopeland?"

"It's Stewart Copeland, Dad. The drummer from the Police."

"Oh. Skinny guy with horse face?"

"He came to school today." I pulled out my treasure. "I have his business card."

Dad took it. He couldn't read English well, but his eyes narrowed as if the card held a secret for him to crack. He gave it back, unimpressed. "So plain. You sure it's the same guy? With the porcupine haircut?"

"He's a famous music producer now."

"Really?" That got his attention. "You met him, you say?"

"He came to school today, to talk about the industry," I said.

"A music producer with so much free time on his hands? I don't believe it."

"That's the thing. People like him make time to come to the magnet school. It's one of the perks of being in the program."

Dad poured himself a cup of tea. "And how did you get to meet this Hopeland, the big-shot music producer?"

I hesitated. He wasn't reacting yet, but the explosion couldn't be that far off. Here goes. "I was accepted into the magnet school at the beginning of the school year."

He stirred the tea, spoon clinking against the sides of the cup in a rhythmic staccato. It felt like forever before he came back to the table, cup in one hand, pipe in the other.

"I see," he said, and lit the pipe.

That's it? I'd prepared for a fight, made a list of solid arguments in my defense. But I had no idea how to handle "I see." To break the uncomfortable silence, I got myself a cup as well, making sure the tea was almost black and very, very sweet.

"Dad," I said, "this school is nothing like the music schools in Moscow. My teacher *suggested* I perform my own composition at the upcoming talent show. I can play whatever I want."

"What's this talent show," he said through pipe smoke. "Next you're going to tell me you've joined the circus. You have to have serious material before playing the stage; it must be exceptional."

In my father's eyes, I was simply never to be mistaken for a real musician. Who knows: had I been born a man, he might've thrust a guitar into my chubby hands and put me onstage next to him before I could walk. So many times I recall my mother begging Dad to teach me instead of the Soviet music instructors, who, though accomplished, all came off the same conveyor belt. I could hear them argue as I plunked away at my piano. "I don't have the patience" was Dad's favorite answer.

"I only want to play the show for practice, to get onstage

again, not because it means anything." It was a little white lie, but I was trying to pad all corners. "Mr. North thinks I have talent."

"Oh. Well. If Mr. North thinks so, then it must be true. Don't worry about what I think."

"Don't say that."

"It's obvious my opinion counts for shit. I *suggested* you learn the craft of divination, but I don't hear you singing praises for me."

"Things are different here. We're not in Russia anymore."

"You're so naïve," he said, shaking his head.

"I want you to be proud of me, and to trust me to do the right thing," I said. "We have to take advantage of being in this country, Dad. There are so many opportunities, but the thing is, we're on our own. Maybe back in Moscow, you and Mom could've used your connections to arrange for the best gigs. But if you haven't noticed, we're not living in Beverly Hills. Here, we're just part of a crowd."

Dad studied his hands for a long time. I'd rarely seen him so contemplative.

"Had I known," he said, "that my children would so easily submit to brainwashing, I never would've left Moscow. At least there I knew the kind of beast I was dealing with."

"So we're supposed to live like it's the eighteenth century?"

"I'm all for progress," he said, raising his fists. "Grab it by the horns, I say. But not at the cost of losing your heritage."

"It's medieval."

"Someday you'll think differently—"

"I really doubt that."

"And it's for that day that I want to prepare you, so you don't blame me for not teaching you anything about the medieval ways of your people." He pushed the chair back, peering at me as if he'd had a revelation. "By the way, that's the most ridiculous notion I've ever heard, especially coming from my own daughter. You do realize there are many professional Roma out there: scholars, business owners, teachers, and scientists. Just because some of us practice fortune-telling doesn't mean we roam the streets and live in fields like rabbits."

"I didn't mean it that way," I said awkwardly. But thanks to Olga, images of colored wagons were never far from my mind.

"You do understand that what Olga and I do is business."

"But you believe in all that stuff. In Baba Varya's curse."

"Millions of people believe in God and in aspirin. Do you call them fools?"

"But it's music I want to learn," I said. "Why can't you teach me that?"

"Oksana, I might've only finished three grades, but I've taught myself six instruments. On my own. I can sight-read any piece of music you put in front of me. If you truly love it, you'll learn with or without me. But I can teach you something more unique, a craft that's part of your heritage as much as the stage. It's what I can leave you. It may not be much. If you want to call my knowledge medieval, that's your choice."

I was subdued by his words, shamed. Even as I didn't think I fit in with my Romani heritage, it fit in with me. I *was* the clay.

"You're right," I said.

"I know," he said. "So. Here's my proposition. I'll teach you the psychic arts, and if at some point you decide they're not for you, I'll respect that."

"What about my school?"

"You can stay, even though you know I won't like it—"

I jumped off my chair and hugged him. "Thank you!"

"And I expect you to do your best."

"So I can play the talent show?"

"Fine, but I tell you one thing. These 'shows' are gonna fill your head with ideas. In real life, you must fight your way to the top. Just because someone said you have talent doesn't mean you've got it made. Talent is only ten percent; the other ninety percent is perseverance. Never forget that."

Even as a little girl, I knew to seek Mom for comfort or encouragement. For the longest time I thought that fathers simply didn't do the whole nurturing bit. Then, when I was eleven, my friend Elisa's mom committed suicide inside their Moscow apartment. Elisa and I found her in bed with a cluster of empty med bottles on her nightstand. Elisa's father—a real-life lumberjack—turned into a drunk after his wife's death, but the agony that crippled him during that time didn't stop him from taking care of his daughter. In fact, he smothered her with affection, transforming overnight into a devoted mother hen. After that I concluded that it must be my dad alone who didn't do mushy. But in his way, Dad loved me. I knew it to be true every time he made me honey tea when I was sick, and when he created a set of illustrated flash cards for my fifth-grade languages-class project, and when he remembered to put on music after tucking me and Roxy in for the night.

It had become a ritual for the three of us. Dad would begin with a story that he'd make up on a spot. Something like "There once lived an old man. He liked to smoke his pipe while taking a walk down the village road every night. And on one of these starless nights, he fell through a hole in the ground, so deep that when he looked up, the opening appeared the size of a saucer." And the old man's adventures took us to magical lands that only my father knew. The music, like Dad's tales, helped my sister and me sleep. Piles of tapes eclipsed our cassette player like plastic mountains above a blacktop lake, but out of all that music I can recall only George Benson's *Breezin'*, Al Di Meola's *Elegant Gypsy*, and, most of all, the home recordings of my own father's music.

———

Dad and I had made our first compromise. Wasn't that proof that there was hope for us still?

I was sure it was as I waited for my turn to go onstage.

As I took my seat at the piano and broke the silence with the first note, the anxiety that normally jerked through my blood during a performance started to fade. The first few measures I treaded with care, the long pauses like tiny trampolines of encouragement. And soon the melody unfolded from the nerves in my stomach, out my fingertips.

There was absolute quiet backstage as the MC announced the first-place winner in the instrumental category. We listened to that voice like it was about to reveal the formula to eternal life. I dragged each breath through a thick brush of panic. If I've messed this up, I thought, I'll be the youngest person to die of a heart attack. A loss to someone more worthy didn't bother me, but I was terrified of losing to myself. In front of Dad.

"And the first-place trophy goes to . . ." Paper rustling.

Applause shook the auditorium, coming from every direction at once. A girl who had sung a Vanessa Williams ballad nudged me. "Hey. Isn't that you?"

Stupefied, I nodded and staggered toward the front of the stage through a tangle of curtains and nerves. How could my piece have won against Mozart's "Turkish March" and three impeccable "Moonlight Sonatas"? When I finally found my way into the spotlight, I took the trophy from the vice principal, who grinned at me and clapped. The sound of his voice congratulating me was drowned out by the applause still rushing the stage. Taking a bow into the auditorium, I gripped my trophy, searching for one face in particular beyond the blinding lights.

After the show, I sat on the concrete steps of the theater, which had long since emptied. Streetlights had flicked on, and the roads buzzed with tourists drunk on Hollywood, blaring TLC or

Mariah Carey or Tupac as they drove past. I watched the cars, my mind drifting.

I'd put the date and time on the calendar in the hallway between the kitchen and the garage, I was sure I had. It was a Russian calendar with jokes and sayings for every day. Some jokes were hilarious; others Dad or Olga tailored to their own brand of funny, which usually involved ass and the many ways of assaulting it.

He must've not noticed the date. Maybe he hadn't checked the calendar that day.

I'd been so absorbed in my thoughts, I hadn't noticed Cruz holding a sheaf of roses a couple of steps down from me.

I suddenly remembered that I'd never mentioned him to my father during our talk. But maybe just as well. He hadn't looked like he was paying much attention, anyway.

Cruz joined me and put an arm around my shoulders. We stayed there for a moment not saying anything, and I lay my head in the crook of his neck. It was one of the many things I loved about him, his easy way with silence.

Later he said, "You know, I recorded the whole thing. In case you want to show it to anybody."

I started to sob.

"Come on," he said. "Let's go home."

COMRADE PUSHKIN

When I was twelve, three of my Russian classmates, Lena, Galya, and Valya, had found it necessary to perform a séance. These girls normally didn't associate with Gypsies, but in this case they'd come to me for help. Back then, though the physical attacks had stopped (Nastya had transferred when her military-pilot father accepted an assignment in the city of Vladivostok near the Chinese border), I was still the official class freak, the Soviet Wednesday Addams, and therefore the only person who might know how to contact someone who'd been dead for a few centuries. I had never actually performed a séance, but it had to be done. For school and a shot at popularity, so elusive.

My parents were away that week, and they had taken Roxy. I was staying with Esmeralda, but she was hardly around, busy trying to get her boyfriend back after breakup number five. In light of all that, my house was the perfect place to convene with the netherworld.

The girls wanted to talk to Alexander Pushkin, the great Russian poet who'd died in a duel for his wife's honor, and whose *The Captain's Daughter* was an assignment in our Russian literature class. Our teacher, Evgeny Vasilyevich, who wore the same brown suit every day, was expecting a three-page essay on the significance of the main character in relationship to the political climate of eighteenth-century Russia. Since none of us had a clue, we had decided to ask the author himself.

After school we ran to my house. Our uniforms, brown with black aprons, created a woolly sheen of sweat on our backs from springtime humidity and excitement.

My stomach swam. I shut the windows, drew the curtains, and locked the doors.

"You sure it'll work?" one of the girls asked as I lit candles around the immediate area.

"I can do this in my sleep," I lied. The girls were very influential in my class and I hoped this favor would be repaid in time.

We sat on the floor in a tight circle in a darkened room. Flickering lights tossed off by the candles reached up to the ceiling and cast an eerie glow, sizzling on occasion. It seemed they made the only noise in the room full of awed expectations (girls) and camouflaged panic (me). I concentrated on the materials: candles—check; spooky, dark atmosphere—check; a piece of white paper with an alphabet circle in the middle—check; the plate, which Dad had strictly forbidden me to touch—check. Dad's divination saucer was marked with a pencil-thin arrow. The girls passed it around, the proof of my family's nuttiness right there in their hands.

"We must begin," I said. "Make sure nobody leaves before we're finished. We don't want the spirit following us around because we forgot to send it back. Do you have the questions?"

Lena handed me a paper. "Copied it straight from Evgeny Vasilyevich's assignment sheet."

I laid it out by the plate and took a deep breath, then exhaled. If I were observing myself from afar, I'd say I was in the zone of deepening spiritual awareness, movements deliberately slow, eyes downcast and heavy. But in truth, I was stalling.

"We are calling to the spirits of the ether world," I said finally, trying to remember the things Dad usually said on such occasions. "Please convene with us."

Nothing. I, for one, was glad.

"We're calling on the spirit of Alexander Pushkin," I said. "Comrade Pushkin, we seek your guidance."

I had always wondered why mediums used such formal language during a séance. I wondered especially because it was difficult for a twelve-year-old to find enough words in that category. After several attempts to convene, and at least a dozen requests for guidance, the girls became restless.

Until a door somewhere in the house, unseen by us, opened. And shut. The candlelight bowed low, never a good sign. No one spoke, always a bad sign. My heart hammered behind my ears.

"Something just brushed against my back," Valya whispered.

That's all it took. The four of us scrambled up at the same time, screeching, arms flapping. Panic squeezed us in her tight fist. Bumping, elbowing, we ran for the front door. Never mind that it was only ten feet away. We crossed Hell to get there, and sprang upon that doorknob.

"Pull," I screamed, but the girls kept pushing, pounding against it as if expecting it to change its mind and open. "You're going the wrong way! The lock. Let. Me. Unlock. The. Door." My fingers, groping for the lock, worked in slow motion against the chaos of screaming faces and wild hair, all erratically seeking safety. Finally I threw the door open and we spilled out.

In the front yard, we took painful breaths, our faces red and sweaty.

"We didn't finish," I panted. "Have to. Go back."

Galya bent over, holding her side. "No way," she said. The other girls agreed.

If I didn't think fast, they'd leave. "Fine," I said. "Just don't blame me if Pushkin follows you home." It took some creative thinking to get them to change their minds and help me. Mentioning the possibility of a wayward spirit playing house under their beds did the trick. I myself wasn't sure if we had in fact made contact with a spirit, but I wasn't taking chances. If something did come through, we had to send it back or I'd be grounded for at least a week.

The problem was that I had no idea how to do that. Dad used to read some sort of an incantation at the end of each séance, but I never got close enough to hear the words. Three faces stared at me expectantly, and I collected my crumbling poise.

"Don't worry, our house is protected. Besides, Pushkin liked kids, right?"

"Probably," Lena said, hopeful. "He did write that *Tsar Saltan* story." To the Soviet kids, *The Tale of Tsar Saltan, of His Son the Renowned and Mighty Bogatyr Prince Gvidon Saltanovich, and of the Beautiful Princess-Swan* was the equivalent of a Mother Goose nursery rhyme, although a bit more violent. Reading this folktale was like watching a modern soap—mystery, betrayal, murder, love, magic, and redemption, it had it all.

In verse it tells of three sisters, the youngest of whom marries a king and by doing so enrages her older siblings to such fits of envy that they conspire to kill her. The lilting prose is as familiar to me as a childhood lullaby.

Three fair maidens, late one night,
Sat and spun by candlelight.
"Were our tsar to marry me,"
Said the eldest of the three,

"I would cook and I would bake—
Oh, what royal feasts I'd make."

Confident of Pushkin's kindheartedness, we advanced toward the house. Once in the foyer, I bounded into the kitchen and raced back with a bundle of kitchen towels. I handed one to each girl. "We must open all windows and doors. Swing the towels in the air like you're chasing a fly. At the same time order Pushkin to get out of the house. Be respectful but firm."

The draft picked at curtains and rustled papers. We tiptoe-rushed from room to room, swatting our towels at the invisible entity. "Please, Comrade Pushkin, get out, go back home, leave us alone, we order you." After what I thought was an adequate time, I announced that the house had been cleansed and hoped for the best.

That was my first and last attempt at leading a séance, and I can still recall the feeling of complete helplessness that had overtaken me. I'd acted brave in front of the girls, but I didn't sleep for days, my blanket stretched tight around my body, waiting for an infuriated genius of Russian literature to turn up in the middle of the night and terrorize me into schizophrenia. I wanted to be accepted by my peers, but I would've preferred to accomplish that by more conventional means—perhaps by letting them wear my Michael Jackson "Thriller" jacket for free. All I knew was that I never wanted anything to do with channeling again.

But in L.A. it was impossible to avoid. Dad's cases became increasingly bizarre, the way he talked about them even more so. Once, he walked away from a channeling session with soot all over his face. "One of the fucking saucers busted into powder," he said, wetting the kitchen towel and dabbing at his eyes.

"Aren't the saucers made of crystal?" I asked.

The towel was turning black as he wiped. "Evil taints everything one shade."

Sometimes I heard screams gust from behind the séance-room doors, or muttering, unarguably even more chilling; other times things shattered against the walls. All of a sudden I was back in Moscow, quaking in my bed with my blanket the only shield against the horrifying sound tracks of some horror flick my parents were watching. They'd marathon three or four films in a row. The groans of the dead, a screen voice splintering me with "Whatever you do, don't fall asleep," would douse me in gallons of sweat. "They're gonna turn it off soon. They're gonna turn it off," I'd chant with my arms wrapped around my knees.

But the show at my father's house did not come with a guarantee that in the morning I'd pick up the VHS tape that had bullied me all night and scold myself for being such a baby. My fears began to resurface, and like back in Moscow, they were compounded by the effects of listening yet being unable to see. For whatever reason, I'd thought that if only I could take one look, my eyes would bring into balance the reality my ears had twisted up. Soon I had my chance.

Tanya, a recent Russian immigrant, had come to my father almost six months earlier, complaining of nightmares that left her physically bruised and mentally exhausted. She claimed to be haunted—terrorized, even—by her ex-husband, who had died in a car accident after a fight over Tanya's infidelity. She believed he was now punishing her for inadvertently causing his death.

Tanya wore her chestnut hair short, in the latest Italian fashion. She worked as a fashion designer, owned a home in Pasadena, and had a fiancé who was a successful screenwriter. Within a few months of her nightmares, all of that had changed. She had lost her job and was on the verge of breaking her engagement.

My father first used hypnosis through guided breathing techniques, in case Tanya's problems stemmed from stress. When that didn't work, Dad and Olga visited Tanya's home and cleansed it by burning sage and sprinkling every corner with holy water the way many spiritual practitioners do. For weeks they chanted and prayed over her. But whoever the malefactor was, it did not relinquish its hold on Tanya.

When my father first heard Tanya's story, he attributed her claims of a possession by her ex's vengeful spirit to feelings of guilt over his death. As time passed, though, he started to consider that she might've been correct all along. There is a widespread Romani belief that we are continuously observed and judged by spirits. Unlike many other cultures that entrust their fate to an ethereal army of gods and angels, Romani culture concedes that our own ancestors and departed relatives hold most of the immediate power over our daily lives. It is the centuries-old concept of karma, only the rewards and the punishments are dished out by our own ancestral spirits. If we live a moral life, these spirits protect and guide us, but if we stray, their retribution can be destructive. According to this belief, intuition is a spirit steering you in the right direction; all you have to do is listen. Therefore, every event in our lives, be it a lucky draw or a deadly accident, is a direct result of our own actions.

Late one evening Tanya stormed into our house uninvited. I was talking on the phone with Brandon but, noticing Tanya's violently shaking hands, quickly told him that I had to go. Olga spoke in quiet, soothing tones as she led the distraught woman to the table and offered her tea.

"Victor left me," Tanya said. She couldn't sit still, like a junkie in need of a fix. She strangled her teacup, barely managing to take a sip. "I can't eat. I can't sleep. I can't look in the mirror."

Olga narrowed her heavily penciled eyes, studying the other woman closely. "We'll call on the spirits and recite the prayers.

I'll give you some more of the cleansed earth to scatter around the outside of the house—"

"It doesn't help," Tanya growled. She leaned across the table, staring crossly at my father. "You're not doing shit. Just taking my money. Using me." Her voice dipped into a lower register on that last word.

Goose bumps fleeted up my arms. I had distinctly heard a man's voice, and I knew I hadn't imagined it. Especially not after the worried looks exchanged between Olga and my father.

He rose with a heavy sigh. "Tanya. We haven't taken your money since our first visit. Here." Out of his wallet he pulled a hundred-dollar bill. "You can have it back. We only want to help."

Tanya snatched the money, ripping the bill into tiny pieces. She stuffed it into her mouth and chewed with satisfaction.

I made a move to leave, but my father motioned for me to hang about and observe. I could feel my bones shaking like dry leaves. Standing in the kitchen doorway, I remained so still that I could feel sweat crawling inside my clothes.

Olga guided Tanya to take another drink of the tea. "We're your friends. We're Tzigane. You know what that means."

Tanya swallowed the last of the bill. "The Devil's people," she said. Face shadowed with sinister delight, she followed my father's every movement as he sat back down. Suddenly she closed her eyes, fighting to stay awake, chest rising and falling with each audible breath. Her sighs boomed in my ears. When she looked up, her features grew hard and pale. "I will never leave, you know," she said.

The experience of seeing a human taken over is nothing like in the movies; reality is more terrifying than artifice. The brain shuts down, its logic shocked into a corner, and the only part still coherent is the most primitive you, the emotional you, the one you can't control. Zhanna and I once had a conversation about what people feel seconds before they die. We were both convinced that even if death is sudden, there must be something inside us, something on the most primal level that senses the end but can do nothing to stop it. Zhanna speculated that the fear gripping a person in that moment is what kills them, before death itself. "It must be the God of all terrors," she would say, "to have that kind of an emotion rip through you." That's what a possession is like, only drawn out into more minutes than you think you can handle in sanity.

We might choose to forget that every human being has a piece of evil stashed inside, but when revealed, it is a possession, an undeniable Hell resurrected if even for an instant. It's Hell gnawing at your skin with the face of a friend. It's yourself resolving into thousands of prayers. And it's you realizing those prayers are like Styrofoam swords that kids wield on the playground.

The weapon is only as strong as the imagination.

Olga poured more tea into Tanya's cup. This time from the cobalt teapot, the one used to calm down the most disturbed. The liquid inside was an infusion of valerian root and lemon balm. "Come on," Olga said. "Try this."

But Tanya's attention centered on my father. Between them a silent dialogue was taking place. "Call any one of your little bitches. They can't make me go. Maybe I'll even stay here. In your house. For a while."

"Nobody's asking you to leave." My father was too calm. He didn't look frightened, but watchful and cautious. "Why not let the girl go? This is Hollywood. Here, your choices are endless."

"She's my wife."

I felt the tension between them, an invisible tug-of-war. The Russian woman gulped the tea with a challenge in her upturned chin and spit onto the floor at my father's feet. He never reacted, just kept making polite conversation.

After a while, Tanya's eyes began to droop. She bared her teeth at Olga. "*Eb tvoyu mat'* (Fuck your mother), you rotten Gypsy bitch. You spiked my drink!" With a string of more colorful expletives than a Russian taxi driver could learn in a lifetime, she finally keeled over, facedown on the table.

My father picked her up and carried her into the séance room.

"Oksana, come," he shouted about halfway down the hall.

Dad instructed me to make sure and stay in the corner no matter what. He then lowered Tanya onto a chair, around which Olga poured a thick rope of salt. "It's okay to be scared— natural," he said to me. "If you know what to do, fear can be dealt with."

"I don't wanna deal with it. She's freaking crazy," I said. "I would rather learn tarot cards and tea leaves, not this."

With a measurable degree of haste, Olga moved about the room, preparing the candles and pouring holy water into tiny saucers. She halted. "Not crazy, Oksana. Tormented. Can't you see how she suffers?"

"I don't care," I said.

"Shame on you, Oksana. You're Romani. Don't forget about our agreement."

"Dad. Please."

"I'll make a circle around you, too," Olga said, and laid a gentle hand on my shoulder in passing. "Just in case."

Though I was ready to protest further, Dad gave me one stony look to indicate the end of the conversation. He pointed to an empty chair and I obliged, mouth dry.

"Before you learn how to swim," he said, "you must first jump in the water." Opening the prayer book, he called to the three spirits and then to the demon residing inside the Russian fashion designer from Pasadena.

At first, nothing happened. The quiet frayed my nerves. Thick, smoky ribbons from the votive candles gathered as though drawn by fear.

Tanya moaned. Then she cackled.

"Dad," I said.

"We should begin." My father turned his attention to the crisp yellow pages of his book—Baba Varya's book, which had always smelled like the inside of a tomb.

Olga picked up a cross from the nearby table and dangled it above Tanya's slumped figure. She recited the prayer of Saint Benedict, patron saint of the poisoned. Her voice floated melodically over another moan.

This is not real, I told myself, shutting my eyes against the being inside the circle. Tanya lifted her head. I knew, because I couldn't quite keep my eyes closed. It is easier to stare fear in the face than to hear it lurk around you. Slowly, her gaze crept about the room.

The candles seemed to be releasing too much smoke, filling my nostrils, creating a stifling cocoon around me. Of course, I knew better than to ask for a cracked window. During an exorcism, all windows and doors must remain shut.

Except for the steady murmur of my father's prayers, the room grew even quieter; so much that my ears went numb. Then I heard another moan. This one more forceful.

Tanya's eyes caught mine. She was right there, hair a bit disheveled, most of the tomato-colored lipstick left back in the kitchen on the rim of her teacup. Yet something else peered out at me from underneath her lowered lashes. Her mouth turned down at the corners, and a long sigh escaped her lips. Everything she did appeared to be in slow motion.

Despite the way my pulse thrashed, I glowered right back at her. What was it Dad had said about not showing fear?

Tanya's gaze slid to my father. "Aren't you going to ask my

name?" she said. Raising her hand, she tried to grab the sleeve of his black jacket. She halted inches away from him, then sneered at the line of salt around her. "Look at me, fucker." She began to hum a song every Russian child knows by heart.

The horned goat is coming to small children. Her legs go . . .
clop, clop!

I clenched my teeth so hard that my jaw pulsed.

Her eyes go . . . blink, blink!

Dad kept chanting.

To those who don't drink porridge.
To those who don't drink milk.
To those children she will go . . . butt, butt, butt!

The moment the spirits entered the room, I felt their presence in the air prickling around my shoulders. Tanya flinched, almost as if she heard an unpleasant noise that hurt her ears.

What the spirits lacked in physical form, they made up for in the powerful presence of their energies. They rode the candles, forcing the flames to bend in obedient horizontal lines.

Tanya jerked her head from left to right, watching something invisible to my eye fly outside her reach.

"I thank you, Avadata, Azhidana, and Kevoidana, for acknowledging my plea," Dad said. Taking the cross from Olga's fingers, he dipped it into the three saucers filled with holy water. He handed it back and came around to face Tanya. "Release the physical body and show your true self."

The voices I heard came from somewhere within Tanya's circle, but none of them sounded like her. Then came the knocking, traveling around the room in an uneven, syncopated rhythms.

"Release the physical body and show your true self."

Tanya's fingers bent into arthritic claws.

Suddenly she crumpled to her knees and started to gag. Her body convulsed with dry heaves. Something invisible to my eyes pounded on her back, but her face remained set in stone, void of any outward signs of agony.

Time dragged. I tried to swallow again, my throat scorched with panic, and wiped the sweat from my palms.

Tanya kept throwing up. After a while, the wooden floor inside her circle was sullied with tiny puddles of bile. My own stomach churned.

It seemed like nothing else could possibly come out of her body when a dense puff of smoke escaped her lips, followed by another. With a sob, Tanya collapsed. The orbs hovered, held captive by the salt.

"In the name of the Father, and the Son, and the Holy Spirit," my father said. The final prayer was recited faithfully. Dad and Olga continued it through the earsplitting wails, the source of which I could not locate. They grew frenzied, like the screeching of cats.

Dad and Olga prayed, their eyes closed, heads bowed in concentration, and I with them. They still murmured after the noise abruptly ended. The candle flames reached their swaying bodies up toward the ceiling once again. The spirits had gone and so had the demons.

Judging by the candles' half-burned stems, a few hours had passed since we started. It felt like an eternity. I raced out of that room as soon as I could move my legs. And from that day on, no amount of Olga's marriage threats and my father's reminders of our deal could make me agree to learn the craft.

PAVEL

The exorcism spooked me for a long time, even more so because it actually worked. Soon after, Tanya moved back to Russia, health and happiness restored. But in Los Angeles, nightmares still drove me to cower beneath my blankets. Every minute of that experience played through my mind like a car crash, frame by frame.

I prayed that my father would stop performing exorcisms, but after Tanya, the word of his expertise spread. Soon more clients came for help. Some demanded he sign a vow of secrecy, to protect their identity lest they end up in *The National Enquirer* under the headline THE BIG HOLLYWOOD SO-AND-SO TURNS TO GYPSY PSYCHICS TO RID HOME OF DEMONIC INVASION.

If done through religious means, an exorcism has to be sanctioned by the church higher-ups. The priest requesting it must attest to the need. On average it takes months to hear back, and frequently the requests are denied based on insufficient evidence. Dad's clients could not wait.

Once, he confided in me that 90 percent of the "possessed" were not possessed at all. Many suffered from psychological disorders such as depression and simply needed a mental nudge in the right direction—a spiritual purge, if you will.

After a particularly draining session, he'd often admit that the line between Hell and neuroses got so blurry that he didn't know what kind of treatment to provide. Regardless, he always advised his clients to see a doctor before his sessions. A strong mind and a healthy body are more likely to withstand possession as well as illness.

When Dad first started getting into the more serious stuff, he took every safety precaution he knew. But like a cop desensitized by the daily atrocities he sees, psychics too frequently experience unwanted aftereffects. Dad and Olga cleansed the house at least three times a week to get rid of any spiritual residue left over from clients. This was done with incantations and the burning of special herbs. But as time passed and they continued to fight, they started to neglect their own rules, and the atmosphere inside the house began to rot.

It is difficult to explain, but if you've walked into a mortuary and felt the heaviness in the air, or if you've ever left a mental hospital and breathed easier, then you'll know what it was like inside that house. It felt like a dumping ground for all the garbage that people carried in their souls. They came, unburdened their troubles, and left happier. Meanwhile, the black muck accumulated in the corners of our house.

I found even more excuses to get out, preferring the company of Cruz and Annie to that of my family when I wasn't at work or school; they'd become my sanctuary. Olga discovered more illicit gambling halls to pour her savings into. When the money ran out, her diamond rings vanished one by one. Dad, preoccupied, didn't seem as keen on teaching me the craft anymore. He found more gigs and more women. On occasion I'd hear him mention Baba Varya's curse. He felt that his neglect of it was bringing this odd unrest into our house. We didn't set the table as often, but then again, the guests didn't stay as long as they used to.

It was during this time, at the beginning of my senior year, that Olga's cousin Pavel finally came to visit from Ukraine. He was tall and thin-boned, with the best posture I'd ever seen in a man, the imaginary string at the top of his head taut all the way to Heaven. A giant bushy mustache drooped over his upper lip. When he ate, some of the food hung off it like a stranded climber. I felt embarrassed to mention it. He was a priest, after all.

"Throw away that book and light a candle at your church" was the first thing he said after Olga gave him the details of her and Dad's business.

We had moved into the living room after dinner one night. Dad and Pavel reclined on one of the leather couches, and Olga took the one across. I'd brought out a tray with tea and pastries and offered our guest a cup, an eldest daughter's duty that I usually disregarded. At this, my father lifted an eyebrow; my noncompliance had become legendary among our guests. But that night I had my reasons. I found Pavel's profession strange but also a most fortunate coincidence. Who if not a priest to talk sense into my father? On several occasions I wanted to ask if Pavel had proof of his vocation, a wallet-size seminary diploma, perhaps.

When I was a little girl, Pavel was one of the best dancers in Grandpa's show. His Gypsy flamenco shook you like a hurricane taunting roof shingles. His polyrhythm (tapping two different rhythms simultaneously) was legendary among the Tzigane.

My first memory of Pavel was of watching him adjust the small oval plates at the bottom of his high-heeled flamenco shoes before one of the shows. He sat in a chair, one foot resting on the opposite knee with a shoe balanced on top of his shin. With a screwdriver, he was loosening the tiny screws on an ivory-colored tap.

"What's that for?" I remember asking.

Pavel lowered the shoe to the floor and beat it against the dusty planks, which produced two sharp raps.

"You see? Spanish dancers. Their sound is thick, heavy, because they use rows of metal tacks. But for a Rom like me to dance a proper *Vengerka*, these loose hollow plastic plates will create a crisper sound, almost like hands clapping."

Pavel was nearly as good at dancing as he was at stealing other men's wives. That's why for the longest time no one believed the rumors of his transformation. I remember the last time I saw Pavel onstage. It was the summer of 1984.

With a delicate caress of the bow, the violin began its song. The *Taborny* dance started off slow, with a woman's graceful hands and the froth of her emerald skirts.

From my usual spot in the wings behind the curtain, I watched the audience, because every time Rubina took center stage, people leaned forward in their seats. Her cat eyes slanted at the corners and she smiled down at the crowd, unfurling her arms with a swan's elegance. And it seemed that was all it took to enchant them further.

Most of the men in the ensemble were either in love or in lust with her. At least that is what Grandma Ksenia said. She did not approve of her presence in the troupe, but since Rubina was one of the most talented dancers, Grandma kept her opinions to herself.

At ten, I was old enough to understand the reasons behind her complaints. When Romani kids grow up on the road, backstage, in hotel rooms, they mature quickly. Not to say that our parents behaved any way they pleased. But when you saw a Romani perform, you experienced the range of pure, untainted emotion. You knew, through her voice, the sorrow for a lost love. Your heart flared at the rhythm with which his feet tapped out the beat of rage itself. Every performance was tears, loneliness, pleasure, delirium.

In a cloud of skirts, Rubina gave the stage one generous turn, her raven hair gleaming in the spotlights. With a shoulder-shimmy and a toss of that mane, she drew delighted shouts from the audience when she bent back until the top of her head brushed the floor and then straightened up in one fluid motion. One more turn around the stage, to catch her breath and for the audience to settle down.

At first Rubina did not notice when another dancer joined her: a tall man with burning black eyes. Tosi was her husband in real life, but during this number, I always forgot that he already had her. They regarded each other like curious lovers. The violin swept down into more opulent registers, and with a strum of fingers, a twelve-string guitar staccatoed underneath.

Husband and wife touched fingertips as the two instruments painted their melody with longing and uncertainty. Draping an arm around Rubina's waist, Tosi was determined to steal a kiss, but she fled his possessive embrace to where I stood hidden in the wings, and I reached out to feel the silk of one beaded sleeve.

Another guitar announced a third dancer. Judging by Pavel's arrogant stance, his polished boots, and a fine shirt the color of garnet, he was rich and wanted for nothing. Until now. The three dancers gathered, Rubina in between her two Romani suitors, and the music ignited like a flash of dynamite, setting the audience ablaze with the struggle of wills onstage.

The men circled. With a sharp whip, a pair of shiny knives appeared in their hands, and they lunged and parried on the wings of jealousy and lust. Rubina drove her way between them. Just as Tosi jabbed his knife.

I heard a collective intake of breath as Rubina's lifeless body slid to the floor and the music dropped away.

The audience was silenced, bound by shock: something every

artist yearns for and dreads. One by one, the people stood, and my heart jumped as if my own life depended on their reaction. The dancers stepped to the rim of the stage to take their bows, faces flushed with elation to mirror that of their admirers, but they didn't hold hands, and I caught Rubina smiling at Pavel the way she should've been smiling at Tosi.

Taborny *dance*

I remember that on the morning after the concert, the ensemble members gathered in scattered groups in the hotel's crumbling courtyard. The bus that would take us to the nearby village for the day's performance waited at the sidewalk. Its faded yellow paint and wide but uncomfortable seats gave an impression of a public bus well on its way to retirement. No surprise there. Not many Soviet artists traveled in style back then.

As I came out of the hotel lobby and headed for the ancient clunker, I felt a nervous kind of energy among the performers. I should've been used to that, since this group's comings and goings resembled a long-running soap opera. I found my mother smoking Cosmos by a white marble fountain of a sputtering merman. Aunt Laura gave me a tight smile as I joined them.

"Gone? Are you sure?" My mother's face registered worry. She glanced back toward the hotel doors.

"Tosi's drunk. You know that's never a good sign," Aunt Laura said, leaning closer with a conspiratorial pursing of lips. "Lenka said she saw Rubina and Pavel talking backstage last night."

"Talking is no crime."

"But the rumors."

"Mom, what happened?" I said.

"We're leaving in a few, Oksanochka. You better go find a seat."

As I started toward the bus, I heard a loud shriek and turned around to see Tosi storming out of the hotel lobby and down its uneven stairs. In one hand he gripped an ax.

Mom pressed me closer to her, hands on my shoulders. "My God, how can this be happening. Who gave him an ax?"

"Probably swiped it from the custodian's closet," Aunt Laura said.

Four men followed behind Tosi as he made for a lonely cluster of taxis at the far end of the parking lot. Like an ocean tide, the rest of us rushed after.

"They're gonna get arrested," someone exclaimed.

I fought my way to the front of the crowd gathering around the taxis, just as my grandfather's voice thundered above our heads. "We have a concert tonight. You're not going anywhere."

Tosi's pupils swayed before settling on my grandfather. "That son of a whore stole my wife."

"We'll deal with this after the concert."

"You think I give a fuck about your concerts?" Tosi said, spittle flying from his lips. "What am I supposed to do, wait until all of Russia knows I've been cuckolded?"

Nobody spoke. Confrontations with the leader were a rare occurrence. The fact that Grandpa stood well over six feet intimidated others enough to think before arguing with the man. But Tosi, who in different circumstances never would have crossed his boss, glared at the older man with a stubborn mix of desperation and principle. "Fire me if you want, but I'm going after them."

My grandfather studied Tosi with a frown that could split an oak.

Ivan, the accordionist, stepped out of the crowd. "Andrei Vasilyevich," he said respectfully to their leader, "I know where they've gone. Pavel's cousin has a house only two hours from here. Let me go with him. We'll be back in time, I promise."

My grandfather raised a hand against an onslaught of incoherent protests. "Quiet! This is not a free show for the *gadjen*," he said. A mute congregation of passersby watched while pretending not to. "All right. You." Grandpa pointed at Ivan. "Make sure you get back to the theater no later than six, and for God's sake, take that ax away from him."

"Got it," Ivan said.

"And don't let him drink any more."

Ivan shoved Tosi into the taxi, but the man refused to give up his weapon. "He'll sober up on the way. Everything will be fine."

"Leonid and Stepan will go with you. No fighting. I'm not bailing anyone out of jail."

Once the taxi disappeared around the corner, everyone piled into the bus. Subdued Roma make for a troubling sight. The theater was about an hour's drive down unpaved roads, and we bounced all the way there. It was a wonder people could actually perform after the miserable experience of that bruising ride, but then again, most of us were used to these conditions. Someone usually found something to complain about, even if only to break the monotony of riding through the bullion-colored fields of wheat stalks shimmying hypnotically in the wind. But not this time.

As was customary, most people were onstage doing one final run-through before the show. Only the kids and a few of those who had finished rehearsing were backstage when the men barged in through the back door.

Tosi dragged his wife by her hair down the dark hallway between the dressing rooms. Shrieking, she fought to steady herself, her fingers clawing at his hand. I was shocked to see that all her beautiful hair was now gone, chopped off into a disheveled mass of uneven clumps. A Romani woman's hair was her pride, her greatest asset. If cut short, it was like the letter "A": a telltale sign of adultery.

Splatters of blood stained Tosi's white shirt. He still had the ax, and Pavel was nowhere to be seen. The men followed behind with somber expressions.

Fear-stricken, I pressed myself against the wall in order to let the group pass. Given the ragged state they were in, my mind immediately painted a picture with Pavel's decapitated body as its focal point, and I made a quick sign of the cross, forcing the image out.

I was about to take off in search of my parents when Aunt Laura rushed by me. "What did you do?" she asked Tosi. In the gloom of backstage lights, her face lacked its normal healthy glow. "Where's Pavel? *Devlo*. Did you kill him, you idiot?"

Ivan tried to get Tosi to loosen his grip, but failed. "Pavel's fine. A few missing teeth and a face not so pretty anymore. But he's fine." He tugged on the ax. "All right, *chavo*. That's enough."

"I'll decide when it's enough." Tosi jerked and shoved his

friend back. "You think I'm drunk?" His lips thinned in a challenge. "I know exactly what I'm doing."

Down on the floor, Rubina sobbed. Between a wail and a cry, she whispered, "What have I done?"

"Shut up, witch," he growled, but his voice came in a hush, drained of the rage I had heard earlier that day. "How could you betray me like this? How could you shame me? I'd do anything for you. Am I not enough that you have to fall for that shit-eating skirt chaser?"

"Please, Tosichka. My love. My golden. Please, forgive me." Rubina's eyes pleaded. She wrapped her arms around her husband's legs. "Let's be happy like we used to be."

"I should've killed the bastard." Tosi tossed the ax to Ivan.

Ivan shook his head as he caught it. "Hospital food will finish him for you."

With the ax gone, Tosi's face softened around the drawn lines of his mouth and eyes. He pulled Rubina to her feet. Tears ran down her flushed face in tracks of black mascara. He wiped at them with the sleeve of his shirt, silent, wide-eyed. He stroked her hair, burying his face in it. By now quite a few people were watching, but the couple might as well have been standing in the cosmos of that wheat field we'd passed on the way. As tension slipped out of the hallway, jokes bounced back and forth.

After the incident, Rubina and Tosi danced with the unbridled fire of newlyweds. After the well-deserved thrashing at Tosi's hand, Pavel never came back. Another dancer took his place. This one was bowlegged and married to a fierce Romani with a gap-toothed smile.

Now a sort of quiet intelligence filled Pavel; a peaceful tranquillity that made people respect him without him uttering a word.

There was nothing left of Pavel the dancer, and I fancied I could see a window in his eyes that led straight to Godly wisdom.

He stayed in L.A. for more than a month and tried to convince Dad and Olga to give up the black craft. Not everything, just the heavier stuff. They might not make as much money playing weddings and reading palms, but at least they'd have their sanity.

Dad resisted, but Olga listened to her cousin intently, her chin propped up in her hand. And so did I.

"It's one thing to toss a card spread or to read a cup once in a while," he said. "But when you engage in demonic communication, you endanger yourself. The control is an illusion."

"He's right, Dad. Don't you feel it?" I said. "I can't even sleep in this house anymore."

Dad fixed his eyes on me. "I made a mistake, I admit. I never should've let you sit in on Tanya's purging."

"You did what?" Pavel crossed himself. "Are you daft, man? She's a child."

"Well, nothing happened. Oksana wasn't ready. Next time—"

"There's no way I'm going through that again." I hadn't expected to speak my mind in front of a guest, but his presence solidified my decision. I would not be learning the craft.

After that conversation Pavel woke up before sunrise and spent his mornings in prayer. The first few times I saw him, head bowed over hands, I thought it was part of his job, an early-morning ritual. But once, I heard him whisper Dad's name, all of our names, and I realized: he was praying for us.

WHERE I FINALLY SAY IT

Pavel returned at last to Ukraine, and to my astonishment Dad was contemplating the man's advice. He finally admitted that he might've gotten himself involved in things better left alone.

It was 1993, my senior year. Finals hovered. My father's question nagged at me. It was one thing to rebel against my family's ideals, but when it came down to it, what exactly did I plan on doing instead?

Strangely enough, it was Brandon who helped me answer that question.

Annie, Cruz, Alison, and I were shooting pool one evening on the back patio of Annie's house.

Brandon showed up wearing a long black dress with lacy trim at the sleeves and the hem. He carried a thick packet under one arm. "So, I've decided," he said, flopping noisily into a lawn chair, then sat up and patted its neighbor, waiting for me to sit next to him.

"To join a convent?" Annie said.

"Bitch." Brandon blew her a kiss and turned back to me. "You, missy, are going to college." He handed me the packet as I sat down.

Dad once told me that when he tried to get into some big-name Moscow university, an admissions counselor told him that Gypsies were better off sticking to what they did best: making the music that Soviets loved so much. Although the man didn't mean to be insulting, my father never forgot it.

"I don't know," I said. "Don't you have to pay like a gazillion dollars for college?"

"Not if you qualify for a Pell Grant," Brandon singsonged.

Alison huffed. "Nice. The foreigners get free school. I was born here and I had to write a fucking essay to get a fucking scholarship." She'd been sitting on the edge of the pool table, uncrossing her legs every time Cruz walked by.

Annie took a shot at a green ball, then straightened. "Don't listen to her. She's bitter because her parents are sending her to Oklahoma State instead of to her grandmother's in France." The ball bounced off one side and came to a stop inches in front of the intended pocket. She stuck out her tongue at Cruz after he nudged the ball in.

"Do you have a major in mind?" Annie asked me.

"You." Brandon snapped his fingers at Annie, shifting his legs under a sea of lacy hem. "Don't pressure her. We still have time."

"Did you guys take that career assessment yet? I got arts," Annie said.

"Me, too," Brandon said. "Way to go, girl. I see a Vegas burlesque in our future."

Alison began preening as Cruz came around the table corner to take another shot. "I got modeling," she said.

"You liar. There's no modeling category in those tests."

"Yes, there is, Brandon. I'll show it to you."

"What about you, Cruz?" I asked.

"Oh, no. You guys leave me out of this."

Once he said that, everyone wanted to know.

"Fine, but don't laugh. Biotechnology."

Brandon pealed with laughter until his eyeliner ran and he started coughing. "Sorry, I'm sorry," he said when Cruz gave him the finger. "It's just . . . I can't even pronounce that . . . without imagining you in one of those cute lab coats and goggles. Okay, okay, I'm stopping." He cleared his throat and took a long drag from the joint Annie passed him. Exhaling slowly, he said, "Right now," and then giggled again.

"Guys, I remembered something funny." Alison jumped down from the table. "When I lived at Grandma's in Paris, we'd go to the local café in the mornings, and every time, a gang of street Gypsies would start begging us for money. Mostly kids. And they'd grope me with their grimy fingers. I'd wonder why their parents didn't make them bathe. But then Grandma told me they stayed dirty on purpose; that way an outsider couldn't identify them if they stole something."

"Alison," Cruz barked. He'd stopped playing, and his cheeks had splotches of red. Something akin to that, red and angry, was spreading inside of me, too.

She continued. "Grandma told me the Gypsies would put a curse on us if we didn't give them something. She also taught me a trick to ward off their curses."

The roof of my mouth grew as ashy as a chimney.

"Every time you walk by a Gyp, you take two fingers and place them here." She started to rub her fingers inside her inner thigh. "Like this."

I jumped her, my breath snagging on flames. My fingers ripped at her silky hair, and when I wrapped my legs around her middle, we toppled over. Everything around me blurred. Only her face remained in focus, like a clear bright chip inside a kaleidoscope. I slapped at her, clumps of her hair tangling in my sweaty hands. I was screaming things in Russian, oblivious to everything else. Alison punched me in the mouth. Pain pricked against my skin. The others were shouting for us to stop. But the loudest noise was my own heartbeat, my own blood.

When Cruz tore me away from Alison, it was only a few moments into the fight, but I felt like we'd been at it for hours. His arms steadied me and my rage retreated.

Alison sobbed on the floor, her face angry pink and bloody where my nails scored tracks. "Get that fucking bitch away from me," she screamed.

Cruz dragged me toward the front door, but all I wanted to do was rip out Alison's tongue by its root. I hoped she knew now that she'd been taunting the wrong Gypsy.

Once on the sidewalk, Cruz firmly led me away from Annie's house.

"My backpack," I said, wiping my eyes with my shirtsleeves.

"I'll bring it by tomorrow. Come on, I'll take you home."

I shrugged away. "You're always taking me home. Is that your answer to everything? In case you haven't noticed, I've been known to find my own way. Isn't that amazing, someone so primitive with the ability to follow a sidewalk?"

"Your lip is bleeding."

"I'm gonna go now." I started down the street. The energy that had propelled my fury earlier had drained. My legs turned cottony. The left side of my face began to throb and I tasted blood.

"You want to talk?" He was following a few feet behind.

"Can't you leave me alone?"

"That's the question of the day, isn't it?"

When we got to my house, lights behind the curtains suggested that people were up. I felt like shit and probably looked worse; no way was I going through the front door.

"My window should be open," I said.

The screen came off easily, and I slipped inside. I turned on the closet light, which glowed softly but wasn't bright enough to be seen from under the door. "Come on," I mouthed, and motioned for Cruz to follow me.

He stood just outside, hands in the back pockets of his jeans. "I should go."

I stuck my head out, elbows on the windowsill. If my father heard voices outside my bedroom he'd definitely investigate, so I whispered, "I didn't mean to go off on you like that."

"Don't worry about it." He crossed his arms. It was the first indication that I might've truly hurt his feelings this time. When I said those petty things I hadn't given a thought to how callous they must've sounded, that here was a guy who'd been listening to my bullshit for three years now and yet was still standing outside my window.

I reached out and wrapped a hand around his forearm. "Please stay."

He didn't say anything, but climbed in. The sill was higher on the inside than it looked and he tumbled to the floor. I grabbed him and we both went down, me shushing, him laughing.

A few minutes later we were sitting on the floor face-to-face while Cruz cleaned the blood off my lip. The closet light drew shadows around us. My face throbbed even more than before, and I winced every time he touched it.

"Hold still. Here's something to distract you."

I felt him press a piece of paper into my hand. "What is it?"

"A surprise," he said.

I scanned the contents of the wallet-size note, barely making out the scribbles. It read:

To Oaksana
Steve Perry
Journey

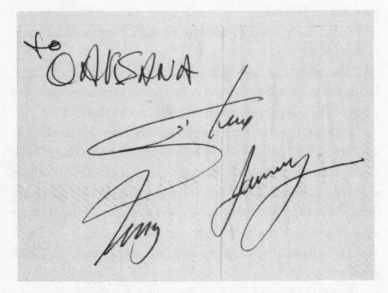

"I can't make out the name."

"It's from Steve Perry. You know, the singer for Journey."

"Oh my God. How did you get it?"

"Believe it or not, we were having lunch at the same restaurant, and I harassed him until he gave in. But he did misspell your name. Sorry about that. I was going to ask him to rewrite it, but he threatened to call security."

"Wow, I have Steve Perry's autograph. Did you touch him? Kidding. This is amazing."

Very gently he felt the puffiness around my lower lip. "I can't believe you jumped Alison like that—not that she didn't deserve it. You're a fierce Gypsy warrior woman."

He dipped a clean tissue in the glass of water sitting on the floor by the bed.

I followed the motion of his hand. It kept me distracted from the way he sucked in his cheeks in concentration. Our knees touched. It felt like I was being pulled to him by a rubber band stretched tight around us. Did he feel it, too? His fingertips brushed my face as he continued his ministrations, leaving strokes of tingle on my skin.

"Sometimes I wonder why you're still here," I said.

"You know why."

"I haven't told my father about us." I had thought earlier that I had the strength, but then the right time never appeared.

Cruz let his hands fall. "There's nothing to tell, is there?"

If I could've come up with a perfect excuse for my silence, I would have. Anything to erase the hurt from his face. But I didn't think that would be fair. "Before, you asked me to be honest," I said. "That's what I'm trying to do here."

"Yeah, I just didn't expect you to be this honest. I thought you'd eventually fall for my animal magnetism." He grinned for a second, then went back to cleaning. "So what now?"

"I don't know. The logical thing would be to stop seeing each other."

"Why?" When I shook my head, he took my face in his hands. "What was the first thing you thought when I asked you that? Don't think about it. Just say it."

"My mother ran away with my father," I blurted out without thinking at all. It came as naturally as if the words had always hovered above my head, waiting to be acknowledged. "She claims it ruined her life. By listening to her impulses, she left herself behind."

Cruz let go. The look on his face startled me, as if I were a fortune-teller who'd revealed a secret of his that no one could've possibly known. It compelled me to load the silence with chatter.

"I've been thinking of moving to Vegas after graduation. Maybe take Brandon's advice. College sounds like something I could do." I didn't tell him that most likely I'd have no choice. My mother would never let me forget our agreement, and besides, someone needed to be there to intercept the liquor bottles.

"Isn't that kind of like running away?" he said, tossing the crumpled, bloody tissue on the floor.

"Don't say that—"

"Come on. Stay here."

"And do what?"

His shoulders tightened and he pulled away from me as if I'd slapped him. "You can be so fucking cold sometimes." Rising from the floor, he pulled the window curtain aside. "I'll see you later."

As always, I'd managed to make a mess of things.

I grabbed him by his shirt. "No, I'm sorry. I didn't mean it that way."

But he wasn't listening, already halfway out.

"Wait. I love you," I blurted out so fast that even I wasn't sure how it happened.

"Say that again."

After climbing back in, he leaned on the windowsill and in a somber tone said, "One more time. I don't think I heard that right."

And so I stopped searching for fault lines in Cruz's belief in our future together. If nothing else, I thought, I could learn a thing or two from him about trust. And when I said, "I love you," I meant it. I loved him the way we do before we learn to classify emotions according to our expectations.

One evening while taking a walk down Hollywood Boulevard, we came across a homeless man propped up against the wall of some posh restaurant. He was missing one sneaker, but his clothes, a denim shirt and jeans, were surprisingly clean of the encrusted grime you'd expect on someone roaming the streets. He peered sightlessly into the distance. People passed, some dropping coins on the sidewalk beside him, but Cruz slowed down and then crouched in front of him.

"Hey. You okay, man?" Cruz touched the man's shoulder. "You need help? Some food?"

The stranger's eyes focused and he sat up slightly. "I'm . . . What day is it?"

Out of the blue, he began to sob, the smell of liquor on his breath like a blow from a shovel. Cruz took him by the elbow and helped him up.

"Come on. It's way too cold out here. My house is just around the corner."

"Are you sure?" I whispered after Cruz had left the man in his kitchen to grab a towel from the linen closet. "What if he's a serial killer or something?"

"Did you see the ring on his finger?" he said. "He's not homeless."

Cruz sat across the table from the man, I leaned on the kitchen counter, hands gripping it at my back, and we listened to the man's story, because there wasn't much we could say to make anything better. He'd been drunk for days over the loss of his wife, murdered a year before.

"I don't know what to do next." Ted rubbed his eyes with the heels of his hands.

"When I was eight," Cruz said, and cleared his throat, "my mom one day left for her sister's house and . . . she was gone."

Tears bloomed in my eyes. Cruz's gaze was fixed on the table's smooth surface. "She didn't just leave. The Manaus police aren't interested in what I think."

I imagined Cruz as a kid, thinking he'd been abandoned until he was told a truth even more terrible.

"I stopped going to school, so Papai sent me here. Before I left, he said, 'Nothing in this life remains unchanged, *o meu menino*. Not even mountains.'"

We didn't see Ted after that night.

But after the revelation of Cruz's secret—his missing mother—many things about him made sense. The snapshot pinned to his bedroom wall was more proof of his state of mind than anything he could've said. I'd never imagined that his sympathetic nature was born out of something more than a carefree upbringing. Instead, it concealed heartbreak. I called Zhanna that very night.

"How do you always manage to fall for these unfinished boys?" she'd said. "Ruslan and now this . . . this *Brazilets*."

"They're not unfinished. What does that mean, anyway?"

"Men without mothers. Their souls are split, unlucky. That's why Ruslan is haunting you still. You're the only woman who loved him."

I rolled my eyes at the phone. "Come on."

"*Bez materinskoy lubvy malchiki stanovyatsa slomannimi muzhchinami* (Without a mother's love, boys grow into broken men)."

"We're in control of our reality no matter what our families are like, and Ruslan is in Russia, all the way across the ocean."

"I told you to get that scarf back," she said.

The conversation was taking a familiar turn, but this time I didn't try to change the subject or make jokes the way I had done in the past.

"I want you to do something for me," I said.

"I'm not digging up graves."

"Can you burn my journal?"

There was a pause, and I waited for her to start cursing in Rromanes the way she did when particularly annoyed.

"Forget the scarf. Burn the book, okay?"

I love my cousin for not seeking an explanation, for not gloating because her crazy ideas might've gotten to me. The burning held meaning in ceremony alone. There was no magic attached to it, but when she called me back some days later to tell me it was done, my room seemed brighter and the colors more solid. My own reflection in the dresser mirror was that of a young woman with fewer shadows in her heart.

With Cruz, for the first time I felt free to remember that trust was as necessary as air. It'd do me good, I finally decided, to try on a bit of happiness. Maybe I was stitching up the tear in my coat, and who knew, maybe I could help Cruz heal, too.

We spent most of the rest of the school year together.

I began to sneak him into my room while my family slept. We broke rules. We were reckless. Cruz brought tapes and books, and bottles of the Yoo-hoo I loved. And I called him a dork for it. We lay on the floor, chilly-hot where our bodies touched. We shared headphones, listened to music, and got drunk on kisses and chocolate.

Cruz kept trying to convince me to tell my family, chastising me for losing my courage.

Turned out I didn't have to, because my father found out for himself.

One February afternoon he woke up early, around five, and walked in on Cruz and me smooching on my bed. He swung the bedroom door against the wall so hard it nearly came off its hinges. Olga peered from around his shoulder, and at the sight of another man's naked chest cried out, *"Nu ty dayosh'* (Well, how about that)!" Cruz had little time to collect himself before my father had him by his hair and me by mine. Olga forcefully nudged him away from us, but nothing could get through to him now.

Roxy, who'd come to visit for a week, ran into the room in the princess pajamas she had on all day, her ponytail skewed to one side.

"Stop, Papa. Stop!" She pulled on Dad's pants, but he didn't even acknowledge her presence.

"*Nu pezdets tebe ublyudok ti yobanniy* (You're fucked, you fucking mongrel)!" He hurled Cruz into the hallway. Before I could run out, he pushed me back into the bedroom and slammed the door in my face.

I scrambled for the window, but before I could climb out, Olga pulled me inside by my hair.

"Let go, Olga."

Roxy, who was still in the room, forgotten by all, squeezed in between us and yelled, "Leave her alone!"

Like Dad, Olga ignored my little sister, yanking at my hair once again. "What do you think you're doing?"

I twisted around, gripping her hands with mine, but no matter how I pleaded with her, she wouldn't get out of my way. When my eleven-year-old sister called our stepmother a bitch, Olga finally threw her out of the room.

Eventually the noise outside the door subsided. I crumpled up on the bed. After a while I stopped wiping away the tears and let them soak into my pillow.

When I woke up, the house was quiet. I was alone. Fear had settled inside my rib cage. Olga came in with a tray of food and set it on the desk.

"Where is he?" I asked.

She clucked her tongue with her hands on her hips. "*Ay-ay-ay*, Oksana."

"What did he do to him?"

"Don't even think about going out that window," she said when I moved. "We know where he lives. Trust me. You don't want your father anywhere near that boy right now. His mood is black enough for murder." My father bellowed for her from the other end of the house. Olga answered and turned to leave. "It's obvious you're ready to marry. But now that you've lain with some *gadjo*, who hasn't as much as a decent family to his name, who'll have you?"

I smashed the tray against the door as she closed it.

For two days I was a prisoner. Dad refused to talk, wouldn't look at me. I was forbidden to go out, even to school—especially not to school. Olga created a long list of chores for me to do as punishment, and that kept me busy: scrub the floors, wash the windows, and serve as much tea as was required. On several occasions I started to explain to them that Cruz and I weren't doing anything wrong.

My only companion was Roxy. We weren't supposed to be talking, so she sneaked into my room when everyone else slept. My little sister did her best to cheer me up with stories of Vegas and her many friends. She told me about our mother building a cardboard prototype of an automated slot machine she called a "talking slut." (I'd tried to correct her pronunciation, but I eventually gave up.) I found the idea brilliant: a customer could play with it as if it were a living person. Quite sure her invention would change Vegas forever, Mom took the talking slut to a casino manager. "He laughed at her," Roxy whispered to me. "Told her that people don't come to Las Vegas to hear machines talk." Several years later talking sluts popped up all over the valley, and Mom was furious enough to boycott casinos for a whole month.

"Let's play video charades," Roxy said.

It was a game we'd made up years ago in Moscow when one of Dad's friends brought a pirated VHS tape with six hours of music videos. They'd been recorded straight from MTV, commercials and all. Roxy and I wore that tape out until we could act out every video. She loved to sit on the floor and guess which singer or group I was. I'd bound up and down as if on coiled springs and shake my imaginary skirt, singing, "Girlz jus vanna hav fu-un." Roxy'd jab a finger at me. "Crazy lady with a partially shaved head!" Or I'd spin around with "Youspinmerountrount bround round round—" "Girlyguy!" she'd scream. "I knew that one right away!"

Our all-time favorite, now that I think back, was my rendition of Def Leppard's "Pour Some Sugar on Me." Wearing a mop head for metal hair and one of Dad's leather vests, I'd squeeze my fists in front of my face and shout, "Put that *shuba* on me." Which literally translated into "Put that fur coat on me."

I wished I could seize those carefree moments and play with Roxy like I used to, but I couldn't get the image of my father beating Cruz out of my mind.

"I don't even remember how to play it anymore," I said.

Roxy frowned and then jumped off the bed to strike a pose that I immediately recognized as a move from Michael Jackson's "Thriller."

"Chamon," she said. "I'll go first."

Three days later my sister went back to Vegas and Dad spoke his first words to me. "You've shamed this family."

I was cutting onions for beef stew on top of the wooden counter extension. The onions intended to squeeze every last tear from my eyes, and a flood of emotion pushed dangerously against the back of my throat. "What family?" I blurted out.

His chair creaked as he leaned back. "What does that mean?"

"The family you walked out on, or the one you and Olga are doing such a great job destroying?"

"Our affairs don't concern you."

"But they do." I left the knife on the board and turned around to face him. "You think because we're kids, we don't understand things. We watch you people rip everything apart without a thought for what it does to us, and we can't do anything about it."

A shadow of sadness flitted across my father's face before it hardened. "Don't try to manipulate this conversation. It won't work. I'm an adult and I know more about such things. Young guys like that have only one thing on their minds."

The floodgate inside of me had been opened and I couldn't contain the stuff spilling out. "All this time you're too busy to talk about anything. You let Olga plan out my life, and now suddenly you have wisdom to share?" I couldn't believe I was talking like this to my own father. He looked as surprised. "I didn't do anything wrong," I said.

"If you think sleeping with some nameless *gadjo* is right, then I should've listened to Olga a long time ago and married you off."

"He's not nameless," I said. My ears burned with humiliation. "You taught him, remember? You, who never let me touch that guitar unless I'm polishing it! I didn't sleep with him. And he's not a *gadjo*, he's Brazilian, and I love him!"

"He's a bastard asshole motherfucker. If I see him again I'll snap his neck like a pretzel."

"Why, Dad?" I sat down across from him. "Why can't you see all the good things I've done? Why is it so hard for you to trust me, to believe I'm smart enough to make the right choices?"

"You're a girl."

"I'm your daughter."

"And your mother's daughter."

"And *your* daughter," I repeated.

"A daughter who disobeys at every turn." He sighed. "Would it be asking too much to have had just one boy?"

"I can do as well as any boy. Look. I found a job, on my own—"

"A job I forbade you to keep."

"—and I got into magnet school without any help—"

"Yet another thing you did behind my back."

"—only because I wanted you to be proud of me," I said.

"Where does the lying end, Oksana? You ask me to trust you. How can I trust a child who cares nothing for my opinion? What else don't I know?"

"You don't know how much it hurt when you didn't come to last year's talent show. I got a personal note from the principal herself, you know. You were supposed to be there."

"Is this what it's all about?" He slapped his knee. "A high-school talent show? That was months ago. What's the use bringing it up now?"

I reached out and covered his hand with mine. His skin was rough, sprinkled with coarse hairs, his fingers square-ended. A tattoo of a lute, hand-poked many years ago, had faded into gray.

"Trust me, Dad. I've got a good head on my shoulders. Even when I argue with you, I still understand that you want the best for me. Everything you say counts. But I'm not going to live your life, or Mom's life. You guys had your chance."

"But you must accept our guidance. You're a girl, and there's an army of assholes out there."

"I will make mistakes. Please, let me. I do love Cruz but I won't act stupid just because of it. And I'm playing this year's show, and I want you to know that if you don't come it's okay. I might even end up working at some Vegas casino for the rest of my life. But that would be my choice. Isn't that what you always wanted from Grandpa?"

With an overcast face, my father stood up and walked away.

Cruz kept calling, but I could never get to the phone before Olga snatched at it. When Annie called I was allowed a five-minute supervised exchange.

"Are you all right?" she said.

"Fine. You guys?"

"Cruz is going fucking berserk here. I haven't heard so much dirty Portuguese since Cousin Roberto's jail stint two years ago."

The phone clicked and bumped.

"Do you want me to come get you?" Cruz's voice. "It's my fault. So fucking stupid."

But I knew if fault were a name tag, it belonged on my chest. No amount of running could separate me from having kept a secret I knew would crush my father.

Dad and I didn't speak to each other for days, and I didn't dare see Cruz. But then one evening Dad called me into his studio. The sun crested the horizon, and the gold-threaded curtains sparkled in its rays. Dad sat at his desk, flyers spread over its surface like a lettered tablecloth.

"I've decided to stop the exorcisms," he said. "You think I should call the newspapers first and change the ad, or reprint the flyers?"

"There's a copier I can use at school on lunch breaks," I said cautiously, and he handed me the master file.

SIGNS

With only two months of school left, Mom began to call more frequently than she had during the entire two years we'd been apart. Every phone conversation, she turned Rumpelstiltskin on me. "Now give me what you promised, little princess!" I think what she enjoyed even more than my impending move was my father's failure to bring me over to the dark side. But she had one, too.

By this time, I had no doubt that Mom was an alcoholic. Roxy often called me in the middle of the night to report Mom's activities, which included hiding out on the balcony in the middle of the night with a snifter and a cigarette. But I could tell Mom wasn't all right, even over the phone. Not only did she slur through the majority of our conversations but her personality changed faster than I could keep track of. Within five minutes Mom could go from loving and enthusiastic to bitter and detached.

My mother had been my idol when I was a kid. Spirited and fierce in her love for her family, the woman could do no wrong, and anyone who claimed otherwise faced my wrath.

"Your mother came home at four in the morning," Grandma Ksenia once said, batting at the flies with a rolled-up newspaper as she, Zhanna, and I walked home from the farmers' market one morning. "She was doing figure eights down the sidewalk. I hope none of the neighbors was awake to see it."

At twelve, I'd grown skin thick as an elephant's as a defense against Grandma's cutting remarks. But telling me I'd have better luck acquiring a well-paying profession (a city bus driver, for example) than a good husband was very different from criticizing my mother's walking, or drinking, habits. Only I could do that.

"She must've tipped at least two bottles of vodka."

"No, she didn't. She made borscht this morning," I said, because no one in their right mind would set out to create Grandpa Andrei's favorite dish while nursing a hangover.

Grandma paused and clucked her tongue at me, then switched the sack from one hand to the other, fanning herself with the same newspaper she'd bullied the flies with.

Zhanna, routinely at the edges of these kinds of conversations, looped her arm through mine and tugged, an intervention she'd attempted too often for someone so young.

"Mom's fine, and maybe you shouldn't spy on people at four in the morning, Grandma."

"She's an alcoholic, that's what she is. That's a sure way to lose a husband. My Valerio could've found himself an actress from the Bolshoi if he wanted to. With a stipend and a vacation dacha out by the lake."

"You're jealous because everyone in the band likes Mom more than you," I said.

"Oh, look, a pigeon." Zhanna tugged harder, but I resisted.

"Your tongue is a kilometer long. Just wait until I tell your father how you disrespect your elders. See if he won't take away that blasted jacket of yours. See if he won't."

For two years, I'd waited for Mom to discover she hated passing out change in casinos, but as the end of the school year approached,

I saw that she had no intention of returning to Los Angeles. I felt guilty even considering going back on my word and worried about her, but I despised the idea of moving to Las Vegas, away from everything I'd come to love.

Then I received a letter of admission from the University of Nevada, Las Vegas. My parents, busy reconstructing their own lives, didn't get involved in my college selection, so the decision was left up to me. UNLV was the only place I'd applied because I had no idea you could apply to more than one school, and I didn't bother to ask a counselor. But maybe on some level I always knew I'd end up in Vegas.

Annie and Brandon were starting general courses that fall at Pasadena City College. Suddenly, we were all growing up.

One evening, in celebration of our imminent descent into adulthood, we went out for sushi. Annie picked a tiny place hidden in the basement of the only apartment building on the block, the rest of the street lined with sagging and decrepit houses.

Cruz came, too, wearing a pair of black slacks and a merino V-neck that matched his eyes.

The atmosphere at the table felt vaguely tense and uncomfortable. We talked about the weather and our Shakespeare teacher, who always smelled of pot. And about our American history teacher, who had asked the question "Is life fair?" on a test, and had taken points off for everyone who answered "Yes," noting "How about now?" in the margin.

Cruz joked around in his easygoing way, but he had bags under his eyes and kept making excuses to leave the table.

Ever since I had told him about my letter of acceptance, he'd acted more withdrawn. We were still together, though we made sure my father had no way of finding out. It wasn't so difficult because Dad now spent so much time in his studio writing depressing love songs and horror-film scores, he wouldn't have noticed a tornado ripping by. Cruz and I avoided many things during those last few months of school. I think we both felt something bad coming. When I brought up Vegas, he'd make a phone call to Pizza Hut and get all buddy-buddy with the person taking the order, or walk out of the room, claiming a headache.

"We can visit," I said once. We were up at Griffith Observatory, on the lawn at the foot of the Astronomers Monument. The night sky slumbered above us, and I leaned back on my elbows to watch it take star-sprinkled breaths.

Sprawled on the grass next to me, Cruz teased the fragrant stalks with his fingertips.

"I might be going back to Brazil."

"Why? When will you come back?" But of course I knew the answer.

"I have some things to take care of."

I turned to look at him. Was he going back for his mother? In the dimness of the observatory lampposts, his face was that last fragment of light before the camera lens twists shut. Soon I'll never see him again, I thought, and blinked to shake it off.

After we were found out by my father, the weight of guilt and the constant presence of "What if?" had packed on me like wet snow on a tree branch. Like my parents had done, I was going against my own parents' wishes, and the fear of someday telling my children "I could've been somebody" began to draw me away from Cruz.

Throughout the meal, the very last we'd have all together, we conversed in a light tone, as if my move to a different state and his return to Brazil didn't spell "breakup" in capital letters. No one at the table asked what we were planning to do.

After hours of strained niceties, Cruz finally laid down his chopsticks. "Can we talk?" he asked me.

We took the stairs up to the sidewalk and began to walk. The air promised rain, and I breathed the dampness deep into my lungs. The houses on this street looked frozen in the fifties, complete with brick trim and giant porches, but many had overgrown front yards.

"Are you mad at me about Vegas?" I finally asked. "Is that why you decided to go back?"

"No," he said. "I saw your father earlier today."

"What?"

"I asked him if we could get married."

I was so shocked, I dropped down on the porch steps of someone's house. "Why would you do something like that? Without asking me first?"

"You drive me crazy, you know that?" He ran a hand down his face and then gestured at me like I was deaf and he had to get my attention somehow. "*Merde!* Did you hear what I said? Your father pulled out a fucking broom when he saw me."

I didn't know what to do, what to say, if I should be mad or flattered.

"What did he say?" I was curious. I couldn't believe Cruz was still alive.

"He said, 'You keep dream, small boy,' and then threatened to call the cops."

I covered my mouth. I couldn't help it. The first giggle rolled out of me, along with some of the tension.

He stuck his hands deep in his pockets and looked around. "I'm glad I can amuse you," he said, trying to hide his own smile.

I went to him, wrapping my arms around his waist. I was still laughing softly, my eyes watery from it. "You are brave, small boy. Brave and completely insane."

"I must be." He pulled away. "So?"

"What?"

"Isn't this what people do when they love each other?"

"And then they divorce—"

"I'm going back to Brazil for sure," he said. "After graduation . . . And I want you to come with me."

Raindrops began to fall softly around us. Goose bumps covered my arms—whether from the sudden coolness or Cruz's offer,
I could not tell. Wouldn't it be something, though? If I said yes,
I'd be the third generation of women in our family to defy her
parents and run away with a man.

"I'll have my own place—our place. I'll buy you a piano and
you can play for me all day." He ran his hands up and down my
arms, palms hot and so familiar. "Come on, we'll be together and
nobody will tell us how to live. I can take care of you."

I closed my eyes against the image. It was dangerously appeal-
ing. But could I really go from my father's house to my husband's?
Not yet.

"I love you so much," I said.

"Don't say that."

I went on, despite him asking me to think about it first. "If we
stay together, we'll burn out. One day everything will spoil and
we'll hate each other."

"Why are you talking this way?" He shook me. "This isn't one
of your Gypsy voodoo tricks, is it? I don't believe in that bullshit,
and neither should you."

He caught my right hand, slipping it under his shirt to his
chest, and held it there.

I pressed my palm to his skin, our fingers intertwined. Spirals
of heat tingled up my hand, his heart lunging at me. His eyes
pleaded, and I begged him to let me go. Instead, he held me in
tight embraces and whispers. These are the things I remember
most: his lips imploring against my ear, in my hair, and the silly
way I kept kissing him and pulling away at the same time.

"It's late," I said. It was a stupid thing to say at that moment, but I couldn't let him change my mind. "We should get back to the restaurant."

His hands fell away, carving an empty space between us. The rain fell harder. For the longest time we stood inches away from each other without touching or speaking. I hugged myself, my body shaking.

He shook his head and walked away without a backward glance.

Within a month I lost more than ten pounds; scrawny did not suit me. For days I wore a shirt Cruz had left months ago under my bed. Sometimes I'd stick my nose in it and try to extract a ghost of his scent from the unwashed fibers. His absence drained every bit of fight out of me.

At the end of the school year I found Mr. North in the main auditorium rehearsing the graduation ceremony with the senior class of 1993. The theater boomed with voices. The chatter of those waiting for their turn onstage kicked up to the rafters. Mr. North clapped the beat to "Pomp and Circumstance" for the piano player, a Korean girl whose lower lip jerked every time she popped a chord. I approached the stage, and when Mr. North saw me wave at him, he broke the melody. "Take five, everyone."

"Why aren't you in cap and gown?" he asked, jumping off the platform.

"I'm not going to the graduation ceremony."

He cocked his head. "You're not?"

"Yeah, you know, there's so much packing to do still—"

"You have to. What will your parents say?"

We took two seats in the front. I hadn't thought our discussion would last more than a minute. Who could expect a teacher tasked with organizing sex-crazed teens into model citizens to play shepherd to one?

"My parents said they're not coming."

What a gifted liar I'd become. I had never actually told my parents how seriously Americans took their high-school graduations, that they wore special gowns, and that the wimpier ones bawled, clutching beribboned scrolls to their chests. If I had, who knows, they might've come. But then again, neither Mom nor Dad was big on ceremony.

In Moscow, at age twelve, I went to my music-school graduation. Solo. Mom was nowhere to be found, and Dad was in a "meeting" bargaining down the price of a Carver amplifier. The main recital hall was a blur of festively adorned families. A music-school diploma in the former Soviet Union was essential when gaining entry to any music conservatory, my mother's dream for me, and the administration went out of their way to show how high *their* diplomas measured. The room, lined with snowy-clothed tables, smelled like a bakery. Every which way you turned, another mountain of *piroshki* or crescent cookies soared above rosy teakettles, matching cups, and real silverware. Parents and teachers mingled over dainty serving plates. Students grinned in clusters of joy. One teenage girl with a giant red Mohawk allowed her mouth to split into a smile when her mother squeezed her shoulder at a teacher's praise.

I'd missed the ceremony, by the looks of it. With a pang of regret, I grabbed a potato-stuffed *piroshki* and zigzagged through the crowd.

Marina Nikolaevna, the school director, saw me and softly clasped her fingers over her middle (she always made the *piroshki*). Her wispy blond bun toppled dangerously to one side as she most likely tried to pin a name to my face. "I didn't see you at the ceremony, Lenochka." And failed.

"Mom and Dad are taking me to Gagri, Marina Nikolaevna, to celebrate the graduation. Could I get my diploma? We're on our way to the train station right now."

It felt perversely satisfying to hold that little black book in my hands.

Perhaps I should've insisted my parents come to my high-school graduation. I still lament not giving them a chance, as I've only recently grasped the significance of memory. Life is made up of sentiment yoked to flashes of recollection.

I took first place during that year's talent show, the last one I'd ever play. This time, as I crossed the stage to accept the trophy, my feet touched ground just fine. I gave a speech. That part is so blank, I fear it never happened and my imagination was shooting home movies behind my back. Cruz wasn't in the audience, and so I felt unfinished. Soul-split. We should've talked it through, made a gentle break instead of shattering apart as if cracked by an ax. Loss scooped me out, and I bowed to my audience with grace and smiles only for the sake of my father, who sat in the front row.

He stood up and clapped as I received the award.

"*Molodets, dochenka* (Good work, little daughter)!" I heard him shout, and the pain that had been suffocating me slunk briefly into the background. His showing up was so monumental that I promptly created an imaginary future where we'd jam during family birthdays and weddings the way many Romani do so effortlessly. Not until later did it come out that Mom had threatened to report Olga to immigration if my father dared skip the concert. For days after, he poked fun at the *samodeyatelnost* (amateur production) of the show. No matter. He was there in the moment with me. And I finally began to accept his nature and his clumsy love.

Later on, backstage, a classmate pressed roses into my hands. They didn't come with a note. I hadn't seen Cruz in weeks and so the flowers filled me with eagerness and anticipation, and I waited until the echoes inside the theater grew cavernous. He never showed. I walked through the dark hallway toward the exit where my father waited to take me home as though I were wading through miles of sand dunes. Cruz was, I was certain, too far out of reach now. But this was also a moment of clarity for me. I finally understood why I hadn't listened to my impulses and followed him to Brazil. Even though I loved him, if I married him I would lose this freedom I was fighting so hard to wrest from my parents. Our independence, our identities, would mesh and soon nothing would be left of me or him. My American goal, I realized quite unexpectedly, wasn't about becoming an American but about doing something I could never do as a young wife. Somewhere in this new landscape I hoped to find just one thing.

PIECES OF ME

The morning of my departure basked in the sublime weather that made California so irresistible. It was late May 1993. Palm trees murmured in the breeze and the distant buzz of traffic reassured all that Hollywood was being worshipped right on schedule.

Mom was driving in from Vegas to pick me up. I had only a few more hours before I'd be gone from Los Angeles for good.

Earlier that day Olga, the wicked witch of every direction on the compass, had tried to make conversation. She hinted that if I wanted to talk, she was there to listen. The notion of opening up to my stepmother was like eating a dish I'd never heard of. Was I famished enough to try?

I'd packed my two suitcases with Olga's help, which consisted mostly of her conducting and talking a mile a minute from the edge of the bed as if we were BFFs. I guessed it was her way of putting me at ease. Too bad she'd picked that particular day, though, when I could manage only short, simple responses without bawling like a seven-year-old whose bike has been stolen.

"All those ripped jeans. So unfashionable." She scrunched up her face at a pair of bell-bottoms I'd placed in my suitcase. "You're a grown woman now."

"I'm moving to Vegas, not Milan."

"It's a classy place. Here. I want you to have these." She shook out a pile of clothes she'd brought in earlier. There were a lot of shiny things with bells and sequins and golden thread. "Look. This one's gorgeous. I got it on sale in Beverly Hills." It was a dress covered entirely in metallic print.

I chuckled, probably for the first time in weeks. "I swear you were a freaking crow in your past life."

"If you must know, I was a Hindu prince with impeccable taste."

"I thought you were a male dancer, or was that in a different lifetime?"

She shrugged and dangled the dress in front of my face as if it were a chocolate bar, and wiggled her eyebrows. "Come on. You know you love it."

I shook my head and stuffed a Slash T-shirt inside my suitcase.

My stepmother looked disappointed, but only for a moment before grabbing something else, a deep blue skirt with splashes of gleaming beads. "What about this one? The color will look amazing on you."

"Maybe," I said carefully, because Olga was being way too nice and I wasn't used to it.

Pressing it against my waist, she said, "You can wear it when you go out to some fancy restaurant with your rich casino-owner husband."

That was a stab in the gut. Immediately the light mood evaporated and I was back to scowling.

She sat back down, hands in lap, mouth pursed. "You can always stay here with us, you know."

After a period of silence, I joined her on the bed, exhausted from thinking heavy thoughts.

"I saw him in the cards, you know," she told me. "Right after he started taking lessons from your father."

"You did a reading on him? You never told me that."

"Well, I did one on both of you. It's a professional habit."

I didn't want to ask, and started to get up in order to resume packing.

Olga squeezed my hand, urging me to stay. "You did the right thing, lambkin. He has a long journey ahead of him, and he must make it alone. Believe it or not, *your* destiny is in Las Vegas."

"Right. That's why you were trying to marry me off to a nice Roma boy."

"Never hurts to try," she said, waving it off like it hadn't created a near disastrous standoff between us. "But this. Yes, I see it so clearly. You will dream about it first."

"What the hell are you talking about?"

Olga wouldn't tell me, claiming she had to set the table for when Mom got there. She had a truce in mind and acted as if she were preparing her home for the queen herself.

I finished packing and came out of the bedroom. Dad was smoking on the living-room couch, staring out the window with a faraway look. Gray peppered his temples and beard more than ever. While studying his profile, I noticed how much he reminded me of Grandpa Andrei. I wondered if he noticed the resemblance when he looked in the mirror or noisily slurped his tea, or when he lectured me on tradition. Did it bother him to be so much like the man with whom he thought he had nothing in common?

Countless times I recall Dad breaking his father's staunchly conservative rules. When he tried, during one rehearsal, to incorporate an electric guitar into his act, Grandpa Andrei shouted from his seat in the empty theater, "Next thing I know, you'll be

Grandpa Andrei in one of his last performances

wearing blue suede shoes, gyrating your ass, with grease dripping off your hair." My grandfather's biggest gripe was how quickly the young generation was drifting away from Romani ways, and if this complaint sounds familiar, it's because it binds every culture like twine binds a broom.

My father strayed, and I after his example, only we did it at different speeds.

Life had a strange sense of humor.

When he heard me come in, he turned. "Ready?"

"Dad, I need to ask you something important."

He patted the couch and I sat down next to him.

"Can I have Grandpa's photo album?"

My father yanked me to him and wrapped his arms around

me as if I were about to go off to war. When he let go, I saw that he was crying.

"You don't have to give it to me. It's not that big of a deal. Really."

His shoulders shook.

"Everything's okay, Dad," I said. I had no idea what had brought him to this state, or how to bring back the pigheaded, wisecracking man I was used to.

He shook a handkerchief out of his breast pocket and blew his nose into it. "It's that blasted mattress. Digs into my back every night and keeps me awake. Might as well sleep on top of a porcupine." He pushed off the couch, stuffing the handkerchief back into the pocket. "I'm fine. Just gonna lie down in my studio for a while. By the way, I left something for you in the kitchen. On the table."

It was the album, tattered and faded to a watery green. I took it back to the bedroom that no longer belonged to me and sat on the floor in the same spot Cruz and I had stood the night I told him I loved him. The album lay open in my lap. My grandparents' faces peered up from a black-and-white photo taken on the set of a film they were shooting. Dressed in period costumes, they looked regal, immortal. And in a sense they were.

With my heart's hand I scooped up the memory of every memento of my remarkable grandparents, and I ran my fingertips over their images before closing the album and laying it on top of my purse with much care.

I left the bedroom when I heard voices, one of them my mother's. All morning, Olga had fluttered—dusting, basting, picking the right dress to wear—in preparation for Mom's arrival. The richest of clients could not bring her to whip out her best china. Not even Grandma Ksenia had kindled such tribute.

"My baby!" Mom waved me over and tugged me onto her lap.

When I was little, her bony thighs provided comfort against every little thing that was wrong with the world. Roxy came scurrying over.

"I'm the baby," she said.

She threw her arms around my neck in that clumsily rough manner kids acquire at the foot of adolescence. Already she stood nearly tall as I did—a legacy of our grandfather, no doubt—but she still smelled like my little sister, of baby powder and bubble gum.

It was mind-boggling to see Mom drinking coffee at the same table with Dad and Olga. No one was fighting. They talked, laughing like the friends they used to be before the affair and the divorce.

"You best take a week off, Nora, 'cause I'm coming to Vegas," Olga said, turning over an empress card and poking at it with a confident finger. "You see?"

Dad propped up on both forearms to peer at the card spread. "What? All this time you've been shitting away your money in the wrong place?"

"Don't fret yourself," Mom said. "This time she'll have help. It'll be over before you have time to wheedle some unsuspecting lounge manager into letting you on their stage."

I never found out what happened to strike peace between the three of them, but I admire my mother for it the most. With dignity, she'd accepted the past. With grace, she'd pieced us together to resemble a family, fragmented as it would remain. For many years the three of them would remain close. At least once a year, Dad and Olga visited us in Vegas. Olga and my mother perfected the art of losing money at slots, and my father now had two women to drag out of casinos in the middle of the night.

Soon it was time to go.

I tossed my stuff in the back of my mother's tank and turned to hug my father.

"If you don't like Vegas . . ." he said, shrugging.

"I'll visit this Christmas," I said, abruptly attached to the house I'd never paid much attention to before.

I held my grandfather's album in my lap and looked back. Dad and Olga stood on the sidewalk, waving. I waved, too, trying to memorize the picture they made together—a giant and a midget huddled close in a way they hadn't in months.

When we passed Annie's house, I watched it with a stab of longing, half expecting Cruz to rush out and say goodbye. But I was lying to myself. Cruz had stopped staying over at Annie's, and after graduation no one knew of his whereabouts. Brandon and Annie avoided me and I them, probably as much for my own benefit as theirs. Of course, I didn't expect them to abandon their loyalty to Cruz, but my eyes stung from crying all the same.

I took mental Polaroids of the entire neighborhood.

And from a distance I noticed someone standing at the corner of our street and Hollywood Boulevard.

My heart almost literally stopped.

He saw me at the same time.

I leaned my forehead on the window and painted a picture of him in my mind: tall, wide-shouldered, long hair nearly golden from the California sun, hands at his sides, wearing all black, turquoise-green eyes never wavering.

As we passed, he stood on the corner like an inkblot against the chalky sidewalk.

Our car slowed down before turning. He moved closer. For a moment I thought he'd changed his mind about Brazil and decided on Vegas instead. But he stopped at the curb.

We turned into the late-afternoon traffic, and I watched him until a city bus erased him from my view.

So there I was, a semi-American teenager leaving L.A.; bereft, but in possession of a substantially finer vocabulary than when I first set foot in Hollywood. The ragged skyline of my old home melted into smog, and the desert, drenched grapefruit-orange by the setting sun, now breathed around me.

"What's with the album?" Mom asked, motioning at my lap. Her voice was balanced like a tightrope walker.

"I'm thinking of doing some family research," I said.

"Really? . . . Why?"

"I don't know. Maybe, if I have kids someday, I could pass it on to them."

Mom turned on the radio where a cowboy crooner was singing that he still believed in me. Roxy was sleeping in the backseat, mouth open and drooling. We sped by a distant mountain with the word CALICO written on it in giant uneven letters.

"That's a ghost town," Mom said. Then she added, "Your father and I have lived through some amazing times. I could tell you stories. You know. If it helps your research."

"It might," I said, surprised by her offer. My mother hardly ever volunteered information on her life with Dad, but over the years, tales of her adventures with the Roma would gush out of her like water from a cracked dam.

"What are you thinking?" Mom asked sometime later. She'd left the windows open, and the air pounced at our hair.

"It's beautiful." I'd never paid attention to this untouched country outside the metropolis. It was a perfectly chiseled sculpture, yet wild and otherworldly. Like all of us.

For the first fifteen years of my life, I was an empty pitcher waiting for some random spout to fill me. What I didn't realize was that I'd made the journey to that water many times over, like the people of Kirovakan ascending the hill of Tetoo Dzhoor. I'd tasted my cultures from the day I was born, and they'd keep me alive until I, too, became an image in an album. A memory. Did I have to choose who I was? At that moment the question sounded absurd. All I could hope for, really, was to improve upon the old design I happened to be a part of. If this meant that I'd someday call myself an American, it'd be a worthy achievement.

But if with time, when a maze of wrinkles claims my skin and the neighborhood strays purr at the sound of my footsteps; long after I've loved eagerly and hated without shame—if even then I am unchanged, unfound, well, perhaps that is simply because I never lost myself in the first place. And that would be just fine by me.

ACKNOWLEDGMENTS

Every one of us has experienced magic, be it a smile, a word, or a deed. We are all magic-makers, and I will forever be grateful to the ones who have walked into my life and helped me along this amazing journey.

My agent, Brandi Bowles, for having killer intuition and a sharp mind at the times when I had neither.

My editor, Courtney Hodell, who has made so many complicated things make sense, in writing and beyond.

Sarita Varma, who has worked hard to make this book seen and heard and not simply shelved away.

Ian Hancock, for being a true role model and for working diligently to bring about much needed change.

Teresa Medeiros, who said yes when she didn't have to.

Mark Krotov, for always being gracious and straightforward.

Lisa McGlaun and Chris Arabia, a.k.a. The Renegades, for being amazing.

Megan Edwards and Mark Sedenquist, for integrity and support.

Charlotte Strick, who designed the most awesome book cover ever.

Carolyn Hayes Uber, whose fortitude and creative energy are contagious.

Amber Withycombe, who kindly pointed me in the right direction.

Bob Mayer, for giving me advice that forever changed my life.

Vegas Valley Book Festival, Henderson Writers Group, and Las Vegas Writers Group, for inspiration.

Jana Cruder, for her shutter talent.

The Farrar, Straus and Giroux team, for making people's dreams come true.

My family. For true love.